# Play, Language, and Stories:
# The Development of Children's Literate Behavior

### Edited by

**Lee Galda**

and

**Anthony D. Pellegrini**

University of Georgia
Athens, Georgia

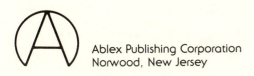

Ablex Publishing Corporation
Norwood, New Jersey

**Library of Congress Cataloging in Publication Data**
Main entry under title:

Play, language, and stories.

Includes bibliographies and index.
1. Language acquisition—Addresses, essays, lectures.   2. Play—Addresses, essays, lectures.
3. Communicative competence—Addresses, essays, lectures.   4. Discourse analysis,
Narrative—Addresses, essays, lectures.   I. Galda, Lee.   II. Pellegrini, Anthony D.
P118.P57   1985   401'.9   85-13396
ISBN 0-89391-292-1

Ablex Publishing Corporation
355 Chestnut Street
Norwood, New Jersey 07648

# Contents

*For Frank and Odet*

# Introduction

Children at play have been the subjects of our scrutiny for many years. We have categorized play, examined social interaction in play, and described how children at play use and play with language. This volume extends the work on the language of play with its emphasis on how the language used in play is similar to more formal, literate uses of language. Use of this formal register is typically required of children in school. The contributors to this volume present original empirical reports from research perspectives as diverse as anthropology and cognitive psychology. These diverse orientations are reflected in varied hypothesized relations between play and language.

We begin with chapters which discuss the influence of knowledge, or scripts, on the use of language in play. Next, several chapters document the development of communicative competence in play, citing the modification of language according to role, the definition of play boundaries, and the use of elaborated language. The discourse-processing skills behind story comprehension, production, and spontaneous play productions are compared. Finally, three chapters depict children at various stages of language development using play and playful routines to help them master new language skills. Together, these studies present a view of the multifaceted nature of the language of play.

That children talk best when they know what they are talking about is thoroughly demonstrated in the chapter by French, Lucariello, Seidman, and Nelson. Reporting data from several studies, they argue that children display language which is syntactically, semantically, and pragmatically more advanced when their discourse topic is knowledge-based, or scripted as compared to nonscripted, and when the context they are in elicits interactions around shared scripts. These data demonstrate the importance of considering script knowledge when inferring linguistic competence. McLoyd, Ray, and Etter-Lewis explore how preschool African American girls use their knowledge of family roles in pretend play. They describe how these children modified their language according to the domestic roles they and their listener assumed. These data show the ways in which young girls' scripts for different family roles are reflected in the language they use when enacting these roles. Knowledge as well as communicative competence plays an important role in preschoolers' increasing facility in sociodramatic play.

Sachs, Goldman, and Chaillé contend that as children's experiences with particular events such as going to the doctor are more numerous, their knowledge about the actions and language surrounding those events grows. Their increasingly richer scripts result in more resources from which to draw when structuring play around a particular theme. This is reflected in more complex play and more communicatively competent players.

Children's script knowledge increases as their language develops. Wolf and Pusch describe how children use language to protect their fantasy play texts from extracontextual interference. They describe how children become progressively more able to keep their texts autonomous as they initially overlook, then transform, and then explain intrusions from the "outside world." These behaviors and other text-preserving strategies indicate that children recognize the specialized nature of their play texts and have a broad understanding of text autonomy. They can separate their play texts from the surrounding context, creating an autonomous text much like those they will encounter in school. Pellegrini discusses how other aspects of children's language in play are similar to the literate language required in school. Defining literate language as narrative, decontextualized language, he demonstrates how the use of explicit and elaborated language and cognitive and linguistic verbs increases with age. The language found in the complex play texts of the older preschoolers is similar to school language tasks such as story comprehension and production. Guttman and Frederiksen's chapter examines the relations between the discourse-processing skills underlying story comprehension and the communication of narrative text in storytelling and play. Their cognitive approach and the text-feature approach of Pellegrini both suggest similarities between the language of play and traditional school narrative language.

Children use play to support them in their language learning. Evans directly examines a school language event, show and tell discussions in kindergarten and second grade classrooms. She suggests that with age children rely less on strategies used in their play to help them meet the demands of the more formal school situation. The narrative play of a preschooler learning English as a second language offers an interesting look at how play is used to gain second-language competence. Heath describes how a young girl incorporated school-language routines and adult-questioning routines into her English-language solitary play and bookreading activities. When the verbal and social demands of cooperative dramatic play were overpowering, she would revert to her first language, continuing to "practice" English in the more manageable solitary situations. The use of language routines in play as practice for handling larger chunks of discourse was clearly one strategy used by this second-language learner. Snow, Nathan, and Perlmann examine how young boys used the book-reading routines of their mothers when they were asked to play at reading a book to someone else. Their data indicate how precisely mothers altered the complexity of their speech during book reading as their children became more competent listeners and discussants. The talk which surrounded the book-reading episodes provided enough experience for some children to competently lead a "pretend" book-reading session.

These nine studies explore aspects of the question of the relation between play and literate language. Together they build a case for both the complexity and the strength of this relation.

*Lee Galda*

*Anthony D. Pellegrini*

# PART I
# KNOWLEDGE BASES AND PLAY

# 1

## The Influence of Discourse Content and Context on Preschoolers' Use of Language*

Lucia A. French
University of Rochester

Joan Lucariello
Susan Seidman
Katherine Nelson
City University of New York

## Introduction

In the last few years, a number of studies have found preschoolers to be much more cognitively competent than a strict interpretation of Piagetian theory would predict. A common thread running through these studies has been an emphasis upon providing an experimental context and/or task content that is "meaningful" for the young child. To a greater extent than is the case for older children and adults, young children's ability to display various cognitive competencies appears to be highly sensitive to both context and content.

Nelson and Gruendel (1981) suggested that general event representations were among the most meaningful contexts for young children. Such a proposal explicitly acknowledges that "context" may be conceived of as internal, or cognitive, as well as external, or environmental. Young children's general event representations are characterizable within the general script model initially described by Schank and Abelson (1977). Scripts are sche-

* Portions of the research reported here were supported by NICHD Grant 5732HDO7196 and NSF Grant BNS 78-25810. Lindsay Evans, Janice Gruendel, and Marylou Boynton aided in the execution of the research. Special thanks are extended to Marylou Boynton and Rosemary Hodges for useful comments on earlier drafts of the manuscript. Address for correspondence: Dr. Lucia French, Center for the Study of Psychological Development, Graduate School of Education and Human Development, University of Rochester, Rochester, New York 41627.

matic representations of events and include information about the temporal and causal organization of a set of related acts, about which components of an event are obligatory and which are optional, and about the props and roles associated with the events. Scripts constitute one of the young child's earliest, most stable, and most richly represented forms of knowledge. In addition to allowing young children to organize and interpret their experience, that is, to predict "when, what, and who" in familiar situations, scripts appear to provide an essential basis for further cognitive development (e.g., Nelson & Gruendel, 1981; Nelson, Fivush, Hudson, & Lucariello, 1983). Finally, scripts constitute a "cognitive context" within which relatively advanced cognitive and linguistic skills can be displayed.

In this chapter, we focus on the latter point and describe several studies that indicate that preschoolers' display of various cognitive and linguistic abilities varies as a function of discourse content and discourse context. For the purposes of this chapter, we define discourse content as the *topic* of a conversational exchange and discourse context as the *setting* in which a conversational exchange takes place.

Results from studies involving four different types of conversational groupings will be discussed; these include experimenter–child, mother–child, and child–child dyads, and groups of children. In experimenter–child interactions, the experimenter interviewed children about their event knowledge. The mother–child dyads were observed interacting both during free play with toys provided by the experimenter and during "nonplayful" participation in a routine event such as bathing or eating lunch. Spontaneously formed groups of preschool children were observed during free play as they interacted in various classroom settings. Child–child dyads were observed playing in various settings established by the experimenter. These quite dissimilar studies converge in supporting the conclusion that discourse context and content have a substantial influence upon the sophistication of young children's language use.

Preschooler's language and conversational skills are relatively advanced when their discourse topic is script-based rather than nonscript-based. The language used by children describing knowledge represented in scripts and by children playing in settings that elicit interaction around scripts is more advanced syntactically, pragmatically, and semantically than language used in other contexts. Additionally, event knowledge facilitates nonliteral play, and the contingency and length of dialogues vary as a function of whether their content is or is not script-based.

## Reporting Scripted Knowledge

Script knowledge can be elicited from children as young as three simply by asking them "What happens when..." they engage in a familiar activity such as getting dressed, eating lunch, or going to a restaurant (Nelson, 1978;

Nelson & Gruendel, 1981). The ease with which these reports can be elicited is somewhat surprising in light of both the general difficulties associated with devising measures to assess preschoolers' knowledge, and preschoolers' reputed difficulties with communicative language. Young children's ready compliance with requests to describe their event knowledge is one indication that such knowledge is well-represented and readily accessible.

Scripts elicited from different children and from the same child on different occasions are highly consistent in terms of both the specific components mentioned and the sequencing of these components (Nelson et al., 1983). This indicates that many scripts are both stable and socially shared, factors that provide important bases for communicative speech and play.

The language preschoolers use when reporting their event knowledge differs in a number of ways from their language in free-play settings, the usual context for sampling productive language. In addition, the temporal structure of their reports and the occurrence of relational terms indicate that knowledge of temporal and logical relationships, and of the vocabulary used to express these, emerges earlier than has traditionally been believed (see French, in press; French & Nelson, 1982, in press).

There are several general features of children's reports of scripted events that are noteworthy given common assumptions regarding young children's linguistic abilities. Such event descriptions do not refer to the "here-and-now," that is, to the immediate temporal/spatial context. The definite article *the* is appropriately used to introduce previously unmentioned nouns that are inherent elements of the events being described. For example, a child might mention "the teacher" when describing lunch at a day-care center. The use of the definite article in such contexts indicates an appreciation of the fact that the whole (e.g., the day-care center) implies the part (e.g., the teacher). The impersonal pronoun *you* is very common in event descriptions, indicating a recognition that scripts apply generally. A high proportion of the verbs are "timeless," that is, do not refer explicitly to the past, present, or future. An utterance such as "You eat and you pay" includes both timeless verb forms and the impersonal "you." These linguistic features suggest that the speaker (in this case a child of 2;11 describing what happens at a restaurant) has a generalized representation of the event being described.

Both mention of things removed from the immediate context and the use of timeless verbs are unexpected in the speech of 3-year-olds. In both naturalistic and experimental studies of language ability, the speech of young children has tended to focus on the immediately present environment (e.g., Brown & Bellugi, 1964; Clark & Clark, 1977; Sachs, 1983), leading some to speculate that preschoolers are unable to engage in displaced reference. The script protocols illustrate that 3-year-olds can talk about their event knowledge in the absence of environmental support. Additionally, Lucariello's data, described subsequently, indicate that under certain conditions even

2-year-olds talk about absent objects and persons and past and future activities.

Noting that timeless verb forms did not appear until about age four in the longitudinal speech samples collected by R. Brown (1973) and his colleagues, Cromer (1968) and McNeill (1979) claimed that the relatively late mastery of this relatively simple linguistic form resulted from an inability to engage in temporal decentration. The script protocols show that 3-year-olds do indeed have the requisite cognitive abilities for such reference. With regard to the use of both displaced and timeless reference, assumptions about the young child's capabilities have been erroneous due to limitations in the types of data available.

The script protocols have also led to a reconsideration of young children's understanding of relational terms such as *because, so, if, but, or, before,* and *after,* which permit the linguistic expression of logical relationships. Most investigations of children's acquisition of these terms have employed comprehension measures. The general conclusion has been that children do not comprehend these terms until age five, eight, or even later.

Most attempts to model noncomprehenders' "partial understanding" of these terms (e.g., Clark, 1971; Emerson, 1979, 1980; Kail, 1980; Paris, 1973) have adopted a "componential model" which holds that semantic components of a given word are acquired in a fixed sequence over time. E. Clark's semantic feature hypothesis is the best known of these models. Clark (1971) claimed that *before* is acquired earlier than *after,* and that there is a period during which *after* is interpreted as if it meant *before.* Componential models arise and gain their support from analyses of error patterns on comprehension tests. If such models adequately reflect young children's understanding of relational terms, then their productions should contain systematic errors. For example, *after* should be used when *before* would be appropriate, *because* and *if* should introduce consequent clauses as often as antecedent clauses, and so forth.

In the course of describing their event knowledge, children produce relational terms several years before "full understanding" of the features is usually attributed to them, and their productions are not in accord with the predictions that follow from the componential models. French and Nelson (1981, 1982, in press; French, 1981), analyzed approximately 700 script protocols produced by 43 children ranging from 2;11 to 5;6. All the relational terms mentioned above appeared in these protocols. The productions were virtually always appropriate; the few "errors" tended to be false starts or semantically uninterpretable rather than reflections of the partial knowledge predicted by componential models. It is important to note that all the children studied by French and Nelson were below the minimum ages at which adequate comprehension was found in the studies cited above.

The componential models derived from comprehension paradigms clearly offer an inadequate characterization of the young child's understanding of relational terms. We believe two factors contribute to the differences in performance with these terms found by ourselves and by other investigators. First, secondary task demands (for example, the metalinguistic demands associated with grammaticality judgments) may mask competency with the terms themselves, while yielding systematic error patterns. These systematic error patterns then provide spurious support for the componential models. Second, production and comprehension may place quite different demands on the young child. The spontaneous production of relational terms involves encoding one's own underlying representation of a relationship linguistically, whereas comprehension involves formulating a mental representation of the relationship on the basis of linguistic input.

Under this analysis, comprehension may be more or less difficult depending upon whether the relationship being expressed matches the listener's prior knowledge. Carni and French (1984) found that 3-year-olds can comprehend *before* and *after* when these terms refer to scripted sequences for which they have stable, preestablished mental representations, but do not seem to comprehend these terms when they refer to sequences having no real-world fixed order, whereas 4-year-olds comprehend *before* and *after* when they refer to either type of sequence. This pattern indicates that despite having a basic understanding of relational terms, young children may experience comprehension difficulties when the terms do not describe previously known relationships. In other words, comprehension of relational terms may initially be limited to content for which the child already has a well-established mental representation of the relevant relationships.

Just as children use linguistic forms previously believed to be beyond their level of competence when describing scripted events, they also demonstrate unexpected cognitive abilities. In addition to those abilities underlying displaced reference and the use of timeless verb forms (discussed earlier), event descriptions reveal preschoolers' understanding of logical relationships, temporal sequencing, and temporal reversibility.

Claims that preschoolers do not understand relational terms often invite the conclusion that they do not understand the logical relationships encoded by the terms. However, preschoolers' appropriate production of these terms when describing their event knowledge reflects a very early appreciation of logical relationships. French and Nelson (1982, in press) have discussed at length the inferences about underlying cognitive representations that can be drawn from the appropriate use of the terms *because, so, if, but, or, before,* and *after.* The appropriate use of *if* and *or* in the context of describing scripted events is particularly interesting because these terms reflect the children's understanding of optional pathways in the instantiation of an event. Consider the following statements:

Well, when the thing that moves doesn't move, sometimes I wanta go up there, if it's not glass. (Speaking of grocery store conveyer belt, age 4;2)

> You could, you could—get in dresses, or, you can get in pants or shorts. But if it's in the summer and you get on pants, too hot. But if you get in pants in the winter, medium. But if you get in a dress in the summer, that's good too. (Getting dressed, age 5;4)

We have suggested (French, 1983, in press; French & Nelson, 1982) that such understanding is the forerunner of hypothetical reasoning. The child's first systematic experience with alternative and conditional relationships may very well be script-based. Repeated encounters with an event lead to an awareness of which elements are constant, which optional, and which dependent upon optional conditions, and so seem an optimal source for the development of an understanding of the hypothetical.

Piaget (1971) and Fraisse (1963) claimed that preoperational children are unable to represent temporal order mentally because they are insensitive to the logical constraints that often govern temporal structure. Research by A. Brown and her colleagues (Brown, 1976; Brown & Murphy, 1975; Brown & French, 1976) demonstrated that preschoolers were sensitive to logical relationships and event order, but did not provide a stringent test of whether young children could independently formulate temporal and logical relationships and remember them over time. In reporting their general event knowledge, young children report the individual components constituting the events in accord with their actual order of occurrence (Nelson, 1978; French & Nelson, 1981, in press). The sequential nature of children's event descriptions shows that they can indeed form mental representations of temporal relationships and maintain these representations over time.

Children can also move bidirectionally within these representations of temporal structure. Occasionally, children, like adults, decide to mention a particular event after omitting it from its proper position in a description. When this occurs, children make temporal repairs. That is, they "backup" their reports to indicate where the omitted act should be inserted. For example, a child of 2;11 effected the following repair:

> She gots something out to bake muffins with. But first, she has to buy some things for muffins.

A more complex temporal repair was produced by a child of 5;4:

> You get the dough, pop it in the oven, and first you roll it then you pop it in the oven. No, I mean, first cookie, first make the dough, flatten it, and then put the cookie cutters out and then press them down...

These temporal repairs seem necessarily to involve both an internal representation of the correct temporal sequence and the ability to move bidirectionally within this sequence. According to Piaget (1971), these are the two abilities which constitute temporal reversibility, a cognitive operation he suggests first appears during the stage of concrete operations and which therefore is unexpected in children under six or seven.

In summary, preschoolers' event descriptions indicate that children possess various linguistic and cognitive abilities at an earlier age than has generally been believed. By encouraging expository descriptions of non-present, but familiar, events, the script elicitation paradigm yields a more complete, and thus more accurate, picture of the young child's competencies. Asking children to describe *nonpresent* events prevented them from limiting their language to the here and now and the *familiarity* of the events undoubtedly contributed to the temporal organization of the descriptions and to the use of the general pronoun forms, timeless verbs, and relational terms. While these data clearly indicate that young children have linguistic and cognitive abilities not generally attributed to them, we are not suggesting that their control of these abilities is identical to that exercised by older children and adults. These abilities are likely to be elicited from—and indeed available to—young children only when they are dealing with familiar, well-established cognitive representations. Important directions for future research include studying young children's limitations in these domains and the processes by which they are overcome.

## Talking to Mothers

Despite a great deal of interest in mother–child communicative interactions (see Snow, 1979, for a review of this research), there has been little consideration of the *content* of mother–child conversations. This issue has been considered by Lucariello, who audio- and videotaped 10 mother–child dyads interacting in three contexts in the home: a familiar, scripted routine such as bathing or eating lunch, novel play with a castle and associated props, and free play with assorted toys (a pull-along train with dessert shapes, a tea set, a stack-toy dog, a bear puppet, and a shape register). The children, 6 males and 4 females, were between 2;0 and 2;5.

Analysis of the transcripts indicated that during participation in a routine situation, the children's language behavior was more sophisticated in terms of object labeling (Lucariello, 1983b), displaced reference, question-answering ability (Lucariello & Nelson, 1982), and conversational skills (Lucariello, 1983a). Conversations such as the following, which occurred during lunch and involved a discussion of future and past activities, were virtually non-existent in the play contexts:

M:  You gonna take a nap after lunch?
C:  No.

M: No? Are you tired?
C: No.
M: Do you remember where you slept last night?
C: In your bed.
(Male, age 26 months, 9 days)

The analysis of language use across settings indicates that language use is generally more advanced in "scripted" settings. But what of mother–child speech in nonscripted settings? Do mothers and children draw on shared event knowledge for the "contents" of discourse in nonscripted contexts, and if so, with what results? These questions were addressed by examining the conversations that took place within the free-play setting.

Speech was analyzed to determine conversational units. A conversation was defined as a segment of the discourse in which the participants demonstrated communicative *and* semantic contingency. Over 85% of the conversations (89 of 103) fell into one of two categories—object talk and fantasy talk. *Object talk* was defined as utterances that drew attention to, named or identified, described, or referred to actions with, objects. *Fantasy talk* was defined as utterances that expressed and supported fantasy play activity.

Object talk reflects one of the most basic functions of language, that is, the literal use of language to refer to the present scene. "Here-and-now" talk is very pervasive in the speech of young children (Brown & Bellugi, 1964; Sachs, 1983) and in the speech of adults interacting with young children (Phillips, 1973; Snow, 1979). Fifty-six percent of the conversations (58 of 103) during free play contained object talk only, indicating the large extent to which conversation in this discourse context referred to the here and now. Object identification is illustrated in the following segment:

M: What does this look like?
C: Umbrella.
M: Umbrella. And what does that look like? (points to second shape)
C: Cake.
(Male, age 29 months, 1 day)

Discussions of object oriented activity also occurred:

M: Doesn't go in there. (Referring to C's attempt to insert shape in slot)
C: (Tries new slot) In there?
M: Not in that one either.
(Male, age 24 months, 22 days)

Object talk was restricted entirely to the here and now and tended to be very repetitive, with identification and placement formats often sustained over many turns.

In contrast to object talk, fantasy talk involves the nonliteral use of language. Because the predominance of a Piagetian orientation in play research has fostered studies examining the emergence of symbolic play in the child as it occurs independently of adult influence (e.g., Fein, 1975; Fenson & Ramsay, 1980; Nicolich, 1977, Piaget, 1962), there have been few investigations of nonliteral mother–child speech. Researchers who have studied fantasy in a social context have focused primarily on the "process" of establishing and maintaining fantasy rather than on the "contents" of pretense episodes (e.g., Dunn & Wooding, 1977; Sachs, 1980; Soderbergh, 1980; Kavanaugh, Whittington, & Cerbone, 1983). For example, Sachs (1980) describes how parental talk scaffolds child play by enriching the child's ongoing actions and providing a more rational structure, a narrative thread, for the child's actions.

Fantasy episodes were analyzed with two aims. The first was to describe the "contents" of mother–child fantasy play activity. Since shared event knowledge has been found to be an important ingredient for successful conversation (e.g., Nelson & Gruendel, 1979; Nelson & Seidman, 1984; Seidman, 1983a, 1983b; French & Boynton, 1984), it was hypothesized that fantasy talk would be substantially based on event knowledge shared by the mother and child. Second, the roles of the two conversational participants in the "process" of initiating and maintaining event-based fantasy episodes was assessed.

Seventeen conversations contained fantasy talk only, and 14 contained a combination of fantasy and object talk. Episodes were defined as groups of maternal–child behaviors related to a single fantasy theme (e.g., having lunch or licking the dessert shapes). There were 33 distinct fantasy episodes. These were analyzed to determine to what extent they were event based, that is, involved behavior and language referring to familiar, routinized activities (e.g., lunch or tea party). Approximately half (15) of these episodes were event based. Thirteen of the 15 event-based fantasy episodes relied upon mealtime scripts, a choice apparently triggered by the availability of a tea set among the toys provided. Thus it appears that the discourse context, which included a tea set, affords particular event-based fantasies. While these data indicate that mothers and children can engage in fantasy play that does not rely upon event knowledge, they also support the hypothesis that event knowledge constitutes an important source for nonliteral play activity.

Studies of nonliteral mother–child play (Dunn & Wooding, 1977; Sachs, 1980; Soderbergh, 1980; Kavanaugh, Whittington, & Cerbone, 1983) have found that mothers play a key role in the "process" of moving interactions away from the here and now and into nonliteral dimensions. A question arises, however, as to whether the mother's role is necessarily so central in event-based fantasy episodes where both mother and child share knowledge of the pretense theme. That is, does "content" affect "process"? In order to address this question, the process by which event-based fantasies were established and maintained was considered.

Event-based fantasies were examined in terms of the components of event knowledge which they contained. Event shemas specify an ordered sequence of actions appropriate to a particular spatial/temporal context, organized around a goal, and include objects and roles associated with the event (e.g., Bower, Black, & Turner, 1979; Mandler, 1983; Nelson, 1981; Nelson et al., 1983; Schank & Abelson, 1977). Accordingly, the event-based fantasies were analyzed for the presence of four components: (a) the mention of goals or themes for the pretense activity; (b) event-related actions; (c) the incorporation of appropriate objects; and (d) the incorporation of event-specified roles (e.g., "waiter" in a restaurant script).

The total number of components (summing across the four types) per fantasy episode was calculated, and it was determined for each episode whether the mother or the child had contributed more components or whether their contributions were equivalent (within a range of plus or minus one). Additionally, these episodes were analyzed to determine who initiated them. Nine of the 15 event-based fantasies were child-initiated. In eight, the child contributed more components than the mother, in four the mother contributed more than the child, and in three the number of contributions was equivalent. In contrast with the general finding that the mother is primarily responsible for moving play interactions to a nonliteral dimension, these data offer strong evidence that these 2-year-olds took an active role in constructing the fantasy episodes. It appears that event knowledge enables very young children to be competent producers of fantasy.

In order to determine how event knowledge served each member of the dyad in creating the fantasies, mother–child contributions of each of the specific types of components were considered. These data are presented in Table 1, which shows that children contributed all four types of components to the pretense episodes and surpassed the mother in the contribution of actions, objects, and actors. The children were particularly adept at contributing object and actor components.

The contribution of object components involved incorporating substitute or imaginary objects associated with a particular event schema into the pretense. For example, in the mealtime or tea-party fantasies, napkins and various beverages (both imaginary) were often incorporated into the play. In

Table 1. Mean Percentage of Types of Components Contributed to Fantasy Episodes by Mother and Child

| Person | Goal/Theme | Actions | Objects | Actors |
|--------|-----------|---------|---------|--------|
| Child  | 28.6      | 56.7    | 70.0    | 76.7   |
| Mother | 71.4      | 43.3    | 30.0    | 23.3   |

considering actor contributions, it was found that the children specified appropriate roles—and supplied actors to fill these roles—in two ways. Using displaced reference, the children proposed actual, but nonpresent, persons to serve as diners. They also attributed agency to available figures, for example, the toy bear and dog became diners wanting tea. The processes of incorporating event-appropriate imaginary objects and of supplying actors through displaced reference to fill the diner roles are illustrated in the following segment. Additionally, this segment illustrates the incorporation and sequencing of event appropriate actions (e.g., setting the table and pouring the beverages), another type of component the children were adept at contributing.

C:  (Holding teapot) Want some juicy?
M:  (Holds out glass) I'll take some juice.
C:  (Pours juice)
M:  Thank you.
C:  (Walks to Daddy's setting) Daddy's cup?
M:  Put some in Daddy's cup.
C:  (Looking at mother) Want some iced tea?
M:  Alright.
C:  Daddy?
M:  Maybe he would like iced tea.
C:  OK.
M:  Should we save it for him when he comes home?
C:  OK. Something else want tea? Something else wants tea, Stacey?
M:  OK, let's set a place for Stacey. She might come over later.
C:  (Picks up cup, walks to table) OK, here's Stace, cup.
(Female, age 25 months, 29 days)

Only seven of the 15 event-based fantasy episodes involved a goal or theme statement. The goal statement, when used, always initiated the pretense episode. Mothers almost always relied on a goal mention to initiate a pretense episode. These mentions took the form "Let's have (or make) a ——." Of the nine child-initiated episodes, only two were initiated by a goal statement. Instead of a goal mention, the children tended to rely upon the three other types of components to initiate their event-based fantasies. They relied most heavily upon object incorporations. For example:

C:  (Picks up teapot) And coffee. Coffee.
M:  Could I have some coffee?
C:  Yeah. (Reaches for cup) And cup?
M:  Mm–huh.
C:  And napkin.
(Female, age 24 months, 20 days)

From these data, it is impossible to determine whether the children failed to grasp the goals of the event enactments or were simply not explicitly mentioning the goals around which the pretense was organized. Additionally, it cannot be determined whether or not the children intended to initiate an entire event-based fantasy activity through the mention of a component. However, in all cases, such initiations were elaborated upon by the dyad so that event-based fantasies evolved.

The final fantasy segment to be presented in this section illustrates many of the processes described here. In this pretense episode the child is doing all the "work." The event schema guiding the pretense is the father returning from work and greeting the child, evidenced in the initiatory goal/theme statement provided by the child. This schema specifies two roles, father and child, and the child utilizes these roles in the pretense activity and provides actors for these roles by assigning relational (i.e., familial) roles to available dolls. The toy train (in which the father comes home) is used as a prop. Additionally, many actions (e.g., riding home, arrival, and greeting—including bits of dialogue) are included and are correctly sequenced.

> C:   (Picks up puppet) The father comes home in the train.
> M:   The father comes home in the train, that's right.
> C:   Want this one ride. (Puts puppet in train) In here. (Pushes train)
> M:   You want that to go. OK.
> C:   (Stops pushing train) And comes home.
> M:   And comes home.
> C:   (Holds puppet up, speaking for puppet) Hi.
>      That took
>      From Minnies
>      Where's other Minnies?
>      (Points to dog) There's the other Minnies. (Walks to get dog)
> M:   Is that the other Minnies?
> C:   (Picks up dog) Yeah.
> M:   Is Minnies your nickname, Alexander?
> C:   (Gives dog to mother) This is the nickname Minnie.
> M:   This is a nickname Minnies?
> C:   Yes.
> M:   What do you think he does?
> C:   (Puts puppet next to dog)
> M:   Oh, you have your puppet and I have mine. Is that what you want?
> C:   (Moves puppet next to dog.)
>      This one talks. (Manipulating the puppet's hat and having a pretend dialogue with the puppet)
>      This way. This way.
>      (Speaking for puppet)

         Fine.
         Yeah.
         Daddy
         comes home.
         Then walk.
         (Points to train) Right there.
    M:   He comes home in the train?
    C:   Yes.
    M:   To this one? (Points to dog)
    C:   Yes (Touches dog) To Minnies.
    M:   To Minnies.
    (Male, age 29 months, 1 day)

Several points emerge from these data. First here-and-now talk, evidenced in terms of object talk, predominates in the mother–child conversations in this free-play context. Mothers and children are, however, quite capable of leaving the confines of the here and now. This is facilitated in large part by the event knowledge shared by the mother and child. Event knowledge provides the "contents" for approximately half of the fantasy episodes. Additionally, and very importantly, such knowledge enables the child to take a very active, in fact the major, role in the "process" of spinning fantasy.

### Talking to Peers

Investigations of mother–child discourse (e.g., Snow, 1979; Bruner, 1981; Ninio & Bruner, 1978) indicate that parents are very sensitive to their young children's communicative level. They adjust their speech to the child's level of syntactic and semantic knowledge, know a great deal about what experiences the child has had and can talk about, and are skilled at "repairing" conversations in which the child does not maintain his/her side of the conversation well. Parents often establish "conversational formats" (Bruner, 1981) in which the child's role is clearly defined and within which the child's responses can be interpreted as meaningful by the parent. The peer speech-partner is probably less skilled and/or knowledgeable along all these dimensions, suggesting that talking to parents and talking to peers probably place quite different demands on the young child. How do children compensate for the conversational support offered by parents when they talk to one another? Here we offer data indicating that shared event knowledge provides the basis for much child–child play and the speech that accompanies it. Shared knowledge minimizes the cognitive demands of interactions and conversations because it establishes a presuppositional base that facilitates the interpretation of an individual's language and actions.

Piaget (1955) claimed that a high proportion of young children's speech was egocentric and reflected a failure to understand the social, communicative function of language. Piaget's characterization of young children's speech as egocentric was based in part on his observations of collective monologues in which children observe conversational turn-taking conventions but violate contingency conventions. As a serendipitous outcome of her investigation of preverbal peer communication, Boynton (1984) videotaped the "emergence" of peer speech among well-acquainted 2-year-olds. This speech was always socially directed and communicative, and these children were never observed engaging in either collective or private monologues (Boynton & French, 1983). These data on the emergence of peer speech offer indirect support for Vygotsky's (1962) view that egocentric, or private, speech does not reflect a precommunicative "stage" in which children do not understand the social, communicative function of language.

Nelson and Gruendel (1979) taped conversations among 4-year-olds in a preschool classroom and found that they had quite extended dialogues which were heavily dependent upon shared, scripted knowledge. These conversations indicate that the children were decidedly not egocentric when they were talking about scripted activities. For example, in one conversation, two 4-year-olds discussed eating at various times during the day (lunch, dinner, snack). Their utterances were contingent and socially directed. The portion of this conversation which follows offers direct evidence of these children's ability to take one another's perspective, in that one child recognizes that the other might be unacquainted with her friend Michael, and the second child affirms this while simultaneously noting that she knows another Michael:

A:   Maybe hot dog (proposing a possible snack food)
B:   But, but, but, Jill and Michael don't like hot dog. Don't you know, but, do you know Michael and Jill?
A:   I know another Michael.
B:   I know, I know another Michael.
A:   No, I just know one Michael. I just know one Michael. (Nelson & Gruendel, 1979, p. 81)

Nelson and Gruendel (1979) suggested that collective monologues might be likely to occur when children were not talking about a topic familiar to each, that is, when they did not have shared knowledge and thus lacked the basis for contingent responding. Most studies of peer communication have involved well-acquainted peers. French and Boynton (1983) hypothesized that collective monologues would be *most likely* to occur among unacquainted children who did not have a history of successful communicative interaction or a great deal of joint experience about which to converse. Free-play period at a preschool that was just opening and served previously unacquainted children (infants through 5-year-olds) was videotaped daily for two weeks. No collective monologues were ever observed. Previously unacquainted children *immediately* engaged in speech that was social, communicative, and topic-constrained, a finding that further weakens the argument that young children are communicatively egocentric. A particularly interesting finding was that the children's language use was quite different, depending upon whether they were participating in activities for which they shared well-established scripts.

The "kitchen corner" constituted a setting about which all participants shared preestablished scripted knowledge. Girls pretended to cook and boys requested things to eat or drink. In addition to mime, there was extensive language use, involving requests for specific foods, negotiations about which pan was appropriate, and so forth. The following conversational segments involve Eddie (3;5), Jared (2;10), Dana (4;2) and Naomi (5;5). Eddie and Jared have been attending preschool for several days, Dana and Naomi are friends who attend another preschool and are visiting the newly opened center for the day; they first met the boys moments before the interaction reported here:

| | |
|---|---|
| D: | Hey, hey, (?) mix this. (Taking can from N) |
| N: | (Mixing motion with spoon) |
| D: | I'm making toaster. (Opening a spice jar) |
| E: | This is making something? What? What are you making? |

(Girls turn toward Eddie)

| | |
|---|---|
| N: | Salad. |
| D: | Do you want to play with us? |
| E: | Do you want to have supper with me? |
| D & N: | What? |
| E: | Do you want to have supper with me? |
| D: | Yes, we're having supper with you. |

(A minute and a half later, Jared has joined the group, and food preparation is continuing)

| | |
|---|---|
| D: | Now, where's the other pan? |
| N: | Right here, I get this pan. (Grabs pan) |
| E: | That's all gone, this all gone (Holds out glass to D, who takes it) |
| J: | It's all gone. |
| D: | OK. |
| J: | It's all gone (extending glass to D, who is working at sink) |
| E: | His pop all gone already (points to J). Pop all gone. |
| J: | Pop all gone already. Pop all gone already. (Dana takes his glass and puts it on sink; J extends apple, but gets no response) |
| E: | (Eats wooden apple dramatically) All done my apple. Here my apple. (Extends to girls) |
| J: | My apple (extends his wooden apple toward D, who takes it) |

D:            I'm gonna put some celery in there, some celery in there (putting "celery" in pots)

Teacher:     What is everybody making?

D:            Snack.

Teacher:     Snack?

E:            I want toast. I want toast. I want toast.

D:            I'm making toast.

N:            Take some of this.

With various participants moving in and out, this pretense episode involved 13 consecutive minutes of contingent dialogue around the theme of preparing and eating food. The interactions here are constrained by roles, and are "role-centric"—that is, not completely flexible and not egocentric. For example, Dana and Naomi have taken over the cooking–feeding roles and respond to the boys and to each other within these roles. They search for pans, plan what goes in them, and dispense food to the boys. Each girl tends to maintain her particular project—making salad or toast—and the boys ask to be fed. This initially emerges as a means of entering the play setting and suggests that the boys recognize the general theme of the girls' play and realize that it can incorporate a "be fed" role. Eddie helps to manage and model entry for Jared. He gets Dana to attend to Jared's statement "pop gone already," and enlarges Jared's role-appropriate act of eating the apple by doing it dramatically. Dana's response to the teacher's question with the term "snack" is interesting, because it names the *overall theme* of the interaction. She could have responded with her prior statement that she was making "toaster." By saying "I want toast. I want toast. I want toast," Eddie displays his memory for her particular job in this "snack," and reinforces the play by reminding her of her self-arranged role and demanding the product of her role from within his role.

These data indicate that even unacquainted children who have not shared particular experiences are able to tap into their shared knowledge of cultural routines to support thematic play. The children all had similar knowledge of the roles and activities appropriate to a kitchen setting. This shared knowledge enabled engagement in cohesive pretense narrated by language. The physical setting provided much more than simply a location and the necessary props for kitchen play. It "afforded meanings" that corresponded to the knowledge the different children brought with them to the school environment. The children could rely upon the meaning inherent in the setting to facilitate their communication. This discourse setting reduced the need to negotiate meanings verbally, thereby reducing both the need for language to be used explicitly to establish meanings and the possibility of misunderstandings occurring.

In settings for which the children did not share preestablished scripts, language was also used communicatively to establish or affirm shared reference. However, conversations in such settings were much shorter and much less rich than those which took place in the kitchen setting. In sharp contrast to a kitchen setting, a block corner or jungle gym does not explicitly offer, and aid in the expression of, a restricted range of meanings. Children were observed using blocks to act out a "Dukes of Hazzard" scenario and using a jungle gym as if it were a car being driven to grandmother's house. In order to achieve joint participation in these activities, at least one child must make explicit the meanings with which he is operating. Although miming the operation of a steering wheel while on a jungle gym may successfully communicate driving, language is necessary to communicate where one is going and what one plans to do upon arrival. Within a kitchen setting, the overall meaning is implicit and language is used to elaborate or comment upon the general theme provided by the setting. In contrast, language is necessary for *establishing* meanings in a block corner or on a jungle gym. Although the children were able to use language in this way, they seemed to find it cognitively demanding, and interactions around a given theme were maintained for only a few minutes. The following is a description of a 4-minute interaction between Jared and Eddie in the block corner:

> J hands E the plow for the dump truck. E smiles, takes it, and puts it on his truck. J gets a plow for his truck, and says "Truck, truck" to himself. E begins a routine of saying "Beep! Beep!" as he pretends to dump from the plow. J watches. Both laugh. E repeats the pattern several times. J says "Beep! Beep!" and loads blocks and the plow into bed of his truck. E and J alternate saying "Beep! Beep!" E continues this while J drives off. J returns and E asks, "Can I have, can I have that?" (referring to block). J hands E the block. E asks for another block: "Can I have that?" E loads the blocks into his truck. Both say "Beep" and watch the blocks fall when E lifts the box of the truck. J drives off. E knocks over a block and looks up, saying "My block fell down. I say Beep! Beep!" E loads blocks into his truck, calls "Beep! Beep!", dumps them and reloads truck. He is playing alone when the teacher calls clean up time.

In this segment, the two boys are clearly engaged with one another part of the time, and their play does have at theme of sorts. However, they signal and maintain the theme primarily through actions (loading and dumping) and through the repetition of a single word (Beep) which marks segments within the play. Such marking was often used within this classroom to establish and maintain interaction in settings that did not clearly suggest and support the enactment of shared themes, and is very similar to the verbal marking that structures mother–infant games such as peek-a-boo (e.g., Boynton & French, 1984).

These observations of a group of children's spontaneous play suggest two conclusions. First, rather than having a monologic quality, preschoolers' speech to peers tends to be socially directed and communicative. Second, the quality and quantity of such speech varies as a function of whether the *content* of the children's play is scripted, which, in turn, varies as a function of the physical *context* in which play occurs. As the studies described below indicate, preschoolers are able to engage in script-based play without the support provided by a setting which conveys and elicits scripted knowledge. However, French and Boynton's (1983) data indicate that such settings are important determinants of the length and quality of peer speech. We suspect that discourse setting may be especially important for children who are not well acquainted, and during the period in which preschoolers are making a transition from talking primarily with conversationally skilled, highly supportive adults to talking with peers who are conversationally unsophisticated. An opportunity to rely upon the physical context to convey the overall theme of an interaction allows children to maintain social and conversational contingency without having to use language in a fully explicit, context-independent manner.

Data from more controlled dyadic interactions also indicate that event knowledge forms the basis for young peers' more elaborated conversations. Seidman (1983a, 1983b; Nelson & Seidman, 1984) carried out two studies designed to extend Nelson and Gruendel's (1979) basic finding that young children's event-based conversations were contingent, cohesive, and organized. It was hypothesized that extended dialogic exchanges would have specific events as their topic, and that the children's scripted knowledge would enable them to activate plans for play. In the first study, the conversations of three dyads (classmates ranging from 4;0 to 4;10) were audiotaped in their day-care playroom. Children participated in three different play sessions—play with two toy telephones, play with Playdoh, and sandbox play. The speech was transcribed and divided into exchanges (defined as a sequence of two conversational turns in which a turn was taken by each partner). Each turn was classified as either contingent (same topic) or noncontingent upon the previous turn. Episodes were defined as sequences of contingent utterances, and noncontingent utterances thus marked episode boundaries.

For each dyad, in each play context, both the longest and shortest episodes were identified. Eight of nine of the longest, and only two of the shortest, episodes were event based. Five of the shortest episodes involved comments on, or requests for, the play materials. The mean number of turns for the longest episodes was 12.6, whereas the mean number for the shortest was 4.8. Shields (1978) reported that when *groups* of 4-year-old children talked, their conversations averaged only four turns. Data from this study of *dyadic* interactions indicates that peers are capable of engaging in longer dialogues, and that event knowledge is the basis for children's extended, contingent exchanges.

Two dyads used the telephones to plan a visit and all dyads enacted food preparation while playing with the Playdoh, and enacted a birthday party while playing in the sandbox. Thus even though the materials offered less direct support for the enactment of particular events than did the kitchen corner or tea set in the studies previously described, it nevertheless appears that specific play materials may prompt children to enact specific themes. However, while play materials may suggest themes for play, the presence of the materials does not explain the elaborated content of the conversations; this can be accounted for only by assuming that the children share similar knowledge of certain events.

A second study was undertaken to describe the interactive goals of dyadic players and to detail the types of knowledge young children express in their play conversations (Seidman, 1983b; Nelson & Seidman, 1984). Ten dyads consisting of same-aged peers ranging from 3;0 to 5;3) were observed and audiotaped during sandbox play. The available props consisted of two shovels, a plastic bucket, a measuring cup, and a large spoon. Utterances were coded for contingency, that is, relevance to an immediately prior utterance. Episodes were again defined as sequences of contingent utterances, and irrelevant utterances thus marked episode boundaries.

Object play and fantasy play were the most frequent interactive goals of these episodes, accounting for over 60% of the discourse in the sandbox setting. Object play was reality based and involved manipulation of and reference to the objects themselves. Fantasy play referred to episodes that evoked a fantasy or imaginative context and involved object substitution or the invocation of imaginary objects. The utterances constituting fantasy play episodes were further categorized as being either scripted (i.e., event-based) or nonscripted. Scripted utterances were those utilized to create an episode of sequentially organized activity based upon event knowledge. Seventy-eight percent of the pretend utterances were script-based, illustrating the large extent to which children of this age rely upon shared knowledge of cultural routines in constructing joint fantasy play.

Seven of the 10 dyads had more than one conversational episode with a fantasy play theme. An average of 83% of their fantasy episodes had event-based play content. Additionally, when fantasy play reemerged in the stream of verbal interaction, 88% of the time it was either a repetition or a development of fantasy content that was proposed in a previous play episode. Thus, a particular event tended to organize pretense across the entire interaction, and the children were able to recover and maintain a given theme, despite diversions to discuss the ownership of play materials or to describe their manipulations of the objects. Such recycling indicates at least a nascent ability to "repair" conversational breakdowns by returning to a prior topic.

A comparison of "cake" episodes of 3-, 4-, and 5-year-old dyads offers some insight into how the use of event knowledge in fantasy play discourse may change with age. The "recycles" represent the reestablishment of a pretense topic after a temporary interruption. As the age of the dyad increased, so did the number of exchanges and the complexity of the created fantasy. In the youngest dyad (mean age, 36 months), one child raises a cake topic, but the other fails to submit another proposal, and this exchange fails to reach the status of shared pretense:

    A:   More. (Requesting more sand)
    B:   What are you doing?
    A:   Get the cake.
    B:   What? Get the cake?
    A:   (?) For real.
    B:   I need that. (Referring to shovel)

The next dialogue was produced by children who were nearly 4 (mean age, 46.5 months). The cake theme was reestablished two times after its initial emergence, and a number of different propositions were established around the general theme. Event knowledge about both baking and birthday parties is integrated into these episodes.

    C:   Yeah, I know. You making cake.
    D:   Yeah! (Chanting) Who wants cake?
    C:   No, it's not finished. You have to get more.
    D:   No, look it!
    C:   OK. (Singing) "Happy Birthday" That cake.
    D:   OK, Oh, Oh.

*Recycle 1*

    C:   You have to pick up all this. No!
    D:   The cake. It all ready. (Singing) "Happy Birthday to FaFa." Look it! OK. I make bigger and bigger and bigger. Oh, Ah!
    C:   OK. (Singing) "Happy Birthday, Happy Birthday to you."
    D:   It's too much.
    C:   I have to make. I'm making. I making coffee.
    D:   Yeah. We're pretending. Pretend.

*Recycle 2*

    C:   Want to put it in? (Reference to pretend cake)
    D:   OK. Hold on.
    C:   (Singing) "Happy Birthday to you." Sing, sing Diana!
    C & D:   "Happy Birthday to you."
    C:   I made Happy Birthday, right?

The oldest dyad's (mean age, 58.3 months) cake-making activity was embedded within an elaborate bakery shop scenario. Unlike the younger children, this pair discussed the cake's ingredients. After the cake was made, it was given to an imaginary delivery truck. The "make cake—give to truck" sequence was repeated in two separate play episodes. Finally, the loaded truck was driven away—a tidy ending to this narrativelike fantasy.

| | |
|---|---|
| J: | Want to play bakery? Want to play bakery shop? Wanna play bakery shop? |
| L: | Then we need something else. |
| J: | A what? |
| L: | Make a cake? |
| J: | Yeah. |
| L: | We can make a cake with the measuring cup. |
| J: | Oh yeah. You have doing, and I'll have doing. |
| L: | Yeah but, we have to play bakery shop. |
| J: | I know. Make the cake. |
| L: | Put in one or more? (Referring to cup of sand) |
| J: | No, put the cake in. |
| L: | OK. I put the cake in there. |
| J: | Put some sugar too. |
| L: | OK. |
| J: | Put some sugar. |
| L: | Have to mix it up. |
| J: | OK. |
| L: | How 'bout some peanuts. |
| J: | No, no peanuts. Just a little peanuts. |
| L: | OK. A little more. |

*Recycle 1*

| | |
|---|---|
| J: | Want to give it to the truck now? |
| L: | OK. |
| J: | Now we have to make another one now. |
| L: | I'll make another. |
| J: | Make believe we have a truck. |
| L: | OK, come on. (Both make truck noises, Brrrooomm!) |
| J: | Now put it in. |
| L: | This is chocolate. Chocolate my flavor. |
| J: | No, don't put in chocolate. |
| L: | A little chocolate. |
| J: | That's chocolate? |
| L: | OK, this, this is grape. |

*Recycle 2*

| | |
|---|---|
| J: | Put it in the truck. Put it in the truck. |
| L: | OK, I get. Truck, I got it in. OK, it's in the truck. |

J:       OK.
L:       Get up on the truck.
J:       Come on, I'm gonna leave you.
J & L:   Brroomm! (driving away)

In both the 4- and 5-year-olds' dialogues, multiple themes were integrated in the creation of the fantasy play. The ability to connect different themes is very important in the development of narrative competence. The fact that Lucariello's 2-year-olds relied on only one event in their event-based fantasies suggests that the ability to integrate different event schemas in pretense play may be a developmental achievement.

Whereas French and Boynton (1984) observed children of varying ages engaging in group play during a preschool's free-play period, Seidman observed same-aged children engaging in dyadic play with a restricted set of objects. Across these different contexts, both sets of investigators found that children's event knowledge often structures their play and conversation with peers. These investigations support and extend prior research (e.g., Nelson & Gruendel, 1979; Garvey & Berndt, 1977), suggesting that event representations are an important source for the content of preschoolers' pretense. Shared event knowledge allows children to interact contingently, to make relevant proposals,, and to incorporate the others' proposals into their own event enactment. In contrast, nonevent-based talk and play were much less likely to support sequentially organized, sustained interactions. Very little research has been directed toward understanding how children use their knowledge when acting in concert. Peer interaction, particularly peer discourse, offers a way of investigating this question. The results reported here indicate that shared event knowledge is basic to young children's complex discourse achievements and to their joint creation of fantasy play.

## Conclusion

In this chapter, we have considered preschoolers' descriptions of their event knowledge, their conversations with their mothers, and their conversations with one another. The specific focus of our discussion has varied across the different studies described, but in all cases we have been concerned with documenting the effects of discourse content and discourse context upon young children's use of language. In describing their scripted knowledge, children between the ages of 2;11 and 5;6 provide evidence that they possess various cognitive and linguistic abilities not generally attributed to children of this age. In talking with their mothers, 2-year-olds display advanced linguistic, representational, and conversational skills as a function of scripted discourse context and content. When preschoolers play and talk with one another, their fantasy play and most complex conversations are primarily script based.

Why should scripts play such a central role in children's language use across these different types of discourse? The most general answer to this question is very simple: Children, like the rest of us, talk best when they know what they are talking about. Scripts constitute one of the child's earliest and most stable forms of knowledge and so provide ideal discourse topics. More detailed versions of this general answer apply within the different discourse domains.

Scripts are temporally and causally organized sequences of activities having both required and optional components. Having a script necessarily involves having a representation of various relationships (temporal, causal, conditional, alternative, and so forth) that hold among the individual elements comprising a script. Repeated experience with an event provides an opportunity to acquire an understanding of these relationships. While event knowledge is probably not the sole source from which children accquire an understanding of logical relationshps, it is undoubtedly a very important source. That the language children use when describing their event knowledge reflects their knowledge of the temporal and logical structure of the events is surprising only in relation to prior research, which has tended to underestimate preschoolers' abilities because it has failed to adequately tap their experientially based knowledge. To suggest that the abilities young children display when describing scripted events are probably fragile and closely tied to specific content in no way discounts the existence of these abilities or their importance as the basis for further cognitive development.

The traditional view that the young child is unskilled in initiating and contributing to fantasy play is challenged by Lucariello's observations of mother–child dyads. The key to the competencies revealed by the 2-year-olds in this study seems to be that the children as well as their mothers had extensive knowledge of the pretense theme. Having a script necessarily involves knowledge of the roles, objects, and activity sequences associated with that event, and the young children were able to draw upon their knowledge of these components in enacting their pretense. In addition to using the available objects, the children invoked imaginary objects (e.g., beverages, napkins) that were event related. They incorporated event-related roles into their pretense by adopting these roles themselves, by using displaced reference to propose nonpresent people to fill roles and by attributing agency to the available dolls. Activities associated with the event theme were enacted and appropriately sequenced. Here again we see that when dealing with familiar well-represented content, young children reveal competencies not previously attributed to them.

All of the data on play interactions indicate the influence of discourse context upon discourse content. In Lucariello's data, much of the mother–child fantasy talk was supported by a discourse context containing props (e.g., the tea set) which elicited shared event knowledge and supported play based upon this knowledge. Similarly, French and Boynton's (1984) observations of spontaneous play in a preschool classroom indicated an interaction among discourse context, event knowledge, and discourse quality. In settings, such as a kitchen corner, which elicited shared event knowledge across participants, conversations were longer and more contingent than in settings, such as the jungle gym, which did not suggest particular thematic content. The extent to which a particular setting is necessary to support conversation about shared event knowledge is an open question, however, since Seidman's research indicates that preschool dyads can engage in complex and lengthy conversational exchanges about familiar events (e.g., food preparation, parties, visits) in play settings which do not offer direct support for the content of their dialogues. At this point we can speculate that while shared event knowledge is an important factor in determining the content of play and discourse throughout the preschool years, physical contexts that suggest and support event based pretense may gradually assume less importance as children become better able to use language to establish the thematic content of their play.

The investigations of mother–child and child–child play reported here demonstrate the powerful role shared event knowledge assumes in children's pretense and the language narrating that pretense. However, the claim that event knowledge provides an important basis for fantasy play is not meant to suggest that such play consists merely of the enactment of scripts. In play, as in fiction, one has the freedom to violate the way things really are in favor of transitory transformations of reality. Nevertheless, nonliteral play necessarily relies upon literal knowledge, and, as Garvey and Berndt (1977) suggest, event schemas contain much of the information and structure needed for symbolic play.

Interviewing children about their event knowledge constitutes a somewhat atypical discourse format in that one participant attempts to elicit information from the other using fairly standardized probes. In true dialogues, the speakers are more equal partners in creating a discourse text, and the assumption, or establishment, of shared knowledge is necessary even for adults to converse readily. Cultural routines such as cooking and birthday parties are among the limited number of topics about which young children share knowledge. We suggest that it is because scripts tend to be socially shared that they assume such an important role in young children's dialogues. Young children are able to be more successful conversationalists when they can rely upon preexisting shared knowledge as a background for their statements rather than having to establish such shared assumptions verbally. By talking about those things for which they have shared knowledge, young children are able to maintain social interaction; this, in turn, undoubtedly contributes to the development of conversational, perspective taking, and negotiation skills.

# References

Bower, G. H., Black, J. B., & Turner, T. T. (1979). Scripts in memory for texts. *Cognitive Psychology, 11,* 177-220.

Boynton, M. (1984) [Signaling shared meaning]. University of Rochester. Unpublished raw data for doctoral dissertation.

Boynton, M., & French, L. A. (1983, October). *Holding it together: Preverbal children's play in a scripted setting.* Paper presented at the Eighth Annual Boston University Conference on Language Development.

Boynton, M. & French, L. A. (1984, April). *Supporting the scaffold.* Paper presented at the Annual Meeting of the American Educational Research Association, New Orleans.

Brown, A. L. (1976). The construction of temporal succession by preoperational children. In A. D. Pick (Ed.), *Minnesota symposia on child psychology. Volume 10.* Minneapolis, MN: University of Minnesota.

Brown, A. L., & French, L. A. (1976). Construction and regeneration of logical sequences using causes or consequences as the point of departure. *Child Development, 47,* 930-940.

Brown, A L., & Murphy, M. D. (1975). Reconstruction of arbitrary versus logical sequencees by preschool children. *Journal of Experimental Child Psychology, 20,* 307-326.

Brown, R. (1973). *A first language: The early stages.* Cambridge, MA: Harvard University Press.

Brown, R., & Bellugi, U. (1964). Three processes in the child's acquisition of syntax. *Harvard Educational Review, 34,* 133-151.

Bruner, J. (1981, October). *The formats of language acquisition.* Paper presented at the Sixth Annual Boston University Conference on Language Development.

Carni, E., & French, L. A. (1984). *Before* and *after* reconsidered: What develops?, *Journal of Experimental Child Psychology, 37,* 394-403.

Clark, E. V. (1971). On the acquisition of the meaning of "before" and "after." *Journal of Verbal Learning and Verbal Behavior, 10,* 266-275.

Clark, H. H., & Clark, E. V. (1977). *Psychology and language: An introduction to psycholinguistics.* New York: Harcourt Brace Jovanovich.

Cromer, R. F. (1968). *The development of temporal reference during the acquisition of language.* Unpublished doctoral dissertation, Harvard University.

Dunn, J., & Wooding, C. (1977). Play at home and its implications for learning. In B. Tizard & D. Harvey, (Eds.), *Biology of Play.* London: Heinemann.

Emerson, H. F. (1979). Children's comprehension of "because" in reversible and non-reversible sentences. *Journal of Child Language, 6,* 279-300.

Emerson, H. F. (1980). Children's judgements of correct and reversed sentences with "if." *Journal of Child Language, 7,* 137-155.

Fein, G. (1975). A transformational analysis of pretending. *Developmental Psychology, 11,* 292-296.

Fenson, L., & Ramsay, D. S. (1980). Decentration and integration of the child's play in the second year. *Child Development, 51,* 171-178.

Fraisse, P. (1963). *The psychology of time.* New York: Harper and Row.

French, L. A. (1981, October). *But of course preschoolers understand the meaning of 'but'!* Paper presented at the Sixth Annual Boston University Conference on Language Development.

French, L. A. (1983, April). Language in Scripts. In K. Nelson (Chair), *Relations between event representations and language use.* Symposium presented at the Biennial Meeting of the Society for Research in Child Development, Detroit.

French, L. (In press). The language of events. In K. Nelson (Ed.). *Event knowledge: Structure function in development.* Hillsdale, NJ: Erlbaum.

French, L. A., & Boynton, M. (1984, March). *The effects of classroom setting upon child–child speech.* Paper presented at the Fifth Annual University of Pennsylvania Ethnography in Education Research Forum, Philadelphia.

French, L. A., & Nelson, K. (1981). Temporal knowledge expressed in preschoolers' descriptions of familiar activities. *Papers and reports on child language development, 20,* 61–69.

French, L. A., & Nelson, K. (1982). Taking away the supportive context: Preschoolers talk about the "then-and-there." *The Quarterly Newsletter of the Laboratory of Comparative Human Cognition, 4,* 1–6.

French, L. A., & Nelson, K. (in press). *Young children's knowledge of relational terms: Some ifs, ors, and buts.* New York: Springer-Verlag.

Garvey, C., & Berndt, T. R. (1977). The organization of pretend play. *Catalogue of selected documents in psychology.* American Psychological Association, *7,* (Ms. No. 1589)

Kail, M. 1980). Etude génetique des présupposés de certains morphèmes grammaticaux. Un exemple: MAIS [A developmental study of the presuppositions of some grammatical morphemes. An example: But] in *Approches du langage, 16,* 53–62.

Kavanaugh, R. D., Whittington, S. & Cerbone, M. J. (1983). Mothers' use of fantasy in speech to young children. *Journal of Child Language, 10,* 45–55.

Lucariello, J. (1983a, April). Context and conversations. In K. Nelson (Chair), *Relations between event representations and language use.* Symposium presented at the Biennial Meeting of the Society for Research in Child Development, Detroit.

Lucariello, J. (1983b, April). *Is the basic level always basic?* Paper presented at the Biennial Meeting of the Society for Research in Child Development, Detroit.

Lucariello, J., & Nelson, K. (1982, March). *Situational variation in mother–child interaction.* Paper presented at the Third International Conference on Infant Studies, Austin, TX.

McNeill, D. (1979). *The conceptual basis of language.* Hillsdale, NJ: Erlbaum.

Mandler, J. M. (1983). Representation. In P. H. Mussen (Ed.), *Handbook of child psychology: Volume III. Cognitive development* (J. H. Flavell & E. M. Markman, Volume Eds.), pp. 420–494). New York: Wiley.

Nelson, K. (1978). How young children represent knowledge of their world in and out of language. In R. Siegler (Ed.), *Children's thinking: What develops?* Hillsdale, NJ: Erlbaum.

Nelson, K. (1981). Social cognition in a script framework. In J. H. Flavell & L. Ross (Eds.). *Social cognitive development: Frontiers and possible futures.* New York: Cambridge University Press.

Nelson, K., Fivush, R., Hudson, J., & Lucariello, J. (1983). Scripts and the development of memory. In M. T. H. Chi (Ed.), *Trends in memory development research.* New York: Karger.

Nelson, K., & Gruendel, J. (1979). At morning it's lunchtime: A scriptal view of children's dialogues. *Discourse Processes, 2,* 73–94.

Nelson, K., & Gruendel, J. (1981). Generalized event representations: Basic building blocks of cognitive development. In M. Lamb & A. L. Brown (Eds.), *Advances in developmental psychology. Vol. 1.* Hillsdale, NJ: Erlbaum.

Nelson, K. & Seidman, S. (1984). Playing with scripts. In I. Bretherton (Ed.), *Symbolic play.* New York: Academic Press.

Ninio, A. & Bruner, J. S. (1978). The achievements and antecedents of labeling. *Journal of Child Language, 5,* 1–16.

Nicolich, L. M. (1977). Beyond sensorimotor intelligence: assessments of symbolic maturity through pretend play. *Merrill-Palmer Quarterly, 23,* 89–101.

Paris, S. G. (1973). Comprehension of language connectives and propositional logical relationships. *Journal of Experimental Child Psychology, 16,* 278–291.

Phillips, J. (1973). Syntax and vocabulary of mothers' speech to young children: Age and sex comparisons. *Child Development, 44,* 182–185.

Piaget, J. (1955). *The language and thought of the child.* New York: World Publishing.

Piaget, J. (1962). *Play, dreams, and imitation in childhood.* New York: Norton.

Piaget, J. (1971). *The child's conception of time.* New York: Ballantine Books.

Sachs, J. (1980). The role of adult–child play in language development. *New Directions in Child Development, 9,* 33–47.

Sachs, J. (1983). Talking about the there and then: The emergence of displaced reference in parent–child discourse. In K. E. Nelson (Ed.), *Children's Language (Vol. 4).* New York: Gardner Press.

Schank, R. C. & Abelson, R. (1977). *Scripts, plans, goals and understanding.* Hillsdale, NJ: Erlbaum.

Seidman, S. (1983a, April). Eventful play: Preschoolers' scripts for pretense. In K. Nelson (Chair), *Relations between event representations and language use.* Symposium presented at the Biennial Meeting of the Society for Research in Child Development, Detroit.

Seidman, S. (1983b, October). *Shifting sands: The conversational content of young peers at play.* Paper presented at the Eighth Annual Boston University Conference on Language Development.

Shields, M. D. (1978). Some communication skills of young children: A study of dialogue in the nursery school. In R. N. Campbell & P. T. Smith (Eds.), *Recent advances in the psychology of language: Language development and mother-child interaction.* New York: Plenum Press.

Snow, C. E. (1979). Conversations with children. In P. Fletcher & M. Garmon (Eds.) *Language Acquisition.* New York: Cambridge University Press.

Soderbergh, R. (1980). Story-telling, dramatic role play and displaced speech in play with dolls. *First Language, 1,* 209–222.

Vygotsky, L. S. (1962). *Thought and language.* Cambridge, MA: MIT Press.

# 2

## Being and Becoming:
## The Interface of Language and Family Role
## Knowledge in the Pretend Play of
## Young African American Girls*

Vonnie C. McLoyd
Shirley Aisha Ray
Gwendolyn Etter-Lewis
University of Michigan

### Introduction

Pretense, like literal behavior, is social only to the extent that the role of "the other" is taken into account (Kerckhoff, 1969). The effective role actor must understand the self–other relationship, role functions, and the suitability of a particular role in a given situation. Social pretense highlights the interdependence of roles and, as such, provides an important context within which children practice and refine interactive rules and role-taking skills (Garvey, 1977; Rubin, Fein, & Vandenberg, 1983). Moreover, because social pretense relies heavily on verbal communication between participants (Pellegrini, 1982; Smilansky, 1968), it may be especially instrumental in the refinement of linguistic aspects of social interaction.

Of the numerous anticipatory roles which children may enact during social pretense, domestic or family roles are immensely popular (Garvey, 1977; Greif, 1976; Stone, 1971). Children's conceptions of the role functions of family members derive from numerous sources including personal interactions with caregivers (e.g., mother, father, grandmother), observa-

---

* Partial support for this research was provided by grants to the first author from The University of Michigan Rackham School of Graduate Studies, the Joint Hampton–Michigan Project, and the National Research Council Postdoctoral Fellowship Program for Minorities sponsored by the Ford Foundation. The authors are grateful to Joyce Cowan and Dwight Walls, preschool administrators; to the children who served as subjects and their teachers and parents; and to Corrine Archie, Sandra Graham, Sarah Howells, Denise Person, Patricia Rich, and Malaika Wangara for transcribing and coding videotapes.

tions of the interactions of family members with one another and with others (e.g., doctors, merchants), and exposure to media representations. They are also informed by social pretense itself, as when one play partner challenges the veracity of the other's role portrayal (e.g., "You're not supposed to iron. You're the daddy.") (Matthews, 1977). Given that the actual behaviors performed during social pretense have been filtered through children's understanding of their social world, children's enactment of family roles provides an opportunity to ascertain "the extent to which children conceive of the family as a system of relationships and as a complex of reciprocal actions and attitudes" (Garvey, 1977, pp. 99–100).

In the research reported in this chapter, we focus on the language which African American preschool girls use during enactment of domestic roles and attempt to gauge their knowledge about the role appropriateness of various linguistic forms. Specifically, we describe the ways in which they modify their speech, first, according to the domestic role they assume and second, according to the domestic role assumed by the listener.

Direct questioning is one strategy researchers have used to assess children's understanding of family roles. Research employing this methodology indicates, for example, that 4- and 5-year-olds tend to distinguish parental roles (i.e., mother vs. father) in terms of nurturance and constraint (Emmerich, 1959), while 6- to 10-year-olds identify power as a critical distinguishing variable (Emmerich, 1961). However, questionnaires or interview protocols which offer a very limited range of possible responses may not capture the breadth or depth of children's knowledge of family role functions and nuances. A potentially richer indicator of how children conceive of this particular aspects of their social world is the language they use during domestic role play.

In a study attempting to disclose children's social knowledge, Matthews (1977) analyzed the domestic role play of same-sex pairs of 4-year-olds. She found that their perception of the competence of males and females varied according to the role relations involved. Specifically, in the role of mother, the female was viewed as highly competent, skillful, and managerial. However, in the role of wife, within which the role relation shifts from the child to the husband, the female was viewed as helpless and inept. The male, in contrast, was viewed as more competent in the conjugal role and less competent in the parental role.

In a study focused directly on speech and sociolinguistic behaviors, Andersen (1977) asked each of 24 3½- to 7-year-olds to "do the voice" for a number of role-specific puppets (e.g., puppets representing mother, father, young child). To elicit contrasting styles, each child was requested to play two roles at a time. Andersen found clear differences between children's representations of mother's and father's speech in style (e.g., fathers spoke in a straightforward, forceful manner; mothers were more soft-spoken, polite, and talkative, tending to explain or qualify almost everything they did or requested), pitch (e.g., fathers had deeper voices than mothers), and repertoire (e.g., fathers used many more imperatives than mothers; mothers used more endearments and baby talk terms than fathers). The speech representation for the young child, in contrast to the representations for father and mother, was characterized by the shortest utterances, use of nonlexical terms representing baby talk, use of directives that described their needs, and a larger number of utterances directed at the mother than the father. Andersen's findings indicate that children as young as preschool age are able to distinguish and use role-appropriate speech in portraying domestic roles. However, the Andersen study does not clarify the extent to which children enacting a domestic role vary their language as a function of the listener's role when the listener is another child who has also assumed a domestic role. Nor does it indicate the extent of speech modification when domestic roles other than mother, father, and young child are enacted.

Further support for the notion that young children are aware of linguistic nuances characterizing various roles comes from the work of Sachs and Devin (1976). They found that preschool children simplified their speech when talking to a real baby or baby doll in comparison to their speech to an adult or peer. For example, a 3 year, 11 month-old child used shorter utterances, fewer utterances which were not present tense, and more repetitions and imperatives when speaking to a baby or a baby doll than when speaking to her mother, suggesting that the child understood the appropriateness of altering speech to meet the needs of the listener, even when the listener was a representational toy. Sach and Devin also found that when children were asked to talk like a baby they indicated a knowledge of phonological and prosodic speech characteristics of babies.

It appears that the kind of knowledge demonstrated by children in Sachs and Devin's study develops from the social interaction that begins with the language behavior of mother and child (Cook-Gumperz, 1981). Snow (1972) reported that mothers use the age of the listener as an important cue in determining their own language production. Mothers' speech to 2-year-olds in comparison to their speech to 10-year-olds is more redundant and simplified regardless of the task or activity they are discussing. Snow suggests that these modifications by mothers provide the young child with comprehensible simplified language which facilitates the acquisition of language. This real-life language modeling by mothers may be incorporated by young children as a role-specific linguistic behavior that they adopt and employ when speaking to children younger than themselves or when enacting the role of mother during domestic pretense.

With respect to children's language in real life, it is worth noting that there is substantial evidence that children possess sociolinguistic knowledge from the very beginning of their communicative development. In an investigation of speech registers, Weeks (1971) found that children between the ages of one and five control a variety of speech styles that they utilize in interpersonal interactions. She identified 10 styles or registers most frequently used including whisper, softness, loudness, clarification, fuzzy speech, high pitch, grammatical modification, phonetic modification, exaggerated intonation, and mimicry. Bates (1976) extended the range of speech styles used by children to include dimensions of politeness. Focusing on very young children (1;8–1;10), Bates found that children not only use polite forms early, but also identified developmental changes. Later development of polite forms such as "please" and language modification include indirect commands, implied threats and promises, and the general softening of commands.

In the present study, we focus on the social role knowlege of African American preschool girls, in part, because of the dearth of research on their sociolinguistic development and socialization with respect to family roles. A consistent theme in research on African American families is the critical role played by women in family maintenance, social support, and child rearing. Particularly in child rearing, the interdependent role interactions of mother–child, grandmother–daughter–grandchild, and of sisters have been identified as central to child development (Aschenbrenner, 1975; Ladner, 1971; McAdoo, 1983; Young, 1970). While this body of literature has begun to document the importance of nurturing females in the development of African American children, it does not clarify how very young children conceive of the roles and duties of significant adult family members.

Building on the observations of Andersen (1977), the study reported in this chapter attempts to extend our knowledge of children's sociolinguistic knowledge by investigating the ways in which girls engaged in domestic role play alter their speech as a function of several listener roles including mother/wife, baby, daughter/big sister, little sister, husband/father, boyfriend, and miscellaneous adults. We analyzed language in the context of these roles and various role relationships in terms of function (i.e., declaratives imperatives, and questions) and complexity (i.e., mean length of utterances and past tense vs. no past tense). In accord with research which indicates that the conceptual notion of nonpresent time and linguistic reference to past events come relatively late in the preschool years (Bloom & Lahey, 1978), we regard the use of past tense as an indicator of greater linguistic and cognitive complexity.

## Method

### Subjects

Nine African American girls who ranged in age from 44 to 65 months were the subjects. Members of triad 1 (mean age = 49 months) were from middle-class backgrounds and attended a college-based laboratory preschool center in a small city in Virginia. Members of triad 2 (mean age = 62 months) and triad 3 (mean age = 62 months) were from lower-class backgrounds and attended a Head Start program in a small industrial city in southeastern Michigan. The girls were randomly assigned to same-age triads and were familiar with members of their respective triad.

## Setting

A trailer with a play room and video equipment/observation room (separated by a one-way mirror) was transported to the Michigan preschool center. The carpeted play room measured approximately 10 ft × 10 ft (3.1 m²) and was equipped with child-sized furniture which included a table, three chairs, and numerous play objects. Most of the play objects had an ambiguous identity and function and lacked a clear-cut referential relationship to objects in the "real" world. The objects included pieces of fabric, cardboard boxes, construction paper, styrofoam cups and cartons, pipe cleaners, paper bags, blocks, cardboard tubes, and round, flat pieces of plastic.

At the Virginia site, partitions were used to define a play area within a larger room. The research assistant who operated the video equipment stood behind the partition but was visible to the children. The play objects were the same as those made available to children in the Michigan preschool center.

## Procedure

Prior to data collection, two research assistants spent approximately four hours per day for two days in the preschool center in order to establish rapport with the children. The children were brought to the play room in random groups of three, allowed to explore the play materials, and told that in the near future they would have a chance to play there.

At the onset of data collection each triad was brought to the play room at the Michigan site where the children were told they could play. The research assistant stated that she would be working in the next room and would check on them periodically or could be summoned if needed. The research assistant then left the children alone and entered the adjoining room where a second research assistant began videotaping the triad's interaction.

At the Virginia site the research assistant who operated the camera brought the children to the play area, allowed them to explore the play materials, and told them that he would assist them if they needed help, but that they were to play on their own. Each play session lasted a total of 30 minutes. However, for the purposes of the present study, we examine a 10-minute (contiguous) segment of the play session, selected on the basis of its richness in cooperative domestic role enactment.

## Data Preparation

A written transcript of each play session was prepared. The transcripts recorded the children's verbatim verbalizations, gestures, and actions. Each transcript prepared by one research assistant was checked by another research assistant by reviewing the videotape and transcript concurrently. In the case of disagreement with the preliminary transcript, the assistant indicated how he or she thought it should be changed. The two assistants then discussed and resolved the discrepancy. If the assistants reached consensus on the speaker's identification but not on all that was said by the speaker, only those portions on which both assistants agreed were retained in the final transcript. If the assistants reached consensus on what was said but not on the speaker's identification, the entire turn (all of what one child said before another spoke) was omitted in the final transcript.

With the exception of baby talk, nonlexical items such as vocalizations directly associated with a sound property of some real or imaginary object such as "ssh" (liquid pouring sound) were omitted. Each child's turn was divided into utterances, and each utterance (conversational equivalent of written sentence or a phrase expressing one complete thought) within a turn was numbered consecutively. The percentage of transcribed words and vocalizations with which a third reviewer agreed ranged from 82% to 95% with a mean of 94%. Percentage of agreement for speaker identification ranged from 90% to 95% with a mean of 94%.

## Coding

Each utterance spoken during the selected 10-minute period was coded in terms of the domestic role assumed by the speaker, if any, and the domestic role assumed by the listener. Our focus on domestic role characters is limited to seven roles, namely, mother/wife, baby, daughter/big sister, little sister, husband/father, boyfriend, and miscellaneous adults (e.g., teacher, doctor, grocer). For the purpose of the present study, only those utterances which were spoken by a child to represent the speech of one of the imaginary domestic characters *and* were directed to a child who assumed the role of a *different* domestic character were regarded as domestic pretend utterances. Thus, utterances spoken by a child in the role of mother, for example, and directed to another triad member who had not assumed one of the seven imaginary roles or who had also assumed the role of mother were excluded.

Each domestic pretend utterance was coded for tense (i.e., past tense vs. no past tense) and length (i.e., number of words). In addition, each domestic pretend utterance was identified as a declarative, imperative, question, or as baby talk and coded for its function. The categories included the following:

1. *Declarative.* An utterance intended to give information to the listener.
   a. *Threat.* The speaker threatens the listener with physical punish-

ment or deprivation of resources (e.g., "You going to get a whipping").

   b. *Advice/instruction*. The speaker counsels the listener or recommends a decision or course of conduct—distinguished from commands which have an authoritarian quality—or attempts to teach the listener how to perform or complete a task (e.g., "You should hold the baby like this").

   c. *Fact/description of action*. The speaker imparts factual information (e.g., "The bus is outside to take you girls to school") or describes past or ongoing or future behavior or intentions (e.g., "I'm going to the store to buy groceries").

   d. *Permission*. The speaker gives permission to the listener to perform a task or behavior (e.g., "Yes, you may go outside").

   e. *Statement of preference*. The speaker expresses a wish or desire (e.g., "I wish that I could play outside").

   f. *Positive reinforcement*. The speaker praises the listener for valued behavior or qualities (e.g., "You're such a good baby 'cause you didn't cry when you got your shot").

2. *Imperative*. An utterance intended to get the listener to act, change behavior, or perform a task.

   a. *Command*. The speaker tells or orders the listener to complete a task or act in a certain manner (e.g., "Put that away").

   b. *Attention-getting*. The speaker directs the listener's attention to interaction (e.g., "Look," "See").

   c. *Prohibition*. The speaker orders the listener to refrain from doing something (e.g., "Don't take the baby outside").

3. *Question*. An utterance intended to solicit information from the listener.

   a. *External environment*. The speaker seeks information about things external to the listener (e.g., "Where is the baby's bottle?").

   b. *Internal state*. The speaker seeks information about the listener's wants, needs, and likes (e.g., "Do you want some?").

   c. *Confirmation*. The speaker seeks approval or confirmation from the listener for a statement or action, often with a tag (e.g., "I'm putting it on, OK?").

   d. *Request*. The speaker draws the listener's attention (e.g., "Know what?"), asks for something or for permission to do something (e.g., "Can I take some more?"), or politely asks the listener to do something or stop doing something (e.g., "Don't do that, OK?")

4. *Baby talk*. Nonlexical items intended to convey the sounds of an infant (e.g., babbling, cooing).

Each utterance spoken during each 10-minute sequence was coded by a research assistant and checked by a second, independent coder. In the case of disagreement, the second coder indicated how she thought the utterance should be coded. Disagreements were then resolved by a third, independent coder.

## Results

The girls produced a total of 807 utterances. Of this total, 616 (76%) were pretend utterances made in the context of domestic role enactment. Of the remaining utterances, 81 (10%) were metacommunications or verbal messages which established the "script" or context for pretend role enactment (e.g., "I'll be the mother, you be the father"), 74 (9%) were nonpretense, and 36 (5%) were uncodable. Compared to the two older triads, the youngest triad produced fewer total utterances (247, 328, 232) and proportionately fewer pretend utterances (85%, 83%, 57%)

### Language as a Function of the Speaker

Table 1 shows the frequency and proportion of pretend utterances made by and directed to one of the seven focal characters during domestic role enactment. The largest proportion of pretend utterances were produced by children in the role of mother, followed by daughter/big sister, baby, little sister, and boyfriend.

**Complexity.** As shown in Table 1, baby had a shorter mean length utterance (MLU) than mother, $t(351) = 5.92 \, p < .001$, daughter/big sister, $t(194) = 4.76 \, p < .001$, and little sister, $t = (75) = 1.91$, $p < .06$. Little sister had a shorter MLU than mother and daughter/big sister, though these differences only approached statistical significance, $t(304) = 1.63$, $p < .10$ and $t(147) = 1.67$, $p < .10$, respectively. There was no difference in the MLU of mother and daughter/big sister, $t(423) = 1.37$, $p < .10$. An analysis of the relationship between role and tense of the utterance indicated that daughter/big

Table 1. Frequency, Proportion, and Mean Length of Pretend Utterances Spoken by Seven Domestic Role Characters

| Character | Frequency | Proportion | Mean Length |
|---|---|---|---|
| Mother | 291 | .58 | 4.29 |
| Daughter/big sister | 134 | .27 | 4.76 |
| Baby | 62 | .12 | 1.97 |
| Little sister | 15 | .03 | 3.00 |
| Boyfriend | 1 | .002 | — |
| Husband/father | 0 | — | — |
| Miscellaneous adults | 0 | — | — |

*Note.* Excluded are (a) utterances made by children who assumed one of the seven roles but directed to more than one pretend character ($n = 99$) and (b) utterances for which the addressee could not be determined ($n = 14$).

sister produced proportionately more past tense utterances than mother who, in turn, produced more past tense utterances than baby or little sister (33%, 9%, 4%, 0%), $\chi^2$ (3) = 47.62, $p < .001$.

Function. Table 2 shows the proportion of declaratives, imperatives, questions, and baby talk spoken by mother, baby, daughter/big sister, and little sister. Mother made more imperatives than baby or daughter/big sister, while both mother and daughter/big sister, compared to baby, asked more questions and made more declaratives. Baby talk was produced by neither the mother nor the daughter/big sister, but constituted slightly less than one third of the utterances made by baby. These differences were highly significant, $\chi^2$ (6) = 138.30, $p < .001$. (Data for little sister were excluded because two of three cells had expected frequencies which were less than five).

There were differences in the type of declaratives spoken by children enacting the mother, daughter/big sister, and baby roles. Compared to daughter/big sister and baby, mother issued more threats (1%, 0%, 16%), offered more advice/instruction (3%, 5%, 17%) and fewer facts/descriptions of actions (78%, 68%, 39%), but gave permission about equally often (.18, .26, .28). These differences were highly significant, $\chi^2$ (6) = 35.10, $p < .001$. However, neither type of imperative nor type of question was related to role enactment.

## Language of Mother, Daughter/Big Sister, and Baby (Speaker) as a Function of the Role of the Listener

In our analyses of how children's language changes during domestic role enactment as a function of the pretend role of the listener, we exclude (a) utterances which were made by children who assumed one of the focal roles but were directed to more than one domestic pretend character, and (b) utterances for which the addressee could not be determined.

Table 2. Proportion of Different Types of Utterances Spoken by Children Enacting Different Domestic Roles

| | Type of Utterance | | | | |
|---|---|---|---|---|---|
| Role | Declarative | Imperative | Question | Baby Talk | Total Frequency |
| Mother | .43 | .40 | .17 | .00 | 260 |
| Baby | .34 | .34 | .02 | .30 | 53 |
| Daughter/big sister | .65 | .19 | .17 | .00 | 108 |
| Little sister | .08 | .58 | .33 | .00 | 12 |

*Note.* Utterances not categorized as a declarative, imperative, question or baby talk are excluded.

Complexity. Of a total of 291 utterances produced by children enacting the mother role, most were directed to baby (41%), followed by daughter/ big sister (39%), little sister (15%), miscellaneous adults (3%), and boyfriend (2%). An analysis of the relationship between mother's MLU and listener indicated that children enacting the mother role did not alter the length of their utterance as a function of whether they were speaking to baby, daughter/big sister, or little sister. Similarly, use of past tense (vs. no past tense) by mother was unrelated to role of the listener when all utterances produced by mother were examined. However, examination of only declaratives produced by mother indicated that mother was more likely to use past tense when speaking to daughter/big sister than when speaking to baby and little sister (combined) (19%, 5%), $\chi^2$ (1) = 4.43, $p < .04$.

Daughter/big sister directed most of her 134 utterances to mother (71%), followed by baby (21%), and little sister (8%). The mean length of utterances produced by daughter/big sister and directed to mother was significantly greater than those directed to baby, $M = 5.29$ vs. 3.25, $t$ (121) = 2.37, $p < .02$. Daughter/big sister was significantly more likely to use past tense when speaking to mother than when speaking to baby or little sister (42%, 15%, 0%), $\chi^2$ (2) = 12.06, $p < .01$.

Baby directed most of her 62 utterances to mother (71%), very few to daughter/big sister (29%), and none to other domestic pretend characters. Neither baby's MLU nor use of past tense differed as a function of whether the listener was mother or daughter/big sister. The low frequency of utterances by children enacting the role of little sister precluded analysis of the relationship between role of the listener and the complexity of speech produced by little sister.

Function. Table 3 shows the proportion of declaratives, imperatives, questions, and baby talk for various speaker–listener relationships. It can be seen that mother addressed more declaratives to daughter/big sister and little sister than to baby, more imperatives to baby than to daughter/big sister or little sister, and fewer questions to little sister than to daughter/big sister or baby, $\chi^2$ (4) = 9.28, $p < .05$. Examination of the relationship between role of the listener and type of declarative produced by mother indicated that mother directed more threats to baby than to daughter/big sister (19%, 14%) as well as more statements of permission (44%, 22%). In contrast, she gave advice/instruction more often to daughter than to baby (22%, 06%) and directed statements of fact/descriptions of action more often to daughter than to baby (42%, 31%), $\chi^2$ (3) = 7.89, $p < .05$. (Declaratives directed to little sister are eliminated because of low cell frequencies.)

Mother directed questions about the external environment more often to daughter/big sister than to baby (59%, 19%), but directed questions about

Table 3. Proportion of Different Types of Utterances Spoken by Mother, Daughter/Big Sister, and Baby as a Function of Listener

| Listener | Type of Utterance | | | | |
| | Declarative | Imperative | Question | Baby Talk | Frequency |
|---|---|---|---|---|---|
| | Mother to | | | | |
| Baby | .33 | .50 | .17 | .00 | 96 |
| Daughter/Big Sister | .49 | .34 | .17 | .00 | 111 |
| Little Sister | .52 | .41 | .07 | .00 | 44 |
| | Daughter/Big Sister to | | | | |
| Mother | .72 | .10 | .19 | .00 | 74 |
| Baby | .61 | .28 | .17 | .00 | 23 |
| Little Sister | .20 | .80 | .00 | .00 | 10 |
| | Baby to | | | | |
| Mother | .34 | .26 | .00 | .40 | 38 |
| Daughter/Big Sister | .33 | .53 | .00 | .13 | 15 |

*Note.* Utterances addressed to boyfriend, husband/father, and miscellaneous adults are excluded.

internal state (44%, 29%) and requests for confirmation (38%, 12%) more often to baby than to daughter/big sister, $\chi^2 (2) = 6.08$, $p < .05$. There was no relationship between role of the listener and type of imperative made by mother.

As shown in Table 3, daughter/big sister addressed more imperatives and fewer declaratives to baby and little sister (combined) than to mother, and about equal proportions of questions to each, $\chi^2 (2) = 13.46$, $p < .001$. An analysis of type of declaratives indicated that daughter/big sister directed statements of fact/descriptions of action more often to mother than to baby and little sister (combined) (69%, 38%), and statements of permission more often to baby and little sister than to mother (25%, 17%) $\chi^2 (2) = 5.57$, $p < .06$. However, neither type of imperative nor type of question produced by daughter/big sister was related to role of the listener.

Table 3 shows that baby directed relatively more imperatives to daughter/big sister than mother, more baby talk to mother than to daughter/big sister, but relatively equal proportions of declaratives to each, $\chi^2 (2) = 4.61$, $p < .10$. Analysis of type of declaratives produced by baby indicated that baby addressed statements of preference more often to mother than to daughter/big sister (78%, 0%), Fisher Exact Test, $p < .003$. There was no relationship between the role of the listener and type of imperative produced by baby.

## Discussion

In the present study, mother was clearly the more dominant, central character. She produced more than twice as many utterances as other pretend characters (most of which were directed to baby) and the greatest number of imperatives, declaratives, and questions. Mother addressed more declaratives to the daughter/big sister, more imperatives to baby, and fewer questions to little sister. Although mother did not alter the length or tense of her utterances overall according to the role of her addressee, she did tend to use more declaratives which were past tense when speaking to daughter/big sister than baby and little sister.

The functions of mother's language also varied as a function of the role of the listener. When speaking to baby, she issued more threats and statements of advice but also asked more internal-state questions, suggesting that both constraint and nurturance are functions salient in African American girls' conceptions of the mother role. This conception probably reflects, to some degree, the real-life experiences these girls have had with their own mothers. Research studies comparing the child-rearing practices of African American parents with those of European American (Bartz & Levine, 1978; Baumrind, 1972) and Chicano parents (Bartz & Levine, 1978) report a distinctive pattern of increased strictness, high control, and high support (nurturance) among African American parents. We are obviously unable to address the question of whether African American children conceive of mothers as controlling and nurturant to a greater extent than do European American children, because only African American children were subjects in the present study. Nonetheless, this question is one which merits study, especially in view of well-documented cultural differences in child-rearing practices.

Our finding that mother directed more internal-state questions to baby is consistent with findings reported by Sachs and Devin (1976). This finding may be one of the most clear-cut indications of the mother's role as caretaker because it reflects the mother's concern for the baby's health, well-being, and happiness. This degree of concern was not apparent in the mother's interaction with older children in the pretend family.

Children enacting the daughter/big sister role also showed meaningful variation in their language as a function of the role of the listener. The utterances produced by this character were more likely to be addressed to the mother. Similar to mother's interaction with baby, daughter/big sister addressed more imperatives to baby and little sister. We found particularly striking the tendency of daughter/big sister (but not mother) to use shorter and less complex utterances when speaking to baby. The speech behavior of daughter/big sister vis-à-vis baby parallels in a significant way that of real-life mothers. Previous studies of the latter show that there is a tendency for mothers to modify their speech to children according to the age of the child in the direction of less complex utterances to infants and younger children (Cross, 1977; Phillips, 1973; Snow, 1972).

The speech modification of children enacting the daughter/big sister role in the present study again may be related to socialization patterns within the African American family. Older children often assume caretaking responsibilities for younger children (Aschenbrenner, 1975; Lewis, 1971; Young, 1970) and, as a consequence, may acquire advanced role-taking skills. It may, therefore, be more appropriate to view the big sister role in African American culture as both an extension of the mother role and an advanced form of the child's role. We believe this interpretation has important implications for the further study of sex role socialization, sociolinguistic development, and culture.

Expectedly, the baby addressed most utterances to mother. There were also more statements of preference and baby talk to mother. In interacting with daughter/big sister, the baby used more imperatives than when interacting with mother. This use of imperatives by children of the pretend family is strikingly consistent. Both baby and daughter/big sister used more imperatives with each other than with mother. The implication is that since mother has a higher status than children, it is less appropriate to direct imperatives to her than to each other. On the other hand, more imperatives are addressed to the baby than to any other family member. This may be due to the baby's assumed lack of knowledge about the social and physical world. Collectively, these findings support Andersen's (1977) assertion that children are aware of many of the sociolinguistic features of social interactions. Their knowledge of social roles tends to parallel real life roles even though the child's social knowledge is still developing.

In the present study, the husband/father role was noticeable by its virtual absence. Other researchers have reported an inability or lack of desire of preschool children to develop adequately the role of father/husband during domestic pretense (Pitcher & Schultz, 1983), leading some to suggest that the dramatic play of American children functions more to prepare girls for adulthood than boys (Stone, 1971). Young children have also been reported to have less knowledge about male sex-linked objects than female sex-linked objects (Vener & Snyder, 1966). These differences in knowledge and preferences may result because the world of children is dominated by females.

Researchers have increasingly applied sequential analysis to real-life mother–child interaction to specify the nature of microlevel contingencies between mother and child during some circumscribed period of time (Maccoby & Martin, 1983). This type of analysis permits assessment of the effects of the mother and child on each other. Moreover, it lends itself to separation of the effects of the individual's own behavior, termed the *self-regulatory component* by Thomas and Martin (1976), from the effects of the behavior of one's partner, termed the *interactive component,* as determinants of an individual's behavior. We believe that use of these statistical procedures would significantly advance our understanding of the interface between children's language during episodes of interactive domestic play and their social role knowledge. For example, it would be possible to determine the extent to which internal-state questions asked by the pretend mother and directed to the pretend baby are influenced by the linguistic behavior of baby (interactive component) versus the pretend mother's own autonomous language cycles.

## References

Andersen, E. S. (1977). Young children's knowledge of role-related speech differences: A mommy is not a daddy is not a baby. *Papers and Reports on Child Language Development, 13*. Stanford, CA: Stanford University.

Aschenbrenner, J. (1975). *Lifelines: Black families in Chicago*. New York: Holt, Rinehart, & Winston.

Bartz, K. W., & Levin, E. S. (1978). Childrearing by black parents: A description and comparison to Anglo and Chicano parents. *Journal of Marriage and the Family, 40,* 709–719.

Bates, E. (1976). *Language and context: The acquisition of pragmatics*. New York: Academic Press.

Baumrind, D. (1972). An exploratory study of socialization effects on black children: Some black–white comparisons. *Child Development, 43,* 261–267.

Bloom, L., & Lahey, M. (1978). *Language development and language disorders*. New York: Wiley.

Cook-Gumperz, J. (1981). Persuasive talk: The social organization of children's talk. In J. Green & C. Wallat (Eds.), *Ethnography and language in educational settings*. Norwood, NJ: Ablex.

Cross, T. G. (1977). Mothers' speech adjustments: The contribution of selected child listener variables. In C. E. Snow & C. Ferguson (Eds.), *Talking to children: Language input and acquisition*. Cambridge, England: Cambridge University Press.

Emmerich, W. (1961). Family role concepts of children ages six to ten. *Child Development, 32,* 609–624.

Emmerich, W. (1959). Young children's discrimination of parents and child roles. *Child Development, 30,* 402–419.

Garvey, C. (1977). *Play*. Cambridge, MA: Harvard University Press.

Greif, E. B. (1976). Sex role playing in preschool children. In J. Bruner & K. Sylva (Eds.), *Play: Its role in development and evolution*. New York: Basic Books.

Kerckhoff, A. C. (1969). Early antecedents of role-taking and role playing ability. *Merrill-Palmer Quarterly, 15,* 229–247.

Ladner, J. A. (1971). *Tomorrow's tomorrow: The black woman*. New York: Anchor Books.

Lewis, D. (1975). The black family: Socialization and sex roles. *Phylon, 36,* 221–237.

Maccoby, E. E., & Martin, J. A. (1983). Socialization in the context of the family: Parent-child interaction. In E. M. Hetherington (Ed.). *Handbook of child psychology (Vol. 4)*. New York: Wiley.

Matthews, W. S. (1977). *Sex role perception, portrayal, and preference in the fantasy play of young children*. Paper presented at the meeting of the Society for Research in Child Development, New Orleans, La.

McAdoo, H. P. (1983). *Extended family support of single Black mothers.* Columbia, MD: Columbia Research Systems.

Pellegrini, A. D. (1982). The construction of cohesive text by preschoolers in two play contexts. *Discourse Processes, 5,* 101–108.

Phillips, J. (1973). Syntax and vocabulary of mother's speech to young children: Age and sex comparisons. *Child Development, 44,* 182–185.

Pitcher, E., & Schultz, L. (1983). *Boys and girls at play: The development of sex roles.* New York: Praeger.

Rubin, K. H., Fein, G., & Vandenberg, B. (1983). Play. In E. M. Hetherington (Ed.), *Handbook of child psychology (Vol. 4).* New York: Wiley.

Sachs, J., & Devin, J. (1976). Young children's use of age-appropriate speech styles in social interaction and role playing. *Journal of Child Language, 3,* 81–98.

Smilansky, S. (1968). *The effects of sociodramatic play on disadvantaged preschool children.* New York: Wiley.

Snow, C. E. (1972). Mother's speech to children learning language. *Child Development, 43,* 549–565.

Stone, G. P. (1971). The play of little children. In R. E. Herron & B. Sutton-Smith (Eds.), *Child's play.* New York: Wiley.

Thomas, E. A. C., & Martin, J. A. (1976). Analyses of parent–infant interaction. *Psychological Review, 83,* 141–156.

Vener, A. M., & Snyder, C. A. (1966). The preschool child's awareness and anticipation of adult sex roles. *Sociometry, 29,* 159–169.

Weeks, T. (1971). Speech registers in young children. *Child Development, 42,* 1119–1131.

Young, V. H. (1970). Family and childhood in a southern Negro community. *American Anthropologist, 72,* 269–288.

# 3

# Narratives in Preschoolers' Sociodramatic Play: The Role of Knowledge and Communicative Competence*

Jacqueline Sachs
Jane Goldman
University of Connecticut

Christine Chaillé
University of Oregon

## Introduction

In this study, we describe some aspects of the sociodramatic play of pre-school children and explore two factors that may account for some of the developmental changes seen in social pretense in this age group. By socio-dramatic play, we mean play in which two or more children jointly enact some kind of pretend activity based on their experiences such as playing tea party, house, or doctor. Such play can be contrasted with another kind of social pretending, thematic fantasy play that is based on fictional narratives (Smilansky, 1968).

By the end of the preschool period, many children engage in sociodrama-tic play frequently and successfully. In advanced sociodramatic play, chil-dren often assume reciprocal roles such as mommy and baby or doctor and patient (Forys & McCune-Nicolich, 1984; Garvey & Berndt, 1977). The ac-tions they carry out in these roles are not limited by the objects available in the play context; rather the children can mentally "transform" objects into those needed or invent imaginary objects (Chaillé, Goldman, & Sachs, 1983; Fein, 1975; Field, De Stefano, & Koewler, 1982; Garvey, 1977). Matthews

* We gratefully acknowledge the contributions of the University of Connecticut Child Development Laboratories, Richard Seewald, Deborah Pierson, James Donnelly, Elaine Dick-inson, Julia Dwyer, Deborah Gabriele, and Bianca Lauro. We also thank Lucia French for her comments on an earlier version of this paper.

45

(1977) introduced the term "ideational play" to identify this developmental trend in pretend play.

In younger preschoolers, the actions carried out in sociodramatic play are related only loosely to the theme of the episode, whereas older preschoolers engage in more structured sequences of actions that create a "narrative line" (Sachs, 1980; Sachs, Goldman, & Chaillé, 1984). This development seems to parallel the trend found at a younger age in solitary pretense. For example, Nicolich (1977) found that toddlers began such pretend play with isolated pretend transformations, but soon created connected sequences of pretend actions such as "cooking food" and then "feeding baby."

A number of aspects of cognitive, linguistic, and social development probably are involved in the changes in sociodramatic play that occur during the preschool period. In this study we examined two factors that seem to relate to the improvement in the ability to create and sustain a narrative line in play.

The first factor relates to the "dramatic" aspect of sociodramatic play: Knowledge of scripted events (Schank & Abelson, 1977) is necessary so that each child in the interaction can generate ideas for actions that are compatible with the theme. The second factor relates to the "social" aspect of sociodramatic play: Communicative competence is necessary so that the children can convey their ideas to one another and come to agreements about what is to be done in the play.

Before discussing each of these factors more fully, we will describe the method used for collecting the samples of play used in this study and then present a brief overview of some characteristics of the pretend play found in the age range we observed.

## Method

Thirty-six children ranging in age from 24 to 64 months were paired in same-age, same-sex dyads. Each dyad was observed in a spontaneous pretend-play situation. The members of each dyad were acquainted with one another, because they were from the same preschool class at the University of Connecticut Child Development Laboratories. Children in each dyad were within 4 months of age and were screened by a teacher for incompatibility.

Three boy dyads started play sessions but were not included in the study. In two cases, the sessions were stopped because of excessive roughhousing, and in one case the data were not used because the boys discovered that they could look through the one-way mirror into the filming room. One dyad of 2-year-old girls was not included because the children were afraid to stay in the room without an adult.

The dyads were taken by a familiar adult to a separate playroom within their preschool building. They were told only that they had a long time to play and that the teacher would come to take them back to their classroom. No specific instructions about what to play were given. The playroom was a small room furnished with two couches, low tables, and a lamp, and had a one-way mirror on one wall. Play objects were arranged on the couches and tables. There were many objects suggesting a doctor theme, such as a toy stethoscope, bandaid box, syringe, medicine bottles, and cotton. Other objects not specific to that theme also were available such as several pieces of fabric, hats, blocks, some pieces of styrofoam, and two dolls (a baby doll and a dog doll).

Toys representing the doctor theme were chosen for several reasons: (a) both girls and boys play the pretend doctor theme spontaneously; (b) children depend primarily on their own experience in playing the doctor theme compared to themes taken from fiction such as super-heroes; (c) the doctor theme has some intrinsic difficulty in that it involves reciprocal roles such as doctor and patient; and (d) the doctor role is generally preferred, leading to some conflict between the children.

The play sessions were videotaped from the next room. Each session was 16 to 30 minutes long, beginning from the time the children entered the room. The data reported here are from the first 16 minutes of each play session.

Using the videotapes, transcriptions of the utterances for each dyadic play session were made by an experimenter who had been present at the taping. Notes describing the nonverbal behaviors of the children and the context for the utterances were also included on the transcripts. Immediate self-repetition was not counted or coded as a separate utterance.

Each utterance on the transcript was coded as to whether or not it was part of a pretend play sequence. Pretend play utterances were defined as those that occurred within sequences of utterances or behaviors showing role-appropriate behavior or nonliteral use of the objects. Coding was done by two raters, each of whom coded half of the transcripts. Both raters viewed the videotapes while coding the transcripts. To assess the reliability of coding for pretend status, a third rater independently coded a 4-minute segment from each tape. The reliability of coding was .87.

## A General Description of the Play Sessions

The total number of utterances occurring during the 16-minute periods ranged from 70 to 388 per dyad. Of these utterances, from 0% to 81% per dyad were coded as part of a pretend sequence. Looking at the 2- to 5-year-old preschoolers as a group, we found that approximately half of their ut-

terances were coded as part of pretend play. This result is consistent with
the findings of other studies of pretend play in similar situations that have
measured the amount of time rather than number of utterances devoted to
pretending (e.g., Matthews, 1977, 1978).

Analyzing the data for the effect of the age of the children, we found that
the children in the older dyads (48–64 months of age) produced more utterances in the 16-minute period than did children in the younger dyads (24–47
months of age) ($t = 2.47$, $p < .05$). Pretending also increased with age independently of the number of utterances produced ($t = 2.48$, $p < .05$). This result also is consistent with findings of studies of the amount of time that
children in this age range spend in fantasy play (Rubin, Watson, & Jambor,
1978; Sanders & Harper, 1976). The biggest change seemed to occur between
2 and 3, with younger 2-year-olds producing almost no utterances coded as
pretending in this dyadic situation.

Another reflection of the older children's tendency to engage in pretend
play was the speed with which they began to play after entering the room.
Most older dyads began pretend play within the first few utterances, drawing upon a preestablished script for doctor play. Here is an example from
two 5-year-old girls who went straight to the doctor's kit upon entering the
room and explicitly mentioned the theme of the play:

> Millie:  (Indicating blood pressure gauge) What's this?
> Mona:   Wanna play doctor?
> Millie:  Well, yeah, Pretend we were both . . .
> Mona:                                              doctors.
> Millie:  Yeah. Will you be the patient for a few minutes?
> Mona:   Um, OK. Then, but then we'll both gonna be doctors.
> Millie:  Yeah.

## Differences Across Three Age Groups

To convey some of the characteristics of the narratives created by these children, we will focus exclusively on the pretend utterances, describing the
sociodramatic play qualitatively. Results will be presented in terms of three
age groups. There were four 2-year-old dyads, six 3½-year-old dyads, and
eight 5-year-old dyads. For each age group, we will focus on the boy dyad
and the girl dyad that exhibited the most pretend play on the doctor theme.

**The 2-year-olds.** The 2-year-olds engaged in very little pretense. They
did not assume roles (Sachs, Goldman, & Chaillé, 1984; see also Garvey,
1982, and Musatti, 1980). They also showed no creation of story lines in their
play. Pretending that involved use of the doctor toys consisted merely of

using the object on the other child or on the self, as in the following two examples:

> Bobbie:   (Puts on stethoscope and "listens" to Lydia's heart) Want your
>           heartbeat? (Bobbie puts the syringe up to her nose) This is my nose
>           medicine.

Contrary to expectations based on notions of egocentrism in young children (Piaget, 1926), the 2-year-olds often did play cooperatively rather than in parallel. Much of the cooperation seemed to be based on attending to what the other child was saying or doing and often imitating utterances or actions.

**The 3½-year-old boys.** In the 3½-year-old age group, the boys did little creation of narratives. In the dyad with the most pretend play involving the doctor theme, all of the pretending involved only object transformations. For example, one boy repeatedly tried to get the other to pretend to "drink medicine." Neither boy was in a role in this interaction. That is, no roles had been explicitly identified and neither boy signaled that he was portraying the doctor or the patient by a shift in tone of voice or speech content.

> Jud:    You want some medicine?
> Sam:    No.
> Jud:    Want some medicine?
> Sam:    No. I don't want any medicine. I have to have some.
> Jud:    Want some? Good for you.
> Sam:    I don't want [          )
> Jud:                 [This one has cookies in it.
> Sam:    Oh. I don't like them chocolate chips. They're chocolate chips? Chocolate chips? I got them at home.
> Jud:    Want some? Good for you. Sip. Just a little sip.
> Sam:    No.

Though the doctor and patient roles never were mentioned by the boys in this dyad, two other roles were referred to briefly but were not followed up by any play relating to the role. Once Jud put on a hat and said "cowboy" and once he said he was a "giant."

**The 3½-year-old girls.** The 3½-year-old girl dyad with the most doctor play was very different from the same-aged boy dyad. These girls took roles such as doctor, patient, mommy, and baby and explicitly talked about their adoption of roles.

Sometimes a 3½-year-old girl invented symptoms, providing a problem element that motivated the treatment. Here is an example of a symptom-treatment sequence.

> Hannah: (Speaking of doll "patient") Oooo. Bleeding. What do you have to do, doctor?
> Sandra: Gonna have to do her blood.

In this particular dyad, suggestions from one child were often blocked by the other child (we will look later at an analysis of disagreements), so that a connected story line failed to emerge in spite of the mention of a problem element that might have served as the focus for plot development:

> Hannah: She's bleeding, I think.
> Sandra: No she isn't.

In spite of the occasional mention of a problem element, most of the doctor play of these girls still consisted of using a doctor toy with a related utterance without linking these behaviors to other actions or utterances in the play:

> Sandra: (Takes "medicine" out of the bottle with the syringe) Now her medicine on her.

**The 5-year-old boys.** The 5-year-old boys differed from the younger children in terms of their elaboration of the story line. For example, they mentioned preparation for the treatment, thereby establishing a setting for subsequent actions, as in "Gotta bring him in the bed first."

Like the 3½-year-old girls, the 5-year-old boys also occasionally mentioned a symptom, providing a problem element motivating a subsequent pretend action, as in "Oh my leg's killing me. Probably because it's broke. Check if it's broke." There was also occasional mention of follow-up care: "Do I hafta sleep over, doctor?"

In spite of these differences between the 5-year-old boys and the younger children, most of their play still consisted of the use of an object paired with an explanation of the use, as in the following three examples:

> I hafta give a shot.
>
> Now I hafta take your heart beat.
>
> We better take my blood pressure up there.

**The 5-year-old girls.** In the 5-year-old girl dyad with the most doctor play, there were far fewer instances of simply using the doctor toys with

accompanying utterances. A frequent element in the 5-year-old girls' play
—not found in the younger children's play and only seldom found in the 5-
year-old boys' play—was a focus on the setting for the play. For example,
at several points during the play (not just at the beginning), utterances were
used to establish the locale, as in

> That's the waiting room.
>
> Yeah, this is the laying down room.
>
> Pretend we needed to put you in the emergency room.

In the play of these girls, there also were more utterances devoted to describing the problem element in doctor play, the symptom. Thus treatments
did not stand alone but were in the context of a story line, as in the following two examples:

> He has a chill. (The doll) Now we'll cover him up.
>
> Pretend you had a bad cut. Real bad. Where's your bad cut, here? (Puts cot-
> ton on knee)

Sometimes the rationale for the present action even was stated in terms
of a pretend past event or state. Such utterances, not found in any of the
other groups, supplied a context for the events to follow. They are especially
interesting in that they require an inference about what would be expected
next, given a certain action or state:

> We both were in a car and we got in a accident.
>
> Pretend I came here, walking home, like this. (Walks with a limp) You said,
> "I'm gonna bring you to the doctor's."

As was the case for the 5-year-old boys, plots sometimes included reference to follow-up care: "I need some things to take home with me, right?"
The episodes of connected actions were somewhat longer and more complex in the 5-year-old girl dyads than in the other children's. Among these
oldest preschool girls, most of the play consisted of repeated rounds of problems and solutions (symptoms and treatments) with some further elaboration. Such rounds are similar to the plots found by Sutton-Smith, Botvin,
and Mahoney (1976) in elicited narratives of 5- and 6-year-olds, which were
made up of repeated rounds with themes such as chase and escape or attack
and defense. These results suggest that there may be parallels between the
skills used in the creation of plots in dyadic sociodramatic play and the narrative skills found in story telling. It would be most interesting to look at the
creation of stories and sociodramatic play in the same children.

## Comparisons Across Groups

In this study, the older dyads also were different from the younger ones in that they marked the distinction between reality and fantasy more overtly (Sachs, Goldman, & Chaillé, 1984). They were more likely to speak about the theme to be played, agreeing or arguing about whether or not they would play "doctor." They also sometimes commented on whether or not actions were part of pretend:

> Jacob: Will it hurt really bad?
> Chuck: It will hurt kinda like—uh—we're just playing, right?
> Jacob: Right.

Galda (1984) has pointed out that there is a parallel between the development of children's narratives and the development of play with regard to the child's awareness of the reality–fantasy distinction. In the development of narrative abilities, there is an increase in the use of devices that serve to mark a story as a special genre. For example, Applebee (1978) analyzed stories for story-telling conventions and found an increase with age in the use of such devices as a formal beginning, a formal ending, and the consistent use of past tense to mark the narrative mode. In children's play, we find a similar development of awareness of the status of pretense. In toddlers, the boundary between reality and fantasy is at first quite vague (Scarlett & Wolf, 1979; Wolf & Pusch, this volume). For example, instead of working out a character's problem within the play framework, the young child may simply solve the problem for the character by intervening. The child does not see that he/she is outside the framework of the pretend play. As children get older, they begin to use various markers that indicate that they know they are pretending. Garvey (1977) argued that this awareness of the fact that actions are not to be taken literally is a crucial step in learning to engage in pretend play. Once again, the results of this study suggest a parallel between narrative abilities and sociodramatic play abilities.

Comparing the boys and girls in the three age groups in this study, it appears that there may be a sex difference in the development of sociodramatic play, with the girls in our sample being somewhat ahead of the boys at each age. In terms of the creation of elements of a narrative line, the play of the 3½-year-old boys was similar to the 2-year-olds' play and the play of the 5-year-old boys was similar to the 3½-year-old girls' play. Such a result would be consistent with some other findings on sex differences in pretend play. Matthews (1977) found that the 4-year-old girls she studied were more ideational than the boys. Similarly, McLoyd (1980), investigating play in 3- to 5½-year-old black children, found more fantasy transformations by girls than by boys. Field, De Stefano, and Koewler (1982), however, have pointed out that the preferred type of fantasy play might be different for boys and girls, because they found that preschool girls engaged in more person fantasy (role play), whereas the boys engaged in more object-based fantasy. Clearly, further research is required to understand whether there are sex differences in the development of sociodramatic play, and if so, what the reasons for the differences are.

With this brief look at the type of play found in the three age groups, let us turn to two analyses that reveal some of the reasons for the nature of the play.

## Knowledge About the Doctor Theme

The first analysis concerning factors that may be involved in the development of narratives focused on the children's knowledge about the doctor play theme. Children build up representations of the events in which they participate. These event representations, called "scripts" by Schank and Abelson (1977), are involved in children's ability to talk about events (Eisenberg, 1982; French, Lucariello, Seidman, & Nelson, this volume; Lucariello, 1983; Nelson & Gruendel, 1981; Sachs, 1983; Seidman, 1983). In this study, children with more complete doctor scripts could presumably use that knowledge in constructing the narrative line in their play. Older children, on the average, have had more opportunity to build up doctor scripts, based on the child's own visits to the doctor, exposure to stories about such visits (e.g., on TV or in children's books), or previous doctor play. Thus, we expected that older children would have more of an internal script that could be used in constructing pretend episodes and would engage in more advanced pretend play around that theme.

Several observations in our study support this hypothesis. First, younger children did less pretend play using the doctor theme. While they explored the various doctor-related objects that were available, when they pretended, they often used different themes. The play of the 2-year-olds did not involve a consistent theme at all. In the 3½-year-old age group, one boy dyad attempted to play doctor, but quickly switched to a theme about killing monsters. A 3½-year-old girl dyad, similarly, gave up the doctor theme and pretended that they were mommies, each with her own baby doll.

Second, in the older dyads, we occasionally found cases in which one child would make up a complete (though brief) story, as in the following example from a 5-year-old girl dyad. In this example, Sheila invented a symptom for her doll, treated the problem, and described follow-up care:

> (Using dog doll) He's sick. He has a chill. Now we'll cover him up. (Collecting objects) There. Aspirins. Bandaids. That's all to bring home with him.

As two indices of knowledge, we looked at the children's use of medical terms and their knowledge of the functions of the doctor-related toys to see whether the older children were different from the younger ones. In Table 1,

Table 1. Mean Number of Medical Terms Used and Functions Known

| Age (years) | Medical Terms | | Functions | |
|---|---|---|---|---|
| | Boys | Girls | Boys | Girls |
| 2 | 1.50 | 2.00 | 1.50 | .50 |
| 3½ | 1.66 | 5.00 | 1.66 | 1.66 |
| 5 | 4.75 | 6.00 | 3.75 | 2.25 |

we see that older children used more words that were related to the medical setting, such as "stethoscope," "emergency room," "pneumonia," and "sore throat."

Knowledge about doctor situations, as reflected in use of appropriate vocabulary, could help a child structure the pretense. In the following example from two 5-year-old girls, each girl was vying to have her doll be the focus of the play. Lana's introduction of the word "pneumonia" guaranteed her success in controlling the subsequent interaction. The two children had shared knowledge that being "pneumonia sick" is a problem deserving immediate attention.

    Lana:   My baby's so sick, my baby (doll). We gotta (          )
    Jean:                                            That's
            the same thing with my baby.
    Lana:   I have something different...
    Jean:                           Mine is sicker a lot.
    Lana:   Mine's pneumonia.
    Jean:   Yours is pneumonia sick, you mean?
    Lana:   Uh huh. Bring her to the hospital. (Girls play with Lana's doll, bring-
            ing it to the couch)

Table 1 also indicates that older children were more likely to demonstrate by their utterances or actions that they knew something about the function of the four toy instruments that were present: a stethoscope, a syringe, a plethysmograph, and a reflex hammer. We mean by "knowledge of function" that the child knew how the piece of equipment was used: for example, putting the stethoscope on the other child's chest rather than talking into it like a microphone. The children often knew that the stethoscope was used on the chest or that it was used for hearing heartbeats. The syringe was well known, often referred to as the "shotter." Some children knew that the plethysmograph was used for taking blood pressure or at least that it was to be wrapped around the arm. Many children knew that the reflex hammer was to be used on the knees.

As well as increasing in knowledge of vocabulary and function, the older children (especially the boys) sometimes invented names for objects that were based on their functions, as in "heart-thing" for the stethoscope, "ouch-thing" for the syringe or "hammer-knee" for the reflex hammer.

As is the case for knowledge of vocabulary, knowledge of the functions of the play objects can have effects on the success of the play. Here is an example in which there was a discrepancy in knowledge about blood pressure between two boys:

Seth: What—how much is it?
John: I don't know, but I took your blood pressure and that's the end of that.

At this point, the two boys broke out of their pretend roles and simply explored the objects for a while before resuming play. Quite often, lack of knowledge on the part of one or both children brought a halt to the development in the play.

Other investigators also have found that doctor play presents some difficulties to children that may be based on the absence of knowledge about the appropriate roles and actions. For example, Andersen (1977) studied children's ability to role-play using puppets representing several different characters. She analyzed various aspects of role-appropriate speech as an index of the child's ability to carry out the role. She found that young children could enact the roles of mother, father, and baby quite well, but had difficulty taking the roles of doctor, nurse, and patient. Snow, Shonkoff, Lee, and Levin (1981) looked explicitly at the effect of the experience of hospitalization on 4- to 9-year-old children's ability to role-play using the doctor theme. They found that preschoolers had much difficulty with role enactment in this situation before they were hospitalized, but improved in their doctor play after their hospital experience. The children's play after hospitalization included more medical vocabulary, reflecting their increased knowledge after the experience.

## Communicative Competence

A second analysis focused on one aspect of the children's communicative competence. Beyond having knowledge about the situation to be enacted, in order to create a story jointly children must communicate their ideas to one another and come to agreements about what is to be done.

Until recently, most researchers, following Piaget's (1926) notions regarding the egocentric nature of young children's communication, have emphasized the difficulty preschoolers have in sustaining conversations. However, several studies now have shown that children do have some skills needed for maintaining a conversation even at a remarkably young age. For example, Mueller (1972) videotaped the interactions of unacquainted 3½-to 5½-year-olds, and found that 62% of their utterances received either a verbal or nonverbal response from the other child. Similarly, Garvey and Hogan (1973) found that familiar 3½- to 5-year-olds were mutually engaged for 66% of their verbal interactions. Garvey and Hogan concluded that although there was some egocentric, private speech of the sort that Piaget had described, most of the children's behavior was social.

One way to assess the child's ability to sustain conversation is to look at the extent to which adjacent conversational turns relate to one another. Halliday and Hasan (1976) have developed formal criteria for assessing cohesion in discourse; some investigators have used formal criteria such as the repetition of a lexical item or anaphora to study the emergence of cohesion in adult–child or child–child conversations (e.g., Bernstein, 1981; Bloom, Rocissano, & Hood, 1976; Pellegrini, 1982). As well as being related through these formal cohesion devices, conversational turns may be related because they make reference to the same discourse topic (Keenan & Schieffelin, 1976). It is this more general type of relatedness that we examined in this study.

To assess the extent to which the two children in an interaction were communicating effectively, we performed an analysis of the degree of relatedness between the children's adjacent conversational turns. In this same analysis, we also looked at the amount of agreement from turn to turn during pretending. Each turn was coded as related or unrelated to the preceding turn, and as agreeing or disagreeing with the preceding turn. Turns were also coded as spontaneous or elicited.

To carry out the coding, at each point in the dialogue where a turn transition took place, the utterance of the child who had just begun speaking was coded with respect to the last utterance of the child who had just stopped speaking. In the following dialogue, the italicized line is the one that would be coded:

> Lana:   My baby's so sick, my baby doll.
> Jean:   *That's the same thing with my baby.*

In this case, we would want the coding to reflect the fact that the second utterance was related in terms of topic to the first (it followed from the turn preceeding) and that it was in agreement. Contrast the following turn transition:

> Lana:   (Talking about "treating" her doll) And I feel bad for his arm. He doesn't feel well.
> Jean:   (Puts on a beret) *My hat.*

Here the transition utterance is not related to the topic of the other child's utterance. In still another case, an utterance might be on the established topic, but disagreeing with the other child:

Lana:   OK, and I'll be the doctor for my baby and you be the doctor for your baby.

Jean:   *No, I have—I'm the doctor for each of the babies. And then next time you're the doctor for each of the babies, right?*

All of these examples are ones in which the second child spoke spontaneously. That is, there was not an obligatory environment for a reply. Such utterances were coded as "spontaneous." Other utterances were "elicited," as in

Jean:   Pretend they were called drops, right?

Lana:   *Right.*

Elicited utterances, like spontaneous ones, could be in agreement or disagreement with the preceeding utterance.

The coding system for turn transitions, then, was as follows:

1.   Related, spontaneous, agreeing (supporting)
2.   Related, spontaneous, agreeing but minimal (e.g., "right" or "yes")
3.   Related, spontaneous, agreeing, but an imitation
4.   Related, spontaneous, disagreeing
5.   Related, elicited, agreeing
6.   Related, elicited, disagreeing
7.   Clarification request
8.   Clarification
9.   Unrelated
10.  Ambiguous or uncodable

The subjects for this analysis were all of the children in dyads in which there was more than a minimal amount of doctor play. There were two 3½-year-old dyads of each sex and four 5-year-old dyads of each sex. Transcripts for all of the dyads were coded by one rater. A subset of the transcripts was coded by a second rater, with a coding reliability of .82.

Table 2 shows the average percentage of utterances that were related to the other child's last utterance (that is, all utterances coded with categories 1–8). A 2 (age) by 2 (sex) analysis of variance on these data indicated that there was no significant effect of age or sex on the overall percentage of re-

**Table 2. The Percentage of Utterances Related to, Supporting of, or Agreeing With the Other Child's Last Utterance**

| Age (years) | Related (%) | | Supporting (%) | | Agreeing (%) | |
|---|---|---|---|---|---|---|
| | **Boys** | **Girls** | **Boys** | **Girls** | **Boys** | **Girls** |
| 3½ | 80 | 71 | 05 | 17 | 15 | 36 |
| 5 | 88 | 73 | 30 | 39 | 56 | 58 |

lated utterances. This result is consistent with the results of Mueller (1972), who found no difference in conversational responsiveness in the 3½- to 5½-year-old range.

The utterances coded in category 1 (related, spontaneous, and agreeing) represent the highest level of utterance relatedness. Such utterances are not only on the same discourse topic, but they *support* the topic. They are in agreement and add something more than a minimal response to the established topic. Looking at this highest level of related utterance, we find that 5-year-olds had more turn transitions of this type (see Table 2). An analysis of variance for supporting utterances yielded a significant main effect for age, $F(1, 23) = 4.91$, $p < .01$. Boys did not differ from girls in their use of supporting utterances and sex did not interact with age.

Table 2 also shows the amount of agreement in the dyads. Here again, the 5-year-olds were different from the younger children. An analysis of variance for the agreement data indicated that the 5-year-olds used significantly more utterances indicating agreement than the 3½-year-olds, $F(1, 23) = 8.75$, $p < .001$. Again no sex difference and no interaction were found.

When the older children did disagree, it appeared that they were more successful in coming to a compromise. For example, some children called on notions of fairness and turntaking when there was a disagreement over roles: "Your turn to be doctor, maybe?" Children in one dyad, who both wanted the doctor role, even agreed that each one would get to be doctor "for five minutes," even though, of course, neither child could tell time.

## The Relationship Between Knowledge and Communicative Competence

Thus far, we have discussed the role of children's knowledge and the role of their communicative competence in the creation of narratives as if these two factors were independent. However, it is quite likely that the two interact. Recent research has shown that it is easier for children to carry on cohesive conversations if the topic of the talk is a familiar, scripted topic. For example, Foster (1982) has examined the conversations of 1- to 2-year-old children with their mothers. She found that when the conversation was about a very familiar topic (a routine or ritualized conversation), the young child could produce a greater number of turns related to the topic than when the topic was novel.

Similarly, Lucariello (1983) recorded the conversations of children between 24 and 29 months with their mothers. Three situations were observed. In one, the mother and child engaged in a familiar, highly routinized situation such as bathtime. In the second, the mother and child played with toys common for young children, such as a tea set and a pull-toy train. In the third situation, the mother and child played with a model castle (it was assumed that the young children did not yet know a "castle script"). Lucariello found that the children's conversations were much more successful in the more familiar contexts. For example, the mean number of turns per conversation for the routine (such as bath time) was 17, whereas the mean number of turns in the castle play was only 9. (See also French et al., this volume, for a discussion of these data.)

Based on such results, we would expect that the older children, with more knowledge of the doctor script, would be able to draw on this shared knowledge and thus construct cohesive conversations more readily. One goal for future research is to assess independently the roles of knowledge and increased cohesion skills for conversational ability in young children.

## Conclusions

In this study of dyadic sociodramatic play in preschoolers, we found that all the children used relevant utterances to accompany their play with the various doctor toys. However, only the oldest children's utterances consistently provided a motivation for the subsequent toy usage. Brief narratives were constructed by the older children. These narratives consisted primarily of repetitive rounds of a "symptom–treatment" theme. Two factors that may contribute to more coherent narrative structures in the older children were examined: knowledge about the play theme and communicative competence.

The older children seem to have had more knowledge of a doctor script and this knowledge contributed to the construction of a narrative line. Knowledge of the doctor script was reflected in the play itself, in the children's use of vocabulary related to the doctor theme, and in their understanding of the functions of the doctor play objects.

The children's increase in communicative competence is reflected in the fact that the older children used more utterances that built on the topic the other child had established and provided support for it. The emergence of greater cohesion in conversation is in itself probably based on a number of changes in children's linguistic and discourse abilities. It is likely that older children are better able to understand the utterance of their play partner, to ascertain an underlying topic from a series of utterances, and to realize that their next utterance should be related to the established topic.

The older children agreed more with one another, whereas the play of the younger children was often blocked by disagreement. While it is not likely that older children are intrinsically more agreeable, they seem to have better strategies for dealing with disagreement and coming to a compromise so that the play can proceed.

Finally, we suggest that knowledge about the play theme and communicative competence interact. It is easier for a child to engage in discourse on a topic when that topic is well known. There are undoubtedly many other aspects of cognitive, linguistic, and social development that underlie the changes that take place in sociodramatic play during the preschool years. Much research lies ahead before we fully understand this complex, intriguing and important part of childhood.

## References

Andersen, E. S. (1977). *Learning to speak with style: A study of the sociolinguistic skills of children.* Unpublished doctoral dissertation, Stanford University.

Applebee, A. N. (1978). *The child's concept of story.* Chicago: University of Chicago Press.

Bernstein, L. (1981). Language as a product of dialogue. *Discourse Processes, 4,* 117–147.

Bloom, L., Rocissano, L., & Hood, L. (1976). Adult-child discourse: Developmental interaction between information processing and linguistic knowledge. *Cognitive Psychology, 8,* 521–552.

Chaillé, C., Goldman, J., & Sachs, J. (1983, April). *Representational object use in the symbolic play of preschool children.* Paper presented at a meeting of the Society for Research in Child Development, Detroit, MI.

Eisenberg, A. (1982). *Language acquisition in cultural perspective: Talk in three Mexicano homes.* Unpublished doctoral dissertation, University of California, Berkeley.

Fein, G. (1975). A transformational analysis of pretending. *Developmental Psychology, 11,* 291–296.

Field, T., De Stefano, L., & Koewler, J. H. (1982). Fantasy play of toddlers and preschoolers. *Developmental Psychology, 68,* 503–508.

Forys, S. K. S., & McCune-Nicolich, L. (1984). Shared pretend: Sociodramatic play at 3 years of age. In I. Bretherton (Ed.), *Symbolic play: The development of social understanding.* New York: Academic Press.

Foster, S. (1982). Learning to develop a topic. *Papers and Reports on Child Language Development, 21,* 63–70.

Galda, L. (1984). Narrative competence: Play, storytelling, and story comprehension. In A. D. Pellegrini & T. Yawkey (Eds.), *The development of oral and written langauge in social contexts.* Norwood, NJ: Ablex.

Garvey, C. (1977). *Play.* Cambridge: Harvard University Press.

Garvey, C. (1982). Communication and the development of social role play. In D. Forbes & M. T. Greenberg (Eds.), *Children's planning strategies (New Directions for Child Development,* No. 19). San Francisco, CA: Jossey-Bass.

Garvey, C., & Berndt, R. (1977). The organization of pretend play. *Catalog of Selected Documents in Psychology.* American Psychological Association, 7, Ms. #1589.

Garvey, C., & Hogan, R. (1973). Social speech and social interaction: Egocentrism revisited. *Child Development, 44,* 562–568.

Halliday, M. A. K., & Hasan, R. (1976). *Cohesion in English.* London: Longman.

Keenan, E. O., & Schieffelin, B. B. (1976). Topic as a discourse notion. In C. N. Li (Ed.), *Subject and topic.* New York: Academic Press.

Lucariello, J. (1983, April). *Context and conversations.* Paper presented at a meeting of the Society for Research in Child Development, Detroit, MI.

Matthews, W. S. (1977). Modes of transformation in the initiation of fantasy play. *Developmental Psychology, 13,* 212–216.

Matthews, W. S. (1978). Sex and familiarity effects upon the proportion of time young children spend in spontaneous fantasy play. *The Journal of Genetic Psychology, 133,* 9–12.

McLoyd, V. C. (1980). Verbally expressive modes of transformation in the fantasy play of black preschool children. *Child Development, 51,* 1133–1139.

Mueller, E. (1972). The maintenance of verbal exchanges between young children. *Child Development, 43,* 930–938.

Musatti, T. (1980). *Social interaction among toddlers during pretend play.* Unpublished manuscript, Istituto di Psicologia, Consiglio Nazionale delle Richerche, Rome, Italy.

Nelson, K., & Gruendel, J. M. (1979). At morning it's lunchtime: A scriptal view of children's dialogs. *Discourse Processes, 2,* 73–94.

Nicolich, L. (1977). Beyond sensorimotor intelligence: Assessment of symbolic maturity through analysis of pretend play. *Merrill-Palmer Quarterly, 23,* 89–101.

Pellegrini, A. D. (1982). The construction of cohesive text by preschoolers in two play contexts. *Discourse Processes, 5,* 101–107.

Piaget, J. (1926). *The language and thought of the child.* London: Routledge & Kegan Paul.

Rubin, K. H., Watson, K., & Jambor, T. (1978). Free play behavior in preschool and kindergarten children. *Child Development, 49,* 534–536.

Sachs, J. (1980). The role of adult–child play in language development. In K. H. Rubin (Ed.), *Children's play (New directions for child development,* No. 9). San Francisco, CA: Jossey-Bass.

Sachs, J. (1983). Talking about the there and then: The emergence of displaced reference in parent–child discourse. In K. E. Nelson (Ed.), *Children's language (Vol. 4).* Hillsdale, NJ: Erlbaum.

Sachs, J., Goldman, J., & Chaillé, C. (1984). Planning in pretend play: Using language to coordinate narrative development. In A. Pellegrini & T. Yawkey (Eds.), *The development of oral and written language in social contexts.* Norwood, NJ: Ablex.

Sanders, K. M., & Harper, L. V. (1976). Free-play fantasy behavior in preschool children: Relations among gender, age, season, and location. *Child Development, 47,* 1182–1185.

Scarlett, W. G., & Wolf, D. (1979). When it's only make-believe: The construction of a boundary between fantasy and reality in storytelling. In E. Winner & H. Gardner (Eds.), *Fact, fiction, and fantasy in childhood (New directions for child development,* No. 6). San Francisco, CA: Jossey-Bass.

Schank, R. C., & Abelson, R. P. (1977). *Scripts, plans, goals, and understanding.* Hillsdale, NJ: Erlbaum.

Seidman, S. (1983, October). *Shifting sands: The conversational content of young children.* Paper presented at a meeting of the Boston University Conference on Language Development.

Smilansky, S. (1968). *The effects of sociodramatic play on disadvantaged preschool children.* New York: Wiley.

Snow, C., Shonkoff, F., Lee, K., & Levin, H. (1981, August). *Learning to play doctor: The acquisition of knowledge about roles.* Paper presented at a meeting of the International Association for the Study of Child Language, Vancouver, Canada.

Sutton-Smith, B., Botvin, G., & Mahoney, D. (1976). Developmental structures in fantasy narratives. *Human Development, 9,* 1–13.

# PART II
# PLAY AND LITERATE LANGUAGE

# 4

## The Origins of Autonomous Texts in Play Boundaries*

Dennis P. Wolf

James Pusch
Harvard University

### The Concept of "Autonomous" Text

As language users we frequently combine what is said or written (a text) with surrounding information (context) in order to make sense. It is this ability to combine text and context which permits us to make sense of all kinds of abbreviations or oddities we meet in language—pronouns, ellipses, the utterances of 2-year-olds or the neologisms of new-to-a-language speakers. For example, a sentence like "Take it from her and put it here" is almost meaningless, until we look around and see who "her" refers to and what "it" is. Similarly, we can only decipher what a 2-year-old means by "That daddy drink" once we see if he is looking at his father's mug or a man across the room having a soda. However, as language users, we are also faced with the necessity of distinguishing or drawing a boundary between text and context. Making this distinction lets us enjoy fiction, catch onto sarcasm, or separate what was stated from what was implied. If I haven't slept for days and someone says, "You look splendid," my ability to perceive the mismatch between text and context lets me in on the speaker's sarcasm.

In cultures, it appears that speakers and writers come to draw this distinction between text and context with a special sharpness. In those cul-

* This paper was originally a part of a symposium, "Play and the Development of Narrative Competence," presented at the annual meeting of the American Educational Research Association, Montreal, Canada, April 11–15, 1983.

We wish to thank the Carnegie Corporation and the Spencer Foundation for funding which supported the Early Symbolization Project. We would also like to thank Sharon Grollman, Pat McKernon, Shelley Rubin, and Jennifer Shotwell for their help in collecting and transcribing the data; Paula Blank for her initial conceptualization of the issues; and Howard Gardner for his comments.

tures, the convention is that "texts"—especially formal written ones—should be composed and responded to as if they were "autonomous" of the situation in which writers set them down or readers encounter them. In other words, book-based cultures teach that well-formed texts convey most of the information a reader needs while depending minimally on information that exists in the surrounding context (Olson, 1977). To illustrate: In reading classes, teachers teach children how to search preceding paragraphs as well as their knowledge of the real world for answers to comprehension questions. Writing instruction is based on learning to communicate with an anonymous and uninformed reader. We have at least one tradition of literary criticism which confines its attention absolutely to the text, shutting out biographical or historical information (Richards, 1929).

### Two Sides of Autonomous Texts: The Lexical and the Pragmatic

A number of different linguistic studies have outlined how speakers and writers use words and phrases to construct an autonomous text. For example, much of the information a listener or reader is to extract must be *in the text* rather than elsewhere (Olson, 1977; Scollon & Scollon, 1979, 1980; Wolf, 1985). Additionally, the different parts of the text should refer to or reflect back on one another in clear and legitimate ways. Thus, speakers and writers must observe the rules for careful anaphoric reference ("One day a boy... That boy... He...") (Bartlett, 1979; Halliday & Hasan, 1976). Finally, in composing texts, speakers and writers can make use of a special set of internal-to-the-text references ("Later in this paper..."; "In conclusion, let me reiterate...") (Halliday & Hasan, 1976).

However, the following example of make-believe play in a 5-year-old suggests that there is a second aspect of autonomous text-making which comes to the fore when we look at oral texts such as plays, lectures, or tales:

M (5;2 years) is playing alone on her living room floor with a pile of blocks and an assortment of small toys and figures. She alternately narrates, speaks for the figures, and performs the actions she describes.

"This is going to be where these people live. They all live in a city. A big, big one." She stands up a tall block: "The church." She lays a line of flat blocks end-to-end. "Some roads for them." "They need a house ... So this way and this one." She builds an arch and fits several little figures under it.

M turns to the observer: "They might be cold in that place (she points to arch openings). She scans her supplies, settles on the shoe box from which the blocks came, and stands it up. "See, there's their house, an apartment house." The box threatens to tip over, but M simply rights it and stabilizes it by placing a block inside. She places a ruler next to the shoe box. "An elevator."

M picks up one of the doll figures and speaks in a high voice for it: "Mommy, mommy, I want to ride in the elevator."

M stands up a taller figure: "Okay, we can do that in a minute. Wait for me."

M: (as child) "No, now, I want to go now."

M: (as mother) "You have to wait for me."

M: (as narrator) "And they talked and talked until they went to the elevator."

M places the figures at base of the "elevator." Again, the whole construction nearly tumbles over.

M: (as mother) "See, it's a dangerous, it's tippy, that's why you have to go with grown-ups."

M reaches over to place the dolls in, and this time the construction does fall down. She turns to the observer, "Say I didn't do it. Pretend it fell down by itself."

M: (as narrator) "So they had to walk up the steps and the girl and her mother were very sad." She moves the two figures up the side of the shoe box in a series of short hops.

In such situations the speaker and listener both have to create and maintain the illusion of a gap between the world of the text and the literal context in which the text is being written or spoken. There should be no references which can be clarified only by turning to the world outside the text. Moreover, events in that contextual world must be kept from barging into and rupturing the text itself. Thus, even in oral narratives, young speakers from literate cultures are mindful of a set of *pragmatic rules* which create and sustain an alledged separation between textual and contextual events.

These pragmatic rules are still more striking in theaters where we create a gap between actors and audience, hide the guy wires and backstage machinery behind curtains, and even turn off the lights. But even in listening to anecdotes or stories, we draw a mental boundary between the words of the text and incidental conversation. In fact, our expectation of such a boundary is so robust that there is even a particular type of folk tale which reflects on and jokes about our belief in and need for this gap:

A traveler lost his way in a great woods. When at last he found a house, he pleaded to be let in. The master answered, "On one condition, that you entertain us with stories the whole night long." The traveler agreed.

When he had rested, eaten, and warmed himself by the fire, he spoke up. "I will gladly entertain you, but I, too, have one condition. If anyone interrupts me, I will not say another word but go right to sleep." All agreed, and the traveler began his tale.

"One day I was lost in a vast forest. I saw a crow and decided to follow his flight, thinking he would lead me out of peril. The crow flew over a tall tree.

Then he flew over two short trees. Next he went round a stunted tree. Again, he flew over a pair of trees..."

"But then what happened?" interrupted an eager listener.

"Ah—then ... good night," said the traveler and laid back closing his eyes.

The pragmatic strictures about the boundary between text and context may seem too subtle either for adults to teach young children or for youngsters to pick up. However, children growing up in highly literate settings are taught about the independence of text and context at a very young age (Ninio, 1980; Ninio & Bruner, 1978; Scollon & Scollon, 1979, 1980; Snow & Goldfield, 1983). In the following conversation, M (1;3) and her mother are looking at a picture book. Whereas her mother recognizes the connections M makes between the text and the surrounding situation, she also shows M how to relate her "comments" to the world *within* her text:

M (1;3):   (Turns to a rabbit picture and sniffs)
Mother:    That's right, who sniffs like that?
M:         (Points to her own nose).
Mother:    Right, M sniffs. Who sniffs *in the picture?* (She points back to the illustration)
M:         (Points to the rabbit and sniffs again)
Mother:    Yes, that bunny rabbit is sniffing his nose.

Similarly, children are also taught that personal narratives and conversations can and perhaps "should" be self-sufficient (Michaels, 1981; Scollon & Scollon, 1979, 1980). Thus, when at 3, M launches into an anecdote with the sentence, "She didn't give me some", her father asks, "Who didn't give you any what?"

## Boundary-Making in Symbolic Play

Book reading and personal narratives are not the only situations in which young children in literate cultures work out the conventional boundaries between text and context. Children from that speech community also develop their understanding of autonomous texts in the course of fictional play. During episodes of pretend play, children as young as five years treat their utterances, not as isolated comments, but as elements in a larger, integrated composition or *text* largely set off from the surrounding, contextual world. The earlier segment of fictional play in which M creates a story about a mother and child trying to ride an elevator suggests just how numerous these kinds of boundary-drawing behaviors can be.

Even in a relatively short episode, M exhibits a number of boundary-making strategies. M uses a set of terms associated with *a* particular situation, which, when used throughout a text, yield a sense of a continuing topic (Halliday & Hasan, 1976). M's description of her city scene includes a number of terms which might appear in stories about villages or cities such as "house," "church," and "road." In terms of preserving her story, M is not distracted by the real-world identities of objects when she meets them. Instead, as she introduces them into her narrative, she transforms those objects into text-relevant props.

Second, M creates a text that can stand on its own, virtually without reference to the spaces, objects, or gestures that form the context of the narrative. Many (although not all) of her phrases are clearly independent of the objects she works with or the gestures she makes (Pellegrini, 1982; Pellegrini & Galda, 1982). Where she wants to abbreviate, M often makes effective use of anaphoric reference (e.g., terms permitting her to refer back to elements mentioned earlier in her narrative). Only after she introduces the figures as "these people," does she refer to them in the body of the text using "they" and "their."

Finally, M monitors and protects the text of her play episode from intrusions which barge in from the surrounding "real" world. On the one hand, she can simply ignore events that intrude into the ongoing narrative (e.g., when the box starts to tip over). Alternatively, when an event occurs which M can use, she reconstrues the intrusion in terms of the fiction she is creating (e.g., when she makes the mother doll describe the tippy construction as dangerous). Where it is difficult to absorb an intrusion smoothly, M uses an aside to explain just how the interruption can/ought to be interpreted (e.g., when she requests that the toppling box be treated as an accident *in* the world of her city). Like many language users in literate settings, M has the notion that a text, like a story, can and often should be "autonomous" from the context in which it is performed. Moreover, M has a number of strategies which permit her to keep her fiction (or text) and the surrounding "real" world (the context) from blurring together.

In this paper, we use longitudinal observations of nine middle-class children to describe how children develop strategies for protecting a text. First, we describe our methods for observing and measuring children's ability to construct a boundary between text and context. Then we present longitudinal data on changes in this ability between the ages of 1 and 5. In closing, we raise some of the implications of our findings for notions of literacy and early education.

## The Design of the Study

As a part of a longitudinal study of early symbolic development, we observed nine children, between the ages of 1 and 7 years, as they acquired the rudiments of symbolic skill in a wide range of domains: music, movement, drawing, three-dimensional construction, quantitative knowledge, and language. The children were visited weekly between the ages of 1 and 3 and twice a month between the ages of 3 and 7. They were seen at home for visits lasting approximately two hours. Each visit contained a free play period, spontaneous play, and structured tasks in two of the seven target domains as well as interview time with parents (Shotwell, Wolf, & Gardner, 1980).

In the arena of language, we focused our attention on the still relatively unexplored problem of children's ability to put sentences together into longer units of discourse. In particular, we examined this ability as it occurs in the context of make-believe play, having discovered that some of children's longest and most proficient texts were performed in that setting. We examined two varieties of play texts: (a) *dramatic play texts* in which children assumed the role of an actor in the play, pretending to a parent, doctor, witch, or pilot; and (b) *replica play texts* in which children (at least eventually) assumed the role of an outside narrator, making toys or dolls take on the part of actors (cf. the earlier example of M at 5;2). We decided to follow both strands in play, treating them as the earliest manifestations of what could, in adults, be thought of as two separate genres: drama and narrative fiction (Scholes & Kellogg, 1966). For our own cataloging and scoring purposes, during the period when these linguistic differences were still clarifying, children's performances were scored as dramatic play if people took the role of actors in the pretense. If these roles were given over to dolls or other kinds of figures, we regarded the performance as a segment of replica play. Where people and figures both had character roles, the performance was viewed as an instance of dramatic play.

We collected observations of both spontaneous play and task responses. Instances of spontaneous play included occasions when a child initiated an episode of dramatic or replica play and instances in which the child chose to play out events based on some materials the experimenter offered. Structured tasks were of two kinds: (a) *implied event tasks* where the experimenter asked the child to play with a set of materials that suggested a possible event (e.g., bowls, spoons, and toy food to suggest a meal scene; and (b) *completion tasks* where the experimenter performed the initial segment of an event and then asked the child to complete the narrative play. The data reported in this paper combines responses on all three types of tasks.

As we wanted to study *children's* text-making capacities through these tasks, we planned to set out our materials and then sit back and record behavior. However, two very natural aspects of the situation intervened. First of all, "on-the-spot" oral composition of fiction requires a certain amount of self-confidence and considerable concentration. Children were often shy or stumped about how to proceed. Second, both dramatic and replica play are often carried out interactively. If an observer sits still taking notes in the corner, the play collapses. On both these counts, we found that children wanted to draw us into play. Rather than refuse and deflate children's interest in the tasks, we revised our earlier commitment to remain invisible. In the event that a child invited us into play, we responded, but stood off from adding novel information or asking leading questions. Thus, our observations come from sessions in which the presence of an interested adult partner provided a kind of focus and scaffolding for narrative acitivity (Bruner, 1975; Vygotsky, 1929). As a consequence, the data presented here are comparable to observations made on parent–child play rather than solitary play or peer play.

## The Problem of Observing an Approach to Texts

Adult speakers and performers are called on to exhibit their ability to separate text and context in a number of situations: Political speakers have to ignore or incorporate hecklers' remarks if they are to carry on. Similarly, actors have to rise above or absorb stage mishaps in order to protect the integrity of the play's fiction. Children's play unfolds in the midst of a larger situation which is somewhat indifferent to their make-believe. Doorbells ring, dinner is called, a baby sister wanders through messing up the "store" or "rocketship." Thus, we reasoned that children's responses to these interruptions provided clues as to how they thought about the problem of maintaining the integrity and autonomy of their texts.

Based on a reading of play session transcripts, we developed a taxonomy of the kinds of "ruptures" or "insults" to which children's play is vulnerable. This taxonomy included: *intrusions* (e.g., the telephone rings nearby; the light bulb flickers); *trouble with props* (e.g., a lid keeps falling into a toy pot; a toy animal won't stand up); *unexpected behaviors on the part of the observer or another person* (e.g., the observer tries to terminate the play in favor of another task; the observer reminds the child of the assigned topic of play in one of the more structured tasks; a sibling asks to play, etc.). Using this coding scheme we isolated all the instances in which a child had to cope with a contextual event which threatened the continuity of the play text.

At a second level, we had to develop hypotheses about the manner in which children's understanding of the boundary between text and context might change. Clearly, one straightforward way of handling intrusions is simply to ignore them or to fix them in some nonverbal manner (e.g., turn your back on your baby sister or choose a less wobbly animal figure). However, we were specifically interested in the set of linguistic strategies children use to set their play "back on track." We reasoned that, with age, children's verbal reactions to outside pressures would provide increasingly explicit transformations of contextual events into text events. We hypothesized, therefore, that children would at first simply acknowledge intrusions, then transform intruding events, and that still later they would exhibit the ability to explain or justify these transformations in terms of the text. The resulting score system is presented in Table 1.

For each child all the play sessions were coded for instances of responses to interruptions. Using this corpus of responses, we looked for the *age of acquisition* for each type of verbal response listed in Table 1. We defined the age of acquisition as the second occasion on which the child exhibited a particular level of response (Phelps, in press). In Table 2 we have displayed these ages, computed in weeks, for each of the children, in both sociodramatic and replica play.

The ages in Table 2 indicate that across both sociodramatic and replica play, children's verbal responses to contextual pressures emerge largely according to the predicted pattern. In dramatic play, eight of the nine children subscribe to the predicted pattern, although Levels 1 and 2 often appear together or in rapid succession. In narrative play, seven of the nine children follow the pattern, with Levels 2 and 3 often occurring together or in close succession.

If we examine the range of all the levels of response used by children in each successive half year of play episodes, it is clear that children are building up a repertoire of strategies for handling contextual pressures. As is indicated in Table 3, the appearance of later strategies does not preclude the use of previously acquired ones.

In fact, our observations indicate that as children acquire new strategies, they may use earlier-acquired or simpler strategies as a groundwork for more sophisticated, final responses. In the following excerpt we can see the microgenesis of a final, rather sophisticated response:

> M, at 4;11, has been acting out a story with a mother doll whom she has been making stomp around. One of the doll's legs comes loose and starts to dangle. At first, M acknowledges this fact without transforming the content in any text-relevant way (Level 1): "Oh, no, her leg is broken." She is somewhat puzzled about how to continue. She then transforms the intruding event, knitting it into the information contained earlier in her text (Level 2): "She broke her leg...when she was stomping." Then M makes the final relation between the contextual event (the discovery of the loose leg) and its textual representation ("She broke her leg...") explicit for the observer: "Pretend she broke her leg and they took her to the hospital and now she's home again. Say I did that part already."

However, the data also contain additional findings. First, children appear to handle interruptions differently depending on the particular kind of fictional text they are creating. Although there is virtually no difference in the rate at which intrusions occur in dramatic and replica-play sessions,

## Table 1. Levels in Verbal Responses to Contextual Pressures

### Level 1: Acknowledgments of Contextual Events

In these statements children acknowledge the contextual event which intrudes into the ongoing text of play. For example, when a toy animal continues to fall over, the child might comment, "That lion keeps falling over." Or, in playing out a dramatic scene, if a co-player insists that the space under a chair be the oven, the child responds, "Oh, okay, that can be the oven."

### Level 2: Transformations of Contextual Events

In these statements children transform the intruding contextual event into material for the ongoing text of play. For example, when a toy animal continues to fall over, the child might comment, "And the lion was so scared he fell over." Or, in playing out a dramatic scene, if a co-player insists that the space under a chair be the oven, the child responds, "Oh, of course, I forgot that we bought this new oven." In this level of statement, the play text "absorbs" rather than acknowledges the interruption. Statements at this level can vary from situation-relevant transformations (e.g., transformations that are simply plausible given the theme of the play episode) to text-relevant transformations (e.g., transformations that build explicitly on earlier statements made in the narrative).

### Level 3: Explanations of Contextual Events in Textual Terms

In these statements children explicitly explain how an intruding contextual event should be taken in relation to the ongoing play text. For example, when a toy animal continues to fall over, the child might comment, "Let's say that he really could stand up." Or, if a co-player insists that the space under a chair be an oven, the child responds, "Yes, that can be the oven, 'cause these (the knobs on a drawer) are where you turn it on. Let's fake that." Such explanations are frequently offered in a lower voice in order to contrast with the delivery of utterances which are a part of the fictional text.

## Table 2. Age of Onset[a] Data for Intrusion Strategies

| Subject | Level 1 | | Level 2 | | Level 3 | |
|---|---|---|---|---|---|---|
| | DP[b] | RP[b] | DP[b] | RP[b] | DP[b] | RP[b] |
| Adrianne | 80 | 123 | 95 | 142 | 142 | 161 |
| Amy | 65 | 152 | 123 | 162 | NE[c] | 162 |
| Heather | 85 | 105 | 109 | 152 | 130 | 156 |
| Jeannie | 121 | 105 | 148 | 154 | 211 | 154 |
| Jonathan | 77 | 104 | 104 | 138 | 129 | 151 |
| Josh | 106 | 94 | 173 | 98 | 217 | 137 |
| Kori | 80 | 115 | 123 | 158 | 125 | 161 |
| Max | 71 | 210 | 150 | 210 | 193 | 210 |
| Maja | 177 | 149 | 177 | 142 | 203 | 149 |

[a]Ages given in weeks.
[b]DP = dramatic play; RP = replica play.
[c]NE = no evidence

71

Table 3. Listing of All Levels of Intrusion Strategies used in each Half Year

| Subject | Half Year 3– (1–1½ yrs) | | Half Year 4– (1½–2 yrs) | | Half Year 5– (2–2½ yrs) | | Half Year 6– (2½–3 yrs) | | Half Year 7– (3–3½ yrs) | | Half Year 8– (3½–4 yrs) | | Half Year 9– (4–4½ yrs) | | Half Year 10 (4½–5 yrs) | |
|---|---|---|---|---|---|---|---|---|---|---|---|---|---|---|---|---|
| | DP[a] | RP[a] | DP | RP | DP | RP | DP | RP | DP | RP | DP | RP | DP | RP | DP | RP |
| Adrianne | — | — | 0,1,2 | 0 | 0,1,2 | 0 | 0,1,2,3 | 0,1,2 | 0,1,2 | 1,2,3 | 0,1,2,3 | 1,2,3 | 1,2,3 | 1,2,3 | NI[b] | 1,2,3 |
| Amy | 0,1 | 0 | 0,1 | 0 | 0,1,2 | 0 | 0,2 | 0,1 | 0,1,2 | 2,3 | 0,1,2 | 1,2,3 | 0,1,2 | 1,2 | 1,2,3 | NI[b] |
| Heather | 0 | 0 | 0,1 | | 0,1,2 | 0,1 | 0,1,2,3 | 0,1,3 | 1,2,3 | 2 | 1,2 | NI[b] | 1,2,3 | 1,2,3 | NI[b] | 1,2,3 |
| Jeannie | NI[b] | 0 | NI[b] | 0 | 0,1 | 0,1 | 0,1,2 | 1,2,3 | 0,1,2 | 1,2 | 1,2 | 1,2,3 | 2,3 | 2,3 | 1,2,3 | 1,3 |
| Jonathan | 0,1 | 0 | 0,1 | 0 | 0,1,2 | 0,1 | 0,1,2,3 | 1,2,3 | 1,2,3 | 1,2,3 | NI | 2,3 | 1,2,3 | 1,2,3 | NI[b] | 2,3 |
| Josh | 0 | 0 | 0 | 0,1,2 | 0,1 | 0,1 | 0,1 | 0,1,2,3 | 0,1,2 | 0,1 | 1,2 | 1,2,3 | 1 | 1,2,3 | 1 | NI[b] |
| Kori | 0,1 | 0 | 0,1 | 0,1 | 0,1,2,3 | NI[b] | 0,1,2 | 0,1,2,3 | 0,1 | NI[b] | NI[b] | 0,1,2,3 | NI[b] | 1,2,3 | 1 | 1,2,3 |
| Max | 0,1 | 0 | 0,1 | 0 | 0,1 | 0 | 0,1,2 | NI[b] | 0,1,2 | NI[b] | 1,2,3 | NI[b] | 1,2,3 | 1,2,3 | NI[b] | NI[b] |
| Maja | 0 | 0 | 0 | 0 | 0 | 0 | 0 | 0,1,2,3 | 0,2,3 | 1 | 1,2,3 | 1,2 | 1,2 | 1,2,3 | 1,2,3 | NI[b] |

[a]DP = dramatic play; RP = replica play.
[b]NI = no instances of intrusions.

children acknowledge these difficulties verbally almost twice as often in dramatic play (where they are typically one of several actors in a scene) as compared to replica play (in which a child is typically the sole author of the fictional action.)

In addition, when we collapsed the play sessions into half-year blocks, we found that a child's most recently acquired strategy provided no simple prediction of either her most frequent or highest level response to interruptions in succeeding periods. This finding may indicate that the development of this text-handling skill is particularly vulnerable to factors like interest, rapport with the observer, and fatigue. However, it may also argue for the complexity of the task of handling intrusions smoothly. Interruptions vary in type. Some intrusions come from objects (toppling, being too large, getting broken or lost). Other threats come from people (asking questions, objecting, suggesting alternative directions for the text). The transcripts suggest that once children acquire Level 3 (explanation of a contextual event in textual terms), they use that strategy more regularly to respond to human intrusions than to troublesome props. Yet even interruptions from the same source vary their degree of intrusiveness. The third time a prop topples is much more intrusive than the first time it wobbles. An interruption can occur at a moment when it is easy or virtually impossible to incorporate (e.g., the development vs. the conclusion section of a narrative). The content of an interruption may mean that it is easily transformed or calls for explanations (e,g., it may be harder to incorporate a phone ringing in a jungle narrative than in an episode of playing store). Hence, the actual pattern of children's responses to intrusions emerges as an interaction between the demands of particular interruptions and children's own capacities.

## Other Aspects of Autonomous Text

These strategies for protecting play texts from intrusions appear to be part of a multifaceted understanding of text boundaries which appears among children who are exposed to books and print-derived conventions prior to reading and writing instruction (Scollon & Scollon 1979, 1980; Snow & Goldfield, 1983). For example, during this same period the nine children we observed also acquired the ability to "stage-manage" and to act as "outside narrators."

"Stage-managing" is the ability to step outside the ongoing fiction of the play and plan how that fiction will continue. By the age of 20 months, children have what might be thought of as an entry-level version of this skill. They can initiate play episodes or pause in the midst of such an episode to offer simple instrumental directives to their co-players or audience such as "Now watch" or "Give me a spoon, I gonna make a cake." By twenty-four months, children's stage-managing grows to include remarks to others about how objects will be used or interpreted in the course of play: "The couch is gonna be the car"; "No, that can't be the cake, we need something round." Finally, between the ages of four and five, children begin to make stage-managing remarks which include detailed or longer-term planning: "I'm gonna be the witch and I'll come out and scare you but not really. You pretend to be scared, but not really, OK?" Our data indicate that these stage-managing skills, like the strategies for responding to intrusions, build up in an additive manner: Children go on using the full range of types, even at age 5. Taken together, children's verbal strategies for handling interruptions and their ability to stage-manage provide a kind of protective zone around the texts they invent. Using these skills, children are free to make use of the worthwhile accidents or hints the contextual world provides; yet they can create and preserve a kind of boundary between the "real world of the kitchen floor" and the fictional world of the text.

As mentioned earlier, young children frequently play at creating fictional texts in two different settings: dramatic and replica play. It is particularly difficult to seal off the fiction from contextual events in dramatic play where the child and co-players assume roles and use full-scale motions, objects, and spaces. However, in replica play children use miniature figures, motions, objects, and spaces. As children learn to project the fiction onto the small figures which they manipulate, they drop out of the participatory role of character and can draw a relatively sharp distinction between the fictional and real worlds. Our longitudinal observations show that until the age of 2, children continue to act as characters in the play, treating the figures only as the passive recipients of their own fictional actions. However, in the ensuing year, two significant events occur: (a) children stop intervening in the play as characters (Scarlett & Wolf, 1979); and (b) children learn to treat the figures as if they were independent agents (Lowe, 1975; Rubin & Wolf, 1979; Watson & Fischer, 1977; Wolf, 1982). As they vest the figures with the ability to speak as characters, children adopt the roles of stage manager and narrator. Between the ages of 3 and 5, children, acting as managers or narrators, respond to intrusions or the necessity of planning in ways that create a sense of a continuous text. In the example of M at 5;2, M does not acknowledge the overturning elevator directly. Instead, she makes the mother figure "speak" to this event. M, acting as the narrator, speaks from outside the event, saying "So they had to walk up the stairs..."

Not surprisingly, children complement these pragmatic text-preserving strategies with a set of text-constructing strategies (Wolf 1984, 1985). In a parallel process, 2- to 5-year-olds learn the linguistic strategies for binding their individual utterances together into longer, cohesive narratives. Thus M exhibits the ability to refer continuously to the same script or situation (collocation), build on earlier substantives (anaphora), and mention the connections between successive events (conjunctive cohension) (Wolf, Grollman, & Scarlett, in press).

## Conclusion: Context and Text

These longitudinal findings suggest that, even before they read and write, children growing up in literate cultures may be sensitive to the expectation that a text can and often should stand apart from contextual events. In the course of their fictional play, these children exhibit a succession of verbal strategies which control the impact of contextual events on their fictional texts. At first, (Level 1), an intrusion has the effect of momentarily fusing the contextual and textual worlds. Slightly later, the play text can withstand interruptions—but by absorbing them (Level 2). At the close of the pre-school years, a child can explicitly acknowledge just how she wants a particular interruption viewed in relation to the fictional text she is developing (Level 3). Through these strategies of overlooking, transforming or explaining children can keep contextual events from barging into their fictions.

Such boundary-preserving behaviors appear to be part of a much broader understanding of text autonomy. By 5, children also exhibit some control of a narrator's stance and the ability to plan for the long-term course of their narratives. Even though the concrete referents for the text (the spaces, figures, actions) are immediately present, children can create chains of utterances which appear to build largely, if not exclusively, on each other rather than on contextually available information. Even in the context of *oral speech* the children studied here may construct a rudimentary understanding of the conventions of autonomous texts.

Thus, there is a remarkable siimilarity between these 5-year-olds' oral narratives and the written texts they will soon work on reading or writing. However, it is crucial to understand the nature of this continuity. The particular children we followed grew up in a culture (or subculture) where even conversations, never mind personal narratives or stories, exhibit some of the specificity and autonomy which is thought to characterize written language. Moreover, these children have language histories which are filled with experiences of *hearing* print: They have been read to, their parents recite familiar stories on long car rides, they retell these stories to younger siblings. Hence, the continuity between these children's play narratives and the stuff of formal language instruction in schools is the result of long instruction, no matter how intimate or informal.

But children in kindergarten classrooms come from a range of language communities. Some of them, like the children in the longitudinal study, have a written text model for discourse. They are lucky, their training dovetails with tasks and materials of formal schooling. But other children may have other equally powerful, yet distinct, models for discourse. Some children learn language in communities where oral, rather than written narrative reigns. In that tradition, speakers and writers often create "joined texts" which are richly and frequently tied to the surrounding situation or performance through exchanges with listeners, gesture and emphatic prosody, subtle allusions to shared past experiences (Michaels, 1981; Wolf, 1985). Often, children who speak or write such "joined texts" have been viewed simply as needing remediation in order to catch up on the conventions of autonomous texts so essential to schooling. However, there is another possibility: Perhaps the educational challenge is to teach children the power of using language in a variety of ways. Written stories, even oral instructions and explanations, often work better if the writer or speaker can think about them in terms of autonomous texts. But secrets, well-known games, personal stories between friends are powerful and effective precisely because of the way in which they fuse the surrounding world of experience and the text world. Sophistication lies in owning both ways of text-making.

## References

Bartlett, E. (1979, April). *Anaphoric references in writing by middle-school students.* In C. Cazden (Chair), Quarterly Meeting of the New England Child Language Association, Cambridge, MA.

Bruner, J. (1975). The ontogenesis of speech acts. *Journal of Child Language, 2,* 1–21.

Halliday, M. A. K., & Hasan, R. (1976). *Cohesion in English.* London: Longman.

Lowe, M. (1975). Trends in the development of representational play in infants from one to three years—An observational study. *Journal of Child Psychology and Psychiatry, 16,* 33–47.

Michaels, S. (1981, March). *Sharing time revisited.* In Ethnography in Education Research Forum, University of Pennsylvania, Philadelphia.

Ninio, A (1980). Picture book reading in mother-infant dyads belonging to two subgroups in Israel. *Child Development, 51,* 587–590.

Ninio, A., & Bruner, J. (1978). The achievement and antecedents of labelling. *Journal of Child Language, 5,* 1–15.

Olson, D. (1977). From utterance to text: The bias of language in speech and writing. In M. Wolf, M. McQuillan, & E. Radwin (Eds.), *Thought and language/Language and reading,* Cambridge, MA: Harvard Educational Review.

Pellegrini, A. D. (1982). The construction of cohesive text by preschoolers in two play contexts. *Discourse Processes, 5,* 101–108.

Pellegrini, A., & Galda, L. (1982). The effects of thematic-fantasy play training on the development of children's story comprehension. *American Educational Research Journal, 19,* 415–428.

Phelps, E. (1984). Methods for the analysis of ordinal data. In D. Wolf and H. Gardner (Eds.). *The making of meanings: Early symbolic development.* Manuscript submitted for publication.

Richards, I. A. (1929). *Practical criticism.* New York: Harcourt Brace.

Rubin, S., & Wolf, D. (1979). The development of maybe: The evolution of social roles into narrative. In E. Winner & H. Gardner (Eds.), *Fact, fiction, and fantasy. New Directions for Child Development, 6,* 15–28.

Scarlett, W. G., & Wolf, D. (1979). Crossing over: The construction of boundaries between fantasy and reality. In E. Winner & H. Gardner (Eds.), *Fact, fiction, and fantasy. New Directions for Child Development, 6,* 29–40.

Scholes, R., & Kellogg, R. (1966). *The nature of narrative.* New York: Oxford University Press.

Scollon, R., & Scollon, S. (1979). Literacy as interethnic communication: An Athabaskan case. *Working Papers in Sociolionguistics, 59.* Austin, TX: Southwestern Educational Development Laboratory.

Scollon, R., & Scollon, S. (1980). Literacy as focused interaction. *The Quarterly Newsletter of the Laboratory of Comparative Human Cognition, 2,* (2), 26–29.

Shotwell, J., D. Wolf, & H. Gardner. (1980). Styles of achievement in early symbolization. In M. Foster & S. Brandes (Eds.). *Universals and constraints in symbol use.* New York: Academic Press.

Snow, C. & Goldfield, B. A. (1983). Turn the page, please: Situation-specific language acquisition. *Journal of Child Language, 10* (3), 551–569.

Vygotsky, L. (1929). The problem of the cultural development of the child. *Journal of Genetic Psychology, 36,* 415–34.

Watson, M. W., & Fischer, K. W. (1977). A developmental sequence of agent use in late infancy. *Child Development, 48,* 828–836.

Wolf, D. (1982). Understanding others: The origins of an independent agent concept. In G. Forman (Ed.), *Action and thought: From sensorimotor schemes to symbol use.* New York: Academic Press.

Wolf, D. (1984). Research currents: Learning about language skills from narratives. *Language Arts, 61* (8), 844–850.

Wolf, D. (1985). Ways of telling: Text repertoires in elementary school children. *Boston University Journal of Education.* In press.

Wolf, D., S. Grollman, & W. G. Scarlett. (1984). Kinds of texts: The evolution of fictional narratives. In D. Wolf & H. Gardner (Eds.), *The making of meanings: Early symbolic development.* Manuscript submitted for publication.

# 5

## Relations Between Preschool Children's Symbolic Play and Literate Behavior

### Anthony D. Pellegrini
University of Georgia

### Introduction

Piaget's (1962) influential book *Play, Dreams, and Imitation* stimulated psychological and educational research into the ways in which children's cognitive and social development is related to and affected by their play. The hypothesized relation between play and aspects of development is based upon a basic tenet of Piaget's (1970) structuralist theory: the synchrony between different aspects of concept development within a developmental stage. According to this theory children's engagement in accommodative symbolic play should result in representational competence and general concept development. In this chapter we will examine the relations between two aspects of children's representational competence: symbolic play and literate behavior.

Literate behavior involves the production and comprehension of decontextualized and narrative language (Heath, 1982; Olson, 1977a, 1977b; Scribner & Cole, 1978; Snow, 1982). Decontextualized language conveys meaning by the linguistic elements within the text. This is contrasted with using shared information between interlocutors or contextual cues to convey meaning. Decontextualized language has also been labeled cohesive text (Halliday & Hasan, 1976), school language (Cook-Gumperz, 1977), and literate language (Olson, 1977b). Olson (1977b) noted that decontextualized language is not typically used in everyday discourse but is used as a tool of literacy in schools. Narrative language involves talking about causally motivated characters acting in temporal sequences (Stein & Glenn, 1979). Children are expected to produce decontextualized and narrative language in their school writing and their talking with teachers. They are also expected to comprehend decontextualized and narrative language in their reading lessons (Olson, 1977b).

In this chapter we will identify those aspects of symbolic play which best relate to a number of measures of literate behavior. First, symbolic play and literate behavior will be defined. In these definitions, similarities between the mental processes involved in both behaviors will be outlined. Second, an exploratory experiment examining the relations between children's play and literate behavior will be reported.

### Symbolic Play

Symbolic play for Piaget (1962, 1967, 1970) reflects children's ability to think representationally. In representational thought children use signifiers (e.g., gestures and words) to designate "signifieds" (e.g., persons). This representational capability is thought to be part of children's general semiotic function; through it they come to realize that signifiers represent signifieds. Indeed, the development of thought, according to the Piagetian model, involves children's gradual differentiation of signifiers from signifieds.

In order to understand fully the relations between representational and intellectual development, some basic levels Piagetian theory must be reviewed. Piaget's (1967, 1970) notions of assimilation and accommodation are essential. In the assimilative mode children interact with objects and people according to predetermined mental plans. The extent to which feedback from these interactions changes the plans is minimal. As such, assimilation alone does not spur development. Accommodation, on the other hand, occurs when mental plans are changed, or modified. Thus, the formation and construction of new cognitive structures is a result, primarily, of the accommodative process.

According to the Piagetian model, development involves *both* assimilation and accommodation; development occurs when equilibration is reached between the two processes. Different activities, however, may be dominated by one of the two processes. Assimilation is dominant in the type of symbolic play in which symbols are egocentric, or autistic (Piaget, 1970). For example, a child may use an idiosyncratic symbol such as clapping to represent a physically absent car. When accommodation is dominant, children imitate someone without being able to relate the imitated acts to their own relevant, or assimilatory, schemas; For example, a child may imitate the word *car* with no knowledge of the word's meaning. In symbolic play, the assimilative process enables children to practice at symbolically representing objects or events. These assimilative symbols, however, are egocentric and cannot be socially communicated. The accommodative process provides children with socially accepted signifiers such as words with which to represent the world to others. Equilibration between assimilation and accommodation occurs when children relate socially defined signs instead of egocentric symbols to their existent concepts.

Children's egocentric symbols become more social, or collective, as children begin to decenter from their own perspectives (Piaget, 1967). That is, children begin to represent symbolic activities with socially defined signs only after they realize that others cannot understand their idiosyncratic symbols; engaging in social–symbolic play with peers facilitates children's accommodation to others' perspectives. These idiosyncratic symbols, then, become replaced by socially accepted signs through the social interaction typical of young children's social–symbolic play.

Social–symbolic play approaches and reaches its peak during the preschool and primary school period, between six and seven years of age (Parten, 1932; Rubin, Watson, & Jambor, 1978; Fein, 1981; Pellegrini, 1982a; Rubin, Vandenberg, & Fein, 1983). Though the literature is discrepant in noting the specific ages of the onset and decline of symbolic play, it is noted consistently that symbolic play follows an inverted U-shaped developmental function: it first appears at approximatley 1½ to 2 years of age, peaks during the preschool and early primary school years, and then declines during middle childhood (Fein, 1981). Aspects of children's social–symbolic play undergo significant change during this period. Play becomes more decontextualized, object substitutions become more abstract, and it becomes more social (Rubin et al., 1983).

### Aspects of Symbolic Play and Literate Behavior

Decontextualized behavior typically has children framing an everyday activity in a make-believe context (Fein, 1981); e.g., a child may pretend to eat when it is not actually dinner time. In order to engage in symbolic play children usually take components of everyday events, or scripts (Nelson & Gruendel, 1979; French, Lucariello, Seidman, & Nelson, this volume), and execute them in the fantasy mode. They use experiences from one realm, the real world, as bases of symbolic play episodes.

The organization of decontextualized play events has been examined by Wolf and Grollman (1982). The organization of decontextualized play, it is suggested, is similar to ways in which narratives are organized. Children's symbolic play can be simply organized by the enactment of schemes (i.e., a single symbolic act), or by the enactment of events (i.e. enacting a number of related schemes), or by episode enactment (i.e., enacting a number of related events). By enacting everyday events in a fantasy context children gain practice at analyzing and reconstructing the temporal and causal structure of these narrativelike events. Children who enact a variety of events will, in turn, have well-developed schemata for those events.

Heath (1982) found that children who enacted a variety of events and story themes were often successful at school-based literacy tasks. She argued that the structural similarities between school-based literacy events (e.g., understanding narratives) and enacting fantasy themes (e.g., enacting little Red Riding Hood) accounts for this relationship. Simply put, children who have a variety of well-developed play scripts usually come to school with a well-developed sense of narrative. This relation is due to the similarity between the rules governing certain play scripts and one aspect of literate behavior, narrative language. Both symbolic play and narrative language events involve telling stories, suspending reality, and ascribing fictional features to everyday objects (Heath, 1982). We would expect, then, that the organization of children's decontextualized play should be related to their literate behavior.

The object substitutions of children's symbolic play become more abstract as their play becomes more decontextualized. Younger children's symbolic play depends on the immediate presence of objects to be used as play props (Vygotsky, 1967; Fein, 1981). They may use an object or an attribute of that object as a play prop. Use of such "object transformations" are less advanced than ideational transformations (McLoyd, 1980). Ideational transformations are independent of physically present objects, e.g., Johnny becoming Batman. By four years of age most children use ideational transformations to enact symbolic play themes (Vygotsky, 1967, McLoyd, 1980; Pellegrini, in press). In social–symbolic play children use explicit oral language to define these ideational transformations (Pellegrini, 1982b, 1983); e.g., "I'm the doctor." The highly symbolic nature of these decontextualized substitutions necessitates children's use of explicit language to define them, if they are to convey unambiguously the meaning of transformations to other players. Thus, one would predict positive relations between ideational transformations and explicit language.

Children's symbolic play also becomes more social during the preschool and early primary school period (Pellegrini, 1982a; Rubin et al., 1983). Young children's symbolic play is generally nonsocial (i.e., solitary and parallel). By the preschool and kindergarten years (3 to 6 years of age), however, solitary pretend play diminishes and only accounts for 1% to 5% of all free play (Rubin et al., 1983). Group pretense, for this age group, accounts for 60% to 80% of all types of play observed (Rubin et al., 1983). The social context of symbolic play may be responsible for children's use of explicit language during play (Rubin, 1980). When children engage in social pretense play, they tend to use explicit and elaborated language (Martlew, Connolly, & McCleod, 1977; Pellegrini, 1982b, 1983, in press). They use complex forms of language so as to convey transformations unambiguously. In such ambiguous situations other players ask for clarification of the ambiguity so that the play episode can be sustained. Indeed, such forms of conceptual conflict between interpretations of play events may facilitate children's accommodation to other players' perspectives. Children tend to resolve such conflicts through clarification and compromise. Children are motivated to resolve conflict and reach a compromise with peers because social compromise is adaptive: Social survival and popularity result from such a behavior (Rubin, 1980). We would predict, then, for social play and conflict resolution to be positively related to literate behavior.

In summary, the social (conceptual conflict among peers and social interaction) and symbolic (decontextualized behavior and substitutions) aspects of play are probably related to children's literate behavior. It was argued earlier that in social–symbolic play, children often encounter conceptual conflict from peers. They use explicit language to define symbolic transformations so as to avoid and clarify ambiguity. In this study we will examine the extent to which these aspects of play (social participation, conflict, decontextualized organization, and object substitutions) relate to literate language.

## Methods

### Subjects

The twenty children, 10 boys and 10 girls, composing the sample all attended a university preschool. Teachers in two classrooms were asked to construct dyad lists of same-age (not more than two months difference) and same-sex children who often played together and who would probably play together in experimental play sessions. Five dyads were randomly chosen from each of the two classroom lists. The children in the younger classroom ranged in age from 47 to 53 months ($M = 51.40$; $SD = 3.23$). The children in the older classroom ranged in age from 56 to 63 months ($M = 59.00$; $SD = 4.51$).

### Setting

The children interacted in an experimental playroom in their preschool. The $14' \times 12'$ room was equipped with two suspended directional microphones and a one-way mirror. Children's play was recorded with a video camera through the one-way mirror; the experimenter operated the videotaping equipment from a separate room. Children were observed playing on two occasions in each of two play contexts.

For the dramatic play context, the following props were set out on a $2.5' \times 3'$ table: two doctors' kits, two dolls, two smocks, blankets, and pill bottles. For the constructive play context, the following props were set out on the same table: wooden and colorful plastic blocks of various sizes, numerous styrofoam shapes, and pipe cleaners.

Only one female experimenter interacted with the children in the experimental contexts. She spent the two weeks prior to data collection interacting with the children in their classrooms so that they were familiar with her. The experimenter escorted each of the sampled dyads to the experimental play-room. Each dyad was observed for four separate 20-minute sessions, twice in the dramatic play context and twice in the blocks context; the order of observations was counterbalanced.

When the children and the experimenter entered the experimental play-room, she told the children, "Play with these toys while I read my book." Each session lasted approximately 20 minutes.

Children's utterances and corresponding actions were transcribed from the videotapes by the experimenter. After the initial transcripts were prepared, the author and experimenter reviewed tapes and transcripts. They attempted to resolve conflicting interpretations of utterances. Where consensus was not reached, those utterances and actions were omitted from the transcripts.

## Measures of Play

In all cases the dyad, not the individual, was the unit of analysis because of the interdependence of behavior in such groupings. That is, frequencies of each category were summed across both members of the dyad and treated as a single score. Four aspects of children's play were categorized: symbolic transformations, social–cognitive organization, narrative organization, and conflicts.

### Symbolic Transformations

Children's use of language to symbolically substitute aspects of play episodes was measured (McLoyd, 1980). All fantasy utterances were first identified and then coded as object (subcategories 1–4) or ideational (subcategories 5–8) transformations. Categories were mutually exclusive. Operational definitions of each subcategory follow.

### Object Transformation

1. *Animation:* Giving inanimate objects living attributes. For example, a child says about a stuffed animal, "My doggie's going for a walk."
2. *Reification:* "Reifying an imaginary object which is functionally related to an existing object" (McLoyd, 1980 p. 1135); for example, a child pretends to drink out of an empty cup and says, "This soda's good."
3. *Attribute of object property:* An object property is attributed to an existent or imaginary object which is functionally related to a real object. For example, a child makes a bang sound while firing a toy gun.
4. *Substitution:* An existing object is given a new identity. For example, a child says about a block, "This is my car."

*Ideational Transformations*

5. *Object realism:* Pretends an imaginary object exists. The imaginary object, however, bears no resemblance to the play object. For example, a child says, "I'm using this brush to cut the grass."
6. *Attribution of nonexistent object property:* A make-believe or substitute object is given a nonexistent property. For example, a child says, "I'm taking my vitamin" as he takes a nonexistent pill.
7. *Situation attribution:* Pretends a make-believe situation exists. For example, "OK, this is the doctor's office."
8. *Role attribution:* Portrays a fantasy role. For example, "I'll be the nurse."

In general, with object transformations children used language to assign an imaginary property or identity to an object; ideational transformations, on the other hand, involved children using language to create fantasy which was relatively independent of objects (McLoyd, 1980).

Interrater agreement for the coding of the transformations was established by, first, having the experimenter code all fantasy utterances according to the verbalized fantasy subcategories. The author, then, randomly chose 10 transcripts and recoded them. The agreement between coders for each subcategory ranged from 81% to 90%, with an overall mean of 86%.

## Social-Cognitive Organization

Social and cognitive aspects of children's behavior were concurrently scored on a nested social-cognitive matrix. The categories, following Rubin et al. (1976) and Smilansky (1968), that comprised the cognitive measures were: (a) functional: repetitive motor activities; (b) constructive: use of objects to build something; and (c) dramatic: transforming a real situation into an imaginary situation. Social categories, following Parten (1932), Rubin et al. (1976), and Johnson and Ershler (1981) included: (a) solitary: playing alone; (b) parallel: playing near, but not with, others; and (c) interactive: interacting with peers in common enterprise.

There were individual scores for each of the nested social-cognitive subcategories, e.g., constructive-solitary. However, interactive-functional behavior was not included in the matrix by nature of the definition: functional play cannot be interactive (Rubin et al., 1976). There were also aggregate social (i.e., separate scores for each of the solitary, parallel, and interactive categories) and aggregate cognitive categories (i.e., separate scores for each of the functional, constructive, and dramatic categories).

Interrater agreement for the scoring of these categories was established by having two observers independently view the videotapes of five dyads. The mean interrater agreement across all categories was 92%. No agreement for a category fell below 87%.

### Decontextualized Organization

The decontextualized organization of play episodes was examined according to a model put forth by Wolf and Grollman (1982). This model describes the extent to which children hierarchically integrate singular fantasy schemes into complex episodes. Operational definitions of each level of organization follow.

*Scheme:* Single fantasy enactments, e.g., holding a spoon to a doll's mouth.

*Event-simple:* 2 or 3 goal-oriented schemes.

*Event-contoured:* At least four different schemes.

*Episode-simple:* 2 simple events.

*Episode-contoured:* More than two contoured events.

Interrater agreement was established by having two observers simultaneously score the transcripts for five dyads. The mean agreement was 83%.

### Conflicts

Children's verbal conflicts were examined following Eisenberg and Garvey (1981), in terms of initial oppositions and others' reactions to the initial oppositions. The subcategories for each form of conflict follow.

*Initial Oppositions*

1. *Simple negation* (e.g., No)
2. *Reason:* Justification for opposition
3. *Countering move:* Substitute for desired object
4. *Temporize:* Postpone compliance
5. *Evade:* Hedge by addressing the propositional content of the utterance rather than acknowledging its illocutionary force.

*Reactions to Opposition*

1. *Insistence:* Supports the same speaker's utterance and adds no new information
2. *Mitigation:* Increased indirection (e.g., please)
3. *Aggravation:* Increased directives (e.g., No)
4. *Reasons:* Explanation or justification given
5. *Counter:* Speaker suggests an alternate proposal
6. *Conditional directive:* A commisive and a directive linked together (e.g., "I'll be your friend, if you come")
7. *Compromise:* Some form of sharing involved
8. *Request for explanation:* Used to elicit reason or explanation
9. *Physical force:* Physical contact with the child
10. *Ignores:* Opponent does not respond

Total number and variety of both initial opposition and reactions to opposition were used in the analyses. Like other measures of play, interrater agreement for conflicts was established by comparing the similtaneous coding of five randomly chosen dyads' transcripts. Agreement reached 83%.

## Measures of Literate Language

The unit of analysis for literate language, as with the play measures, was the dyad. Frequencies of utterances across dyads were categorized according to: conjunctions, noun phrases, reference, and individual verb types.
*Conjunctions:*

1. *Temporal:* Connects events in a time-related manner, e.g., "and then"
2. *Causal:* Connects events in cause–effect manner, e.g., "because"

*Noun phrase:* Individual noun phrases were coded according to aspects of the nominal group (Hawkins, 1973).

1. *Modifiers:* Word(s) in noun phrase immediately preceding the head (e.g., *The red* dog).
2. *Head:* The only obligatory component of the nominal group is the head: nouns or pronouns (e.g., The red *dog*).
3. *Qualifiers:* Word(s) in noun phrase immediately following the head (e.g., The red dog *in the window*).

*Reference:* Endophoric and exophoric reference were examined (Halliday & Hasan, 1976). *Endophora* is defined as a linguistic tie between presupposed and presupposing elements (e.g., a noun and pronoun). *Exophora* exists when the presupposed element is not linguistically encoded.

*Verbs:* Verbs were defined according to mental and linguistic processes denoted and according to tense.

1. *Mental/linguistic verbs:* Denote cognitive and linguistic processes (e.g., *think, say*)
2. *Verb tense:* Present, past, and future.

Interrater agreement for the literate language categories was 98%.

## Results/Discussion

Data were analyzed in two steps. First, zero-order correlation coefficients were calculated for relations between predictors (measures of play) and criterion variables (measures of literate language).

Table 1. Significant Inter-Correlations Between Measures of Play and Literate Behavior[a]

|  | Verbs | | | | Noun Phrase | | Cohesion | | |
|---|---|---|---|---|---|---|---|---|---|
|  | Linguistic | Cognitive | Past | Future | Modifier | Qualifier | Endophoric | Temporal | Causal |
| *Conflicts* | | | | | | | | | |
| Number | | | | | | | | | .75 |
| Variety Initiate | | .62 | .66 | .75 | .72 | | .75 | | .65 |
| Reason | | | .74 | | | | | | .67 |
| Request Explanation | | | .77 | | | | | | |
| *Transformations* | | | | | | | | | |
| Substitutions | | | | | .65 | .85 | .63 | | |
| Situation | | .93 | .77 | .86 | .75 | | .93 | | |
| Number Objects | | .70 | | .69 | .75 | .62 | .84 | | .69 |
| Number Ideas | | .88 | .79 | .77 | .70 | .69 | .93 | .87 | .70 |
| *Social-Cognitive Play* | | | | | | | | | |
| Constructive | | | | | .82 | | -.62 | | |
| Dramatic | | .70 | | .85 | .83 | .77 | .79 | | |
| Social | | | | .86 | | | .80 | | |
| Social Dramatic | | .62 | | .84 | .86 | .63 | .72 | | |
| *Narrative* | | | | | | | | | |
| Contoured Event | .65 | .64 | .69 | .63 | .70 | | | | |
| Episode | | .63 | .63 | | .67 | | | | |
| Contoured Episode | | .89 | .75 | .65 | .78 | | .86 | .71 | |

[a]Critical values for correlation coefficients, $df = 8$; $p < .05 = .63$; $p < .01 = .76$.

In the second stage of analysis, step-wise multiple regression procedures were used to determine the aspects of play which were the most potent contributors to aspects of literate behavior.

These analyses should be interpreted cautiously for two reasons. First, caution is needed in the interpretation of these results in that many individual predictor variables were significantly interrelated; this was also the case with many criterion variables. To correct these problems of colinearity

### Table 2. Summary of Regression Analyses

| Criterion | Step Entered | Variable Entered | $R^2$ | F | P |
|---|---|---|---|---|---|
| *Cohesion* | | | | | |
| Endophora | 1 | Transform: Situation | .88 | 58.92 | .0001 |
| | 2 | Narrative: Scheme | .93 | 52.49 | .0001 |
| | 3 | Conflict: Variety Initiate | .98 | 125.84 | .0001 |
| | 4 | Transform: Role | .99 | 251.52 | .0001 |
| *Conjunctions* | | | | | |
| Causals | 1 | Transform: Substitution | .85 | 45.30 | .0001 |
| | 2 | Conflict: Reason | .92 | 45.27 | .0001 |
| | 3 | Conflict: Compromise | .97 | 70.79 | .0001 |
| | 4 | Transform: Situation | .99 | 267.46 | .0001 |
| Temporals | 1 | Transform: Situation | .84 | 43.91 | .0002 |
| | 2 | Social-cognitive: Social-dramatic | .94 | 56.10 | .0001 |
| | 3 | Social-cognitive: Social | .96 | 59.41 | .0001 |
| | 4 | Narrative: Contoured Event | .98 | 119.60 | .0001 |
| *Noun Phrase* | | | | | |
| Modifiers | 1 | Social-Cognitive: Dramatic | .78 | 29.75 | .0006 |
| | 2 | Narrative: Event | .92 | 45.09 | .0001 |
| | 3 | Narrative: Contoured Event | .96 | 56.92 | .0001 |
| | 4 | Narrative: Scheme | .98 | 86.43 | .0001 |
| Qualifiers | 1 | Transform: Situation | .73 | 22.51 | .001 |
| | 2 | Transform: All ideas | .89 | 28.9 | .0004 |
| | 3 | Transform: Substitution | .94 | 33.60 | .0004 |
| *Verbs* | | | | | |
| Linguistic | 1 | Narrative: Contoured Episode | .43 | 6.11 | .03 |
| | 2 | Conflict: Variety Resp. | .66 | 6.96 | .02 |
| Cognitive | 1 | Transform: Situation | .87 | 53.24 | .0001 |
| | 2 | Transform: Substitution | .94 | 60.88 | .0001 |
| Past | 1 | Conflict: Request Explanation | .83 | 18.24 | .001 |
| | 2 | Conflict: Variety Response | .91 | 20.90 | .001 |
| | 3 | Conflict: Contoured Episode | .96 | 30.86 | .001 |
| Future | 1 | Social-cognitive Dramatic | .75 | 24.00 | .001 |
| | 2 | Narrative: Contoured Episode | .84 | 19.29 | .001 |

with principal components or factor analyses, a larger sample would have been needed. Second, these data are correlational, and therefore, causality and directionality cannot be inferred.

## Play and Endophora

Endophora is an aspect of language commonly associated with literate language (Snow, 1982; Olson, 1977a, 1977b). Endophora measures speakers' linguistic rendering of meaning. Results of regression analyses indicated that endophora was most likely to co-occur with ideational transformations (i.e., situations and roles) in complexly organized play episodes. That is, two categories of ideational transformations, situation and role transformations, set in a complex play script accounted for most of the variance in endophora. Further, variety of conflicts initated were also significant predictors of endophora.

These relations of the play variables and endophora support the conclusions of previous observational work of children's fantasy play (Pellegrini, 1982a, 1983). It was argued that if highly abstract play transformations are to be unambiguously communicated to other players, children should use explicit language, such as endophora, to encode the transformations. For example, in the block-playing context a child wanted to use a block to introduce a house-moving script: "How about you being the moving man." In this case the child explicitly defined (through an endophoric reference) her playmate's role in the play episode. Ambiguity may have resulted in this situation if the role transformation was not explicitly defined. In such a script the possibility for ambiguity exists because a player could take any number of roles. Such abstract transformations are likely to elicit endophoric reference because of the possibility for ambiguity. Less abstract transformations, such as object transformations, did not co-occur with a high incidence of endophora. Examination of less abstract forms of play supports this interpretation; constructive play was a negative predictor (− .62) of endophora.

Endophora occurred in elaborately organized play scripts. It may be that the use of endophora was necessary for play to reach the contoured episode level; the use of unambiguously defined transformations was necessary for the sustenance of play at this level. If children defined transformations ambiguously, disjointed episodes may have resulted. As a result of this ambiguity, the play episodes would not have reached the complex level of contoured episodes. This interpretation is supported to the extent that less complexly organized play scripts (schemes and events) were negatively, though not significantly, correlated with endophora, (− .36 and − .15, respectively).

Children's use of endophora also tended to co-occur with a variety of initial conflicts. That is, when members of the dyad initially disagreed they also tended to use endophora. We can speculate, following Rubin (1980) and Pellegrini (1982b), that these initial conflicts were the result of the ambiguity and conceptual conflict inherent in social–fantasy play. Initial conflict often resulted from the misunderstanding of the meaning of a transformation (Pellegrini, 1982b). For example, when two girls were doctoring a doll, one of them said, "My bandaids." The other child said: "These not bandaids." The first child then resolved the conflict, and as part of the process used endophora: "These are my bandaids."

It should be noted, however, that a high frequency of conflicts did not predict endophora. It seems that a low level of conceptual conflict and rapid conflict resolution (initial opposition) co-occurred with use of endophora, whereas a high level of conflict (e.g., a number of conflicts) did not. An examination of Table 1 illustrates this point; variety of initial conflicts correlated with a number of measures of literate language. Those types of conflict which indicated sustained and unresolved conflicts (i.e., variety of responses and number of conflicts) were not significant predictors of literate language. Thus, only those conflicts that are initiated and resolved quickly seem to be beneficial to certain aspects of development. As has been suggested by Piagetian-oriented research (e.g., Rubin, 1980; Pellegrini, 1984b), the conceptual conflicts that characterize peer interaction are adaptive only when the conflicts are resolved. In resolving conflicts themselves, children accommodate to each others' perspectives. The short duration of the conflicts in the present study suggest that children did just that: They disagreed, then accommodated to each others' perspectives by resolving conflicts. They used endophora in the process. Use of this strategy enabled them to communicate in an unambiguous, sociocentric manner.

## Play and Elaborated Noun Phrases

Like endophora, elaborated noun phrases (e.g., modifiers and qualifiers of nouns) are also used to render linguistically explicit meaning (Bernstein, 1971; Hawkins, 1973). Indeed, Bernstein (1971) and his colleagues (e.g., Cook-Gumperz, 1973, 1977; Hawkins, 1973) have included both measures as indicators of elaborated code. Like endophora, modifiers and qualifiers co-occurred with ideational transformations and initial conflicts. Again, abstract transformations and initial conflicts are dependent upon verbal elaboration, if they are to be communicative. Further, the highly positive and significant intercorrelations between endophora and modifiers (.79) and endophora and qualifiers (.87) suggest that they may compose a common factor, which could be named elaborated language. However, further research, with a larger sample, is needed to determine the psychometric reality of such a factor.

Elaborated noun phrases, unlike endophora, however, were used with both object and ideational transformations. The elaborated noun phrases were probably used to extend the meaning of an object to its transformed fantasy identity. For example, when a child gave an inanimate doll animate qualities she used elaborated noun phrases: "Here's another baby. She's the good baby." Children's use of elaborated noun phrases helped transform the object to its fantasy role by embellishing, or extending, its existent perceptual and functional qualities.

The use of modifiers was most likely to occur in social-dramatic play. In social-dramatic play, by definition, children must communicate their fantasy transformations to other players (Smilansky, 1968). The fantasy component of social-dramatic play has players executing symbolic transformations; the social component has children communicating the transformations to other players. The use of modifiers helps children execute both these components unambiguously. Again, the combination of fantasy transformations in a social context results in players generating elaborated language.

## Play and Conjunctions

Another important aspect of children's literate language is the way in which they are able to use language to organize their world causally and temporally. This ability is particularly important in the school-based literacy events of young children. Literacy events can be defined as "occasions in which written language is integrated to the nature of participants' interactions and their interpretive processes and strategies" (Heath, 1982, p. 50). Young children's literacy events typically involve their producing and understanding various forms of narratives (Heath, 1982). In narratives, fictional characters encounter problems, set goals, and attempt to reach these goals through a series of causally and temporally related events (Stein & Glenn, 1979). As was noted in the introduction, we hypothesized a positive relation between narrativelike organization of decontextualized behavior and literate behavior. This hypothesis was based on Heath's (1982) observations of the structural similarities between both events. In both situations they: tell stories, make believe, and fantasize. Generally, our data supported this hypothesis; highly organized play was structured with temporal and causal conjunctions. In the present study we examined the extent to which children used temporal and causal conjunctions to organize their fantasy play.

The presence of causal and temporal conjunctions in children's play indicates the extent to which their play is organized in a narrativelike way; narratives, primarily, are organized temporally (Applebee, 1978). In the present study temporal conjunctions were elicited by social-dramatic play when players were transforming real situations to fantasy situations. Temporals were used to define the situational background against which children's play occurred. For example, in an episode where children were using blocks to represent cars, Anna used a temporal conjunction as part of the transformation of a fantasy road and a fantasy gas station: "I gotta get some gas before I can push——before I have to push the car." As can be seen from the fourth variable entered into the temporal conjunction equation, contoured events, temporals were used in well-developed play scripts.

Causal conjunctions seemed to be used in two ways in the present study: to transform objects and events (substitution and situation, respectively) and to resolve conflicts. In the former case, causals were used as part of the transformational utterances. For example, a child used a causal as part of the substitution of a yellow plastic block for a piece of cheese: "Don't eat that cheese 'cause it's poison." In this case, and similar cases, the fantasy characters acted in a logical, cause–effect manner. Children's use of cause–effect motivations indicates that they are using the characters' psychological motivations to enact the story (Scarlett & Wolf, 1979). Such cases indicate that children understand story characters as abstract entities; they understand *why* characters do things, not only that characters' activities and events follow a specified temporal sequence (Scarlett & Wolf, 1979).

In addition, causals were used to settle conflicts: they were used as part of reasoning and compromising statements. When children of equal status (as measured by age) engage in conflict, they tend to use reason, in the form of causally related arguments, to settle conflicts. Equal-status peers use reason, rather than force, to settle disputes, because they want to sustain the play (Piaget, 1970). Antisocial behavior is not engaged in frequently by most children because children want play to continue and because they probably realize that consistent disagreements reduces their popularity (Rubin, 1980).

## Play and Verbs

Verbs will be the last set of variables to be discussed. These variables will be discussed in terms of their use as indicators of children's "metanarrative" awareness (Scarlett & Wolf, 1979). Use of past and future tenses indicated that children, in their play, were consciously manipulating the temporal aspects of play scripts. It also indicated that their play was going beyond immediate environmental stimuli (Scarlett & Wolf, 1979); past and future event references were used to complement the present actions. Children in the present study typically used the future tense in social–dramatic contoured episodes. They often used future-tense markers to plan or organize the enactments, e.g., "I'm gonna eat one of these." We can speculate that when groups of children enact complex play themes such as contoured episodes, a fair amount of planning is needed. Sachs and her colleagues have shown that most of preschoolers' fantasy play language is indeed dedicated to planning (Sachs, Goldman, & Chaillé, 1984). In order for children to sustain an abstract and complex play episode, their role transformations and object transformations must be decided in advance. If children do not know their expected sequence of actions or how to respond to other players, they cannot sustain the enactment. Future tense verbs helped to plan such future actions. Future tense verbs served an explicit planning function (e.g., "Let's pretend that this is a truck") and helped to announce what would happen next (e.g., "I'm gonna go to bed"). In both cases future tense verbs helped orient players to their appropriate next move.

Like future-tense verbs, past tense verbs occurred in contoured play episodes. However, past tense verbs were used in parts of the episode involving conflict (requesting explanations and variety of responses to initial conflicts). Past tense verbs may have served the function of providing children with the background information for aspects of the play episode for which there were conflicting interpretations. It seems that the use of past tense, like future tense, verbs served an organizational function. Children used these verb tenses to direct other players in complex play episodes. In less complex episodes (e.g., scheme and events) there was less need to orient other players and, as a result, there was less of an occurrence of future and past tense verbs.

Players' use of these verbs indicated their conscious awareness of the processes involved in enacting complex play episodes (Scarlett & Wolf, 1979). Their use of future and past tense verbs to manage ongoing interaction indicated their awareness of the components of play scripts. Such an awareness has been labeled "metanarrative" (Scarlett & Wolf, 1979). Indeed, Flavell (in press) has noted that individuals who interrelate past, present, and future events are likely to have metacognitive knowledge about that event.

We can make further inferences about children's metacognitive knowledge of a specific area by examining their generation of cognitive and linguistic verbs (e.g., think, say) in that context (Torrance & Olson, 1984). In the present study cognitive and linguistic verbs co-occurred with contoured play episodes in the midst of situational and substitution transformations. Utterances such as "Pretend this is the hospital," showed that children used their knowledge of everyday scripts to enact play episodes (French et al., this volume; Nelson & Gruendel, 1979). When a possibility for ambiguity and uncertainty existed, as it did when transformations were being made, children used their knowledge of similar events to guide the enactment of the present play events. Individuals tended to engage in metacognition when they experienced conflict and had to explain and justify their behavior to others (Flavell, in press).

## Summary

The discussion of the relations between symbolic play and literate language is still speculative to the extent that the directionality of the relations is unclear. Given the previously described analyses, there are at least two explanations for the results. The first, as suggested earlier, is that certain forms of play elicit literate language. It may be, however, that children who exhibited literate behavior also tended to engage in specific forms of play. Results of a play-training study may help clarify the directionality of the issue. Pellegrini (1984a) trained groups of children in various aspects of story enactment, one of which was thematic–fantasy play. He examined their use of two aspects of literate behavior in their story retellings (endophora and conjunctions). The training of children to enact fantasy themes resulted in their increased use of endophora but not in their use of temporal or causal conjunctions. Exposure to play, then, did result in the improvement of one aspect of literate behavior, elaborated language, but not in another aspect. Such mixed results raise the competence-performance issue (Flavell & Wohlwill, 1969). Children in the play-training conditions were trained to use both endophora and a variety of conjunctions. They did not use them, however, in a related task (retelling the story). This suggests that they had some level of competence in the use of these forms. However, this competence was not realized, in terms of their performance, on the retelling measure. The results, then, may be an artifact of the criterion variable, story recall.

The results of the described study indicated reliable relations between certain forms of play and aspects of literate behavior. More experimental work with a varied sample age (i.e., preschool through the primary grades) needs to be done before the directionality of the relations is determined.

## References

Applebee, A. (1978). *The child's concept of story*. Chicago, IL: University of Chicago Press.

Bernstein, B. (1971). *Class, codes, and control (Vol. 1)*. London: Routledge & Kegal Paul.

Cook-Gumperz, J. (1977). Situated instructions: Language socialization of school-age children. In S. Ervin-Tripp & C. Mitchell-Kernan (Eds.), *Child discourse*. New York: Academic.

Fein, G. (1981). Pretend play in childhood: An integrative review. Child Development, *52*, 1095–1118.

Flavell, J. (in press). Speculations about the nature and development of metacognition. In R. Kline & F. Weinert (Eds.), *Metacongition, motivation, and learning*.

Flavell, J., & Wohlwill, J. (1969). Formal and functional aspects of cognitive development. In D. Elkind & J. Flavell (Eds.), *Studies in cognitive development*. New York: Oxford University Press.

Halliday, M., & Hasan, R. (1976). *Cohesion in English*. London: Longmans.

Hawkins, P. (1973). Social class, the nominal group and reference. In B. Bernstein (Ed.) *Class, codes, control, (Vol. 2)*. London: Routledge & Kegan Paul.

Heath, S. B. (1982). What no bedtime story means: Narrative skills at home and school. *Language in Society 11*, 49–76.

Johnson, J., & Ershler, J. (1981). Developmental trends in preschool play as a function of classroom program and child gender. *Child Development*, 1981, *52*, 995–10004.

Martlew, M., Connolly, K., & McCleod, C., (1977). Language use, role and context in a five-year-old. *Journal of Child Language, 5,* 81–99.

McLoyd, V. (1980). Verbally expressed modes of transformation in the fantasy of black preschool children. *Child Development, 51,* 1133–1139.

Nelson, K., & Gruendel, J. (1979). At morning its lunchtime: A scriptal view of children's dialogues. *Discourse Processes, 2,* 73–94.

Olson, D. (1977a). From text to utterance: The bias of language in speech and writing. *Harvard Educational Review, 47,* 257–281.

Olson, D. (1977b). The language of instruction: The literate bias of schooling. In R. Anderson, R. Spiro, & W. Montague (Eds.), *Schooling and the acquisition of knowledge.* New York: Wiley.

Parten, M. (1932). Social participation among preschool children. *Journal of Abnormal Psychology, 27,* 309–314.

Pellegrini, A. (1982a). Development of preschoolers' social-cognitive play behaviors. *Perceptual and Motor Skills, 55,* 1109–1110.

Pellegrini, A. (1982b). The construction of cohesive text by preschoolers in two play contexts. *Discourse Process, 5,* 101–108.

Pellegrini, A. (1983). The sociolinguistic contexts of the preschool. *Journal of Applied Developmental Psychology, 4,* 397–405.

Pellegrini, A. (1984a). The effects of dramatic play on children's generation of cohesive test. *Discourse Process, 1,* 57–67.

Pellegrini, A. (1984b) Identifying causal elements in the thematic-fantasy play paradigm. *American Education Research Journal, 21,* 691–703.

Pellegrini, A. (in press). The effects on play contexts on the development of preschool children's verbalized fantasy. *Semiotica.*

Pellegrini, A., & Galda, L. (1982). The effect of thematic-fantasy play training on the development of children's story comprehension. *American Educational Research Journal, 19,* 443–452.

Piaget, J. (1962). *Play, dreams,* and *imitation.* New York: Norton.

Piaget, J. (1967). *The psychology of intelligence.* London: Routledge & Kegan Paul.

Piaget, J. (1970). Piaget's theory. In P. H. Mussen (Ed.), *Carmichael's manual of child psychology (Vol. 1).* New York: Wiley.

Rubin, K. (1980). Fantasy play. Its role in the development of social skills and social cognition. In K. Rubin (Ed.), *Children's play.* San Francisco, CA: Jossey-Bass.

Rubin, K., Watson, K., & Jambor, T. (1978). Free play behaviors in preschool and kindergarten children. *Child Development, 49,* 534–536.

Rubin, K., Vandenberg, B., & Fein, G. (1983). Children's play. In E. Hetherington (Ed.), *Manual of child psychology: Social development.* New York: Wiley.

Sachs, J., Goldman, J., & Chaillé, C. (1984). Planning in pretend play: Using language to coordinate narrative development. In A. Pellegrini & T. Yawkey (Eds.), *The development of oral and written language in social contexts.* Norwood, NJ: Ablex.

Scarlett, W., & Wolf, D. (1979). When it's only make-believe: The construction of a boundary between fantasy and reality in story telling. In E. Winner & H. Gardner (Eds.), *Fact, fiction, and fantasy in childhood.* San Francisco, CA: Jossey-Bass.

Scribner, S., & Cole, M. (1978). Literacy without schooling: Testing for intellectual effects. *Harvard Educational Review, 48,* 448–461.

Smilansky, S. (1968). *The effects of sociodramatic play on disadvantaged preschool children.* New York: Wiley.

Snow, C. (1982, March). *Literacy and language.* Paper presented at the annual meeting of the American Educational Research Association, New York.

Stein, N., & Glenn, C. (1979). Analysis of story comprehension in elementary school children. In R. Freedle (Ed.), *Advances in discourse process: New directions in discourse processing (Vol 2.).* Norwood, NJ: Ablex.

Torrance, N., & Olson, D. (1984). Oral language competence and the acquisition of literacy. In A. Pellegrini & T. Yawkey (Eds.) *The development of oral and written language in social contexts.* Norwood, NJ: Ablex.

Vygotsky, L. (1967). Play and its role in the mental development of the child. *Social Psychology,* 12, 62–76.

Wolf, D., & Grollman, S. (1982). Ways of playing. In D. Pepler & K. Rubin (Eds.), *The play of children.* Basel, Switzerland; Karger.

# 6

## Preschool Children's Narratives: Linking Story Comprehension, Production, and Play Discourse

Marilyn Guttman
Carl H. Frederiksen
McGill University

### Introduction

It is generally assumed that children begin their formal schooling with well-developed oral communication skills, sufficient to cope with the communicative demands of their home and neighborhood environments. Motivated by the view that the acquisition of literacy skills involves more than the decoding of orthographic symbols and the transfer of already established oral discourse skills to reading and writing, investigators have recently concerned themselves with two issues. The first has focused on a general contrast between oral conversational discourse on the one hand and written school texts on the other, and concerns the proposition that there are fundamental differences between the two. It has been asserted that young children entering school must adjust to new demands of literate written texts, demands which entail basic changes in language and thought (e.g., Olson, 1977). However, this emphasis on a simple oral–written language dichotomy has been criticized by researchers who have suggested that variables other than modality such as function, genre, context, or register may account for differences between the two (Scribner & Cole, 1981; Rubin, 1980; Tannen, 1982). This latter view emphasizes the multiple varieties and functions of both oral and written discourse and similarities as well as differences between the two.

The second issue concerns the sources of skills underlying children's ability to comprehend and/or produce literate school texts. These sources are sought in the various early language experiences of the preschool child. The suggestion is that certain typical discourse activities such as various forms of play may be similar to activities associated with literacy, and hence, may facilitate the development of these skills (Gundlach, 1981). The challenge facing researchers concerned with this issue is to specify the similarities and differences between these early discourse activities and those that children will encounter in their early school experience (Rubin, 1980). Characteristically, research concerned with this issue has emphasized similarities and differences in the linguistic structures children produce rather than the cognitive representations and processes involved in generating discourse in different situations of oral language production and to relate these to processes underlying the comprehension and production of literate school-type discourse.

The present research is concerned with both of these issues. First, by comparing preschool children's productions across a range of play and story production activities, we seek an understanding of the discourse structures and processes underlying children's ability to communicate text structures in situations of discourse production that span the oral/literate and play/school dichotomies. Second, we attempt to link these production abilities to story comprehension. We focus on imaginary (dramatic, pretend) play, because among the early language experiences of the preschool child, this activity has been identified as a fertile context for studying children's development of narrative skills (e.g., Sachs, 1980). We concentrate on storytelling, because stories represent a literate school-related genre which is within the experience of the preschool child. For example, cognitive studies of text comprehension indicate that children as young as 4 years of age have developed a schema for conventional story structures (e.g., Wimmer, 1980).

In the first part of this study, we examine issues that have arisen from diverse studies of children's imaginary play. Next, we summarize recent theoretical and methodological developments in research on text comprehension and how they pertain to analyzing the cognitive structures and processes involved in children's comprehension and production of story texts across tasks. The theoretical foundation on which the present research rests is a model of constructive processes in discourse comprehension and production that emphasizes the cognitive processes employed by children in building and communicating conceptual (frame) representations for different discourse genres. The methodological techniques involve methods of discourse analysis motivated by this model that provide the basis for explicit descriptions of structures and processes at different levels of semantic representation and text structure.

The application of these techniques to the comparative analysis of discourse production across a range of play and story production tasks is the subject of the present research. By analyzing in detail children's comprehension and production, we hope to be able to compare directly the cognitive processes they employ in different discourse tasks, and to link these to their story comprehension. Put simply, we would like to answer the following two questions: Do children display the same pattern of discourse production skills in play and story production? Is the ability to produce narrative discourse related to the ability to comprehend narrative text structures?

## Play as Discourse and Social Construction

Two main empirical approaches to questions concerning the nature of play and its role in children's development can be distinguished (Sutton-Smith, 1979, 1980). The first views play as a voluntary activity that results in advances in cognitive development; the second stresses play as a form of social communication that reflects children's knowledge of cultural norms and values. In this selective review, we consider research that stems from these two approaches and that has implications for the study of discourse processing in preschool and early elementary-school-aged children. We focus on one type of play, namely, imaginary play, which has also been referred to as symbolic, pretend, pretense, imaginative, or dramatic play (Golomb, 1979). Studies of children's discourse for this age range have concentrated on descriptions of dyadic or social play; with few exceptions (e.g., Martlew, Connally, & McCleod, 1978), monologic or solitary play has not been the object of study.

In the first approach, researchers have focused specifically on the role of play in the cognitive development of preschool and elementary-school-aged children (Feitelson & Ross, 1973; Singer, 1973; Smilansky, 1968). A limited number of studies have attempted to link components of pretend play—such as role enactment, the transformation of objects, and peer negotiations—to the ability to comprehend and compose literate school texts. In one line of research, play training studies have explored the facilitative effects of imaginary play on selected measures of comprehension and production competency (Pellegrini, 1984; Pellegrini & Galda, 1982; Yawkey & Silvern, 1979). A second line of research, focusing on analysis of textual surface devices (cohesion and topicalization patterns) of play discourse, has emphasized similarities between children's play texts and "decontextualized" written school texts (Pellegrini, 1982). The suggestion is that play fosters the ability on the part of young children to explicitly express their meaning in language, a skill associated with the comprehension and production of literate texts. That dramatic play elicits cohesive text in contrast to constructive play (Pellegrini, 1982) and that the use of cohesive devices within the context of this form of play increases with age (Wolf & Pusch, this volume) has been shown. It may well be that play discourse has features in common with written discourse and that such a contrast may have implications for a description of literacy development. The present research shares an interest in this issue but emphasizes instead the comparative analysis of play discourse and narrative discourse in terms of the cognitive structures and processes associated with different levels of text and semantic representations.

The second approach emphasizes the communicative strategies underlying children's appropriate use of language in social settings. One line of research has employed observations of children's play involving peer interactions (Garvey, 1974, 1977; Sachs, Goldman, & Chaille, 1984) and adult-child interactions (Sachs, 1980) in both laboratory (Garvey, 1974, 1977; Sachs, Goldman, & Chaille, 1984) and home settings (Keenan, 1974, Sachs, 1980). These studies have explored children's developing knowledge of conversational discourse rules and structures as reflected, for example, in their ability to: (a) sustain topically related coherent discourse (Keenan, 1974); (b) apply principles of turn-taking (Garvey & Hogan, 1973); and (c) interpret and respond appropriately to each other's speech acts (Garvey, 1975). More recently, these researchers have drawn attention to play as a useful context for exploring the early manifestations of children's stories, described as "story lines" or "action plans" (Garvey, 1977) and as containing elements analogous to those proposed in story grammars (Sachs, 1980). Emerging from this perspective is the concept of play discourse that is jointly constructed by participants within a communicative context and that reflects shared knowledge of normative roles and "story lines" or "action plans" (Garvey, 1977; Sachs, 1980).

A second line of research focuses on the processes involved in the production of discourse in face-to-face interactions and provides a framework for inquiring into the role of children's world knowledge in guiding their communicative efforts (Cook-Gumperz & Corsaro, 1976; Corsaro, 1983). Central to this approach is the notion of a frame (schema) that is mutually constructed by participants during the course of an interaction and that reflects both world knowledge and features of the social environment. Recent microethnographic studies of spontaneous peer interactions within a preschool setting (Cook-Gumperz & Corsaro, 1976; Corsaro, 1983) have investigated the verbal and nonverbal strategies (often prosodic in nature) by which children interpret, negotiate, and construct their shared meaning and have demonstrated that children's expression of their knowledge of social roles and normative behavior is dependent on features of the social–play environment (e.g., playhouse vs. sandbox) (Cook-Gumperz & Corsaro, 1976) as well as on the structure and nature of different role play activities (e.g., family role-playing vs. fire fighting) (Corsaro, 1983).

In summary, studies of play discourse conducted from a cognitive perspective have attempted to associate selected surface features of play texts with those of "literate" school texts but have not provided for an analysis of the cognitive processes and structures involved in the construction of play texts at different levels of text representation. Studies conducted from a social perspective have emphasized the social knowledge and communicative strategies involved in the cooperative construction of play texts. To date, the discourse structures and cognitive processes underlying children's ability to construct their "story lines" have not been the focus of study.

## Text Comprehension

Both of these issues have concerned researchers in the area of text comprehension and, more recently, text production. Research, inquiring into the knowledge structures and cognitive processes underlying children's ability to comprehend and/or generate stories, has been conducted within the framework of three main theoretical approaches: (a) text-based theory (Frederiksen, 1975, 1977; Kintsch, 1974; Kintsch & van Dijk, 1978); (b) knowledge-based (schema) theory (Mandler & Johnson, 1977; Rumelhart, 1977; Stein & Glenn, 1979); and (c) frame construction theory (Frederiksen, 1985, in press; Frederiksen, Frederiksen, & Bracewell, 1984, 1985). Initially, studies employing methods of free recall focused on the discourse structures and propositional knowledge underlying children's ability to comprehend text. Text-based approaches have emphasized the effect of surface textual features and propositional structures on comprehension processes; knowledge-based approaches the extent to which comprehension is influenced by the listener's or reader's goals, prior knowledge, and expectations about discourse structures. Current frame-construction approaches to comprehension stress the centrality of inferential processes involved in building a conceptual representation for a text that reflects both textual information and the language user's world knowledge.

Text-based approaches to comprehension have examined how knowledge acquired from text is influenced by aspects of its surface realization such as topicalization patterns (Clements, 1979), cohesive devices (Halliday & Hasan, 1976), and propositional structures (Frederiksen, 1975; Kintsch, 1974). Analysis and classification of inferences which connect propositions within a text have enabled researchers to characterize the internal coherence of a text (Frederiksen, 1977, 1981) and analysis of inferences connecting text propositions to propositions produced during story recall have enabled the study of text-based inferences in comprehension (Frederiksen, 1977; Tierney, Bridge, & Cera, 1979). To account for processes by which a reader or listener builds a conceptual structure for a text, operations have been specified (Kintsch & van Dijk, 1978) in the form of macrorules which operate on the propositional content (microstructure) of a text to enable the construction of a macrostructure that represents the gist, topic, or essence of a conventional discourse type (e.g., stories, psychological reports). Text-based approaches to comprehension have described inferences involved in the comprehension of various types of texts but have failed to adequately explain how a reader or listener generates inferences specific to a particular text or context or why particular inferences are made and not others (Frederiksen, 1981; Frederiksen et al., 1985).

Knowledge-based approaches have emphasized the use of prior knowledge and expectations in comprehension. Within this approach, researchers have employed the notion of suprapropositional structures for stories called story schemas (Mandler & Johnson, 1977; Stein & Glenn, 1979; Thorndyke, 1977) or event schemas (Rumelhart, 1977; Wimmer, 1980) to explain how children's expectations concerning the structure of simple conventional stories serve to organize and generate their representation of stories. Comprehension, here, is viewed as a form of pattern recognition, achieved through recognizing features of a text's content that are instances of the language user's internalized schema for a story. Empirical research has demonstrated that well-structured stories are better recalled than ill-structured ones and that inferences are generated to make ill-structured stories conform more to a "canonical" story structure (Mandler & Johnson, 1977; Stein & Glenn, 1979; Thorndyke, 1977). Current work has shown that even children of about 4 and 5 years of age reveal the ability to recall a well-structured story (Wimmer, 1980), but that their spontaneous productions lack many of the components specified by the story schemas (Stein & Glenn, 1979; Stein, 1982). Research in this area, however, has not provided for direct comparisons of children's competencies in comprehension and production to explain this differential performance. Moreover, these studies have been limited to a consideration of the structure of conventional single-protagonist stories, a characterization that itself has been criticized (Brewer & Lichtenstein, 1980) and their applicability to text production has been questioned (Hidi & Hildyard, 1983; Scinto, 1983). Furthermore, they have not accounted for the role of textual features and text-based processes in comprehension (Weaver & Dickinson, 1982) and have encountered difficulty in explaining how children can comprehend an unfamiliar text for which they do not possess a preexisting schema (Frederiksen, 1981). Finally, the results of these studies may also be consistent with models of story structure other than those postulated by these researchers.

In summary, attempts to specify the role of text-based and knowledge-based processes in comprehension have motivated a considerable amount of experimental work. While differences still exist between researchers over the extent to which comprehension is influenced by the features of a text or the language user's prior knowledge and expectations, current work in the area is characterized by an emerging consensus that comprehension is a process by which children construct a suprapropositional conceptual representation (schema, frame) for a text that reflects both propositional information derived from properties of the text and the world knowledge they bring to the comprehension task (Frederiksen, 1977, 1981).

### Frame Construction Processes in Children's Story Production

The third approach emphasizes processes of frame construction (rather than frame instantiation) that are involved in building suprapropositional conceptual representations for different discourse genres and that reflect both text-based and knowledge-based processes. For example, both Bruce (1980) and Trabasso and Nicholas (1980) have examined how children build high-level representations for stories, the former investigating inferences children must make to comprehend a protagonist's plans and the latter, the inferences necessary to connect event chains in narrative discourse. Frederiksen has developed a theoretical and methodological framework that enables the comparative analysis of children's frame construction processes in both discourse comprehension and production tasks and across different genres, and that accounts for the knowledge underlying the generation of a particular type of text (Frederiksen, 1985, in press; Frederiksen et al., 1984, 1985). The current approach to frame construction was suggested in a study of a teacher–child conversation in a directed nursery-school activity (Frederiksen, 1981). Conversational inferences generated by participants reflected both text-based (local illocutionary and propositional) constraints and global frame-based constraints associated with the directed task. Later, Frederiksen (1985, in press) postulated frame grammars, formalized as recursive transition networks, for different types of frame structures, and methods of frame analysis were applied to the investigation of children's comprehension of different discourse genres (Frederiksen & Frederiksen, 1982) and school-aged children's story productions (Frederiksen et al., 1984, 1985). The grammars define the rules by which frame elements are linked to form higher-order structures, and the child is assumed to possess such rules which he uses to construct frame structures of a given type such as narrative, conversational, problem, procedural, and descriptive.

This theoretical approach begins with the assumption that a text consists of both a conceptual (semantic) structure and a textual structure. Semantic representations for texts occur at two levels: a propositional level which specifies the semantic content of clauses and a suprapropositional level which represents the high-level meaning structure of a text. Propositions instantiate frames and make them expressible in language. Text structures also are characterized by two levels: clause structures, which encode propositions and text-level linguistic devices such as topicalization and cohesion structures. Interrelationships among propositions are signalled through such cohesive relations as reference, ellipsis, conjunction and substitution, while topicalization patterns reflect frame level structures by controlling the sequence and introduction of topics as old and new. Methods of established discourse analysis techniques, motivated by this model (Frederiksen et al., 1984, 1985), provide the basis for explicit descriptions of these structures and inferences concerning processes associated with the production/comprehension of different levels of text (including surface-level textual and clausal structures) and semantic structures (including propositional structures and conceptual frame structures). In addition, inference analysis permits precise analysis of subject's text and frame-based inferences (Frederiksen, 1985, in press) as well as for the analysis of interpropositional coherence within the text.

This study employed the theoretical model and discourse analysis techniques of Frederiksen (1985, in press; Frederiksen, et al., 1984, 1985) to an analysis of preschool children's discourse. It was concerned with preschool children's ability to produce narrative text structures in both their elicited story productions and in their spontaneous imaginary play and with the relationship of this *production* ability to *story comprehension*. The first concern was addressed by obtaining children's text productions in the following two sequences of experimental situations: (a) story task condition: story comprehension, picture-elicited story production, and free story production; and (b) imaginary play: monologic and dialogic. Thus, tasks within each experimental condition were varied, enabling the systematic investigation of the effects of task constraints on selected measures of text production ability. Content was controlled by employing a large floor toy, pictures, and texts, all involving the same characters, objects, and scenes. The second concern was met by relating these measures of text production competency to children's overall comprehension, as measured by propositional recall on a story comprehension task (involving the same controlled content).

Our overall research goal is to examine children's production of story and play discourse at each level of semantic and textual structure. This study focuses on findings resulting from the analysis and comparison of relatively low-level linguistic and semantic structures, clausal structures, propositional structures, and their relationship, as measured by an index of propositional density. Analyses of propositional and clausal structures permit inferences concerning children's production of these aspects of discourse structure. Analysis of propositional density enables inferences concerning the processes involved in encoding propositions as clauses. Propositions represent the semantic content of clauses and instantiate conceptual frame information; clauses encode propositions while reflecting text-level structural choices (such as cohesive devices). Subsequent analyses will investigate frame-level conceptual structures and how they are represented in text.

## Method

### Subjects

Six boys and 6 girls were tested. Subjects ranged in age from 4.8 years to 5.4 years. Children lived within a central middle-class Montreal area, were native speakers of English, and were attending an English-language cooperative nursery school. The school followed a child-centered program that included daily scheduled periods of free play, allowing for varied types of play activities. All 12 children participated in the story task condition. The children were randomly assigned to one of two experimental imaginary play conditions: (a) solitary play ($n = 4$, 2 boys and 2 girls) and (b) social play condition ($n = 8$). The 8 subjects within the social and play condition were randomly assigned to 4 same-sex dyads (2 male and 2 female). Only results from the social play condition are presented here.

## Materials

Materials for the imaginary play and story task conditions were adapted from commercially produced Richard Scarry toys and books. These materials were selected because they depicted social scenes, characters in normative roles, and themes typically found in children's stories. Characters were changed from the original version to provide for more equal male and female representation. The identical scenes, objects, and characters were portrayed within the story task and imaginary play conditions using the materials described below.

**Imaginary play.** The large detachable floor toy ($1.5 \times .75 \times .24$ m) placed in the center of the room included (as depicted in Figs. 1 and 2): (a) four city and country scenes; (b) road tracks on which cars and trucks were placed, and (c) figures (about 7 cm in height) portraying characters in familiar social roles such as a "grocer cat" and a "taxi fox." It was expected that the imaginary play toy would elicit play episodes consisting of narrative episodes (e.g., going to the store) similar to those depicted in the story tasks.

**Story task.** The materials employed in the story tasks included: (a) two oral stories, (b) two picture booklets, and (c) a single picture. A brief description of the materials follows:

1.  Stories: Two texts written and taped by the female experimenter, "Mr. Fumbles" and "Mrs. Goat," were adapted from several Richard Scarry books. Each story depicted a protagonist who is involved with various townspeople in a series of mishaps that finally result in the destruction of his/her car. The first story featured the central character in a series of car crashes; the second, a central character who by mistake drives other people's cars. Each story consisted mainly of a narrative and conversational event sequence. Conversational events accounted for approximately 34% of the content of each story. The oral texts, each approximately 390 words in length, were matched for number and type of major and secondary clauses, coded according to Winograd's (1972) system of clausal analysis. They differed slightly in terms of the average number of propositions encoded per clausal segment (propositional density). The measure of propostional density for Mr. Fumbles was 3.28; for Mrs. Goat, 2.86.

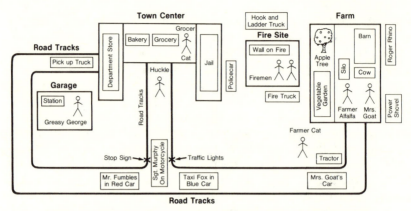

Figure 1. Diagram of floor toy used in imaginary play condition.

Figure 2. Photograph of child playing with imaginary play toy.

2.  Picture booklets: Two original picture booklets, each consisting of 12 clearly interpretable colored pictures (11 × 20 cm) were assembled from Richard Scarry books to create picture sequences that corresponded to the series of events depicted in the two oral versions. The pictures were placed in individual plastic covers and presented in loose leaf binders.
3.  Single picture: A single picture (11 × 20 cm) depicted three characters in nonaction poses. These characters were prominently featured in the two story and picture-booklet versions.

Subjects were randomly assigned to one of two groups, and the two versions of stories and picture booklets were counterbalanced across the story comprehension and picture-elicited production tasks. All children received the same picture for the third and final task.

## Procedure

To reduce the possibility of subject reaction to an unknown person, the experimenter (an experienced teacher) served as an aide with nonauthoritative status in the nursery school for two days a week over the two month period preceding the presentation of the experimental conditions. All children were tested/observed in a small room which adjoined the main classroom and in which small group activities took place daily. The room provided a familiar setting for the children and enabled the experimenter to collect protocols free from the main classroom noise and distractions.

Children were tested in the following sequence of experimental conditions: (a) imaginary play: monologic and dialogic; (b) story tasks: story comprehension, picture-elicited story production, and free story production. A brief description of the procedures used in each task/play condition follows.

**Imaginary play.** Three 10-minute videotape and audiotape recordings of 4 same-sex dyads engaged in spontaneous play with a large floor toy were made at intervals of one week over a three-week period in the presence of the female experimenter. Children were familiarized with the toy and recording equipment and told they could play with the toy in any manner they chose. The presence of the experimenter and recording equipment situated in the far corner of the room proved to be unobtrusive. Only one child displayed any curiosity with the equipment, and this interest was momentary. Interactions with the experimenter were minimal and consisted mainly of requests for help in fixing or arranging the toy.

Since, over the course of their play within a social setting, children engage in various types of solitary and social play (e.g., Doyle, Connolly, & Rivest, 1980), sampling of both monologic and dialogic discourse is possible.

Distinctions between monologic and dialogic discourse can be noted in terms of (a) input information, and (b) intended audience. Participants, engaged in dyadic play, receive information as well as clarifications, confirmations, and negations over the course of their interaction. Within this context, the child alternates roles as speaker and audience. Monologic discourse, on the other hand, appears to be characterized by the absence of both input information and an intended audience.

**Story tasks.** Audiotaped protocols were obtained for 12 children one week following completion of the imaginary play observations. Children were familiarized with the tape-recording procedures by the experimenter, who then explained the directions and presented the materials. Each child individually completed the three story tasks over one session—approximately 25 minutes in duration in the following order of presentation:

1. Story comprehension: Children listened to a taped story while looking through a picture booklet. Beeps on the track of the audiotapes served as cues for turning the pages. Children then gave an immediate recall, prompted by the pictures.

   All our subjects expressed reluctance to perform this task. Their typical complaint was that they could not remember the story. Encouragement on the part of the experimenter took the form of nondirective prompts such as "Tell me whatever you can remember" and "Tell me what happened." Despite this initial hesitation, all the children proceeded to complete the task.

2. Picture-elicited story production: After looking through a second sequence of pictures, children turned to the beginning of the booklet and told a story to accompany the sequence of pictures.

3. Free story production: Children told a story of their own choosing about one or more of the three characters depicted in a single picture.

The story tasks, similar to those developed by Bracewell, Frederiksen, and Frederiksen (1982) and Frederiksen et al., (1984), were designed to vary in terms of the textual information and pictorial information made available to the child prior to and during production. The first task differed from the second task in terms of the textual information (oral story) presented to the child immediately preceding his/her production. The third task differed from the second task with respect to the pictorial support offered both preceding and during production. Within this design, the story comprehension task may be regarded as both a recall and as a production task which differs from other production tasks in terms of task constraints that operate to influence comprehension and production processes (Bracewell et al., 1982).

All tasks were similar in that they required the child to generate a story in the presence of an experimenter who, after giving instructions, restricted interaction to minimal feedback (e.g., "OK," "That's great"), despite some children's efforts to draw her into a conversation.

### Data Source

Audiotaped protocols obtained under the story task situation and audio- and videotaped recordings of spontaneous play sessions were transcribed by the experimenter. Transcriptions of videotaped recordings included notes of nonverbal behavior. Verbal protocols were then segmented into clausal units corresponding to main clauses and any embedded clauses (Winograd, 1972). Only major clauses and bound adjuncts were considered to be independent clauses. Fragments, onomatopoeic sounds, rhyming words, and interjections spoken in isolation (a pause of more than one second) were counted as separate segments. False starts and information that was unclear were noted in the transcripts but for the purpose of this study were not analyzed as separate segments. Play protocols included a total of 1,850 segments, an average of 154 segments for each 10-minute play session.

The corpus of protocols analyzed in this study included: (a) 36 story productions obtained under the story task situations; and (b) 8 "monologic" and 8 "dialogic" imaginary play productions obtained from play protocols. Our objective underlying our choice of play productions was to select for each child a topically related stretch of monologic and dialogic discourse that met established criteria for imaginary play. The decision procedure for selecting each play production was as follows:

**1. Identification of topicality related discourse units.** Coding of all segmented play protocols in terms of lexical cohesion was established by employing identical lexical items, superordinates, subordinates, synonyms, and repetitions (Fine, 1976). This linguistic analysis is based on the contextual category of field (Gregory, 1967; Gregory & Carroll, 1978). Field, a diatypic variety of language, represents the linguistic reflection of recurrent characteristics of the use of language in a situation. For example, a child when playing with a car uses words and sounds such as *road, drive, crash, beep-beep,* and words such as *food, eat,* and *yum* when playing with grocery store items. In some contexts, field has been thought of as accounting for the topic of a text (Martin, 1983), i.e., in situations that closely reflect occurrences in the nonverbal context (Gregory & Carroll, 1978). Topics which occurred with the greatest frequency across the three sessions for the four dyads were (a) cars; (b) fire-truck ladder; (c) jail; (d) policeman; (e) farm animals; (f) vegetable garden; (g) going to town-center stores; and (h) Roger-Rhino (a rhinoceros characterized as a construction worker). Activities can and often do incorporate more than one topic. For example, a child can put farm animals in jail. When two such topics overlapped, their segments were included as part of both topics.

**2. Identification of monologic and dialogic discourse.** Topically related discourse units were coded for the occurrence of (a) monologic discourse (discourse occurring during children's solitary or parallel play); and (b) dialogic discourse (discourse occurring during children's social play). Thirty-three percent of discourse was coded as monologic; 67% as dialogic. Solitary play was assessed by collapsing Parten's categories (Doyle et al., 1980): (a) solitary play (the child is alone and engaged in independent activity); and (b) parallel play (the child is physically close to the other child and plays with similar toys, but the play is independent). Social play was defined by employing Parten's categories of: (a) associative play (the child plays actively with the other child); and (b) cooperative play (the child's play with the other child is organized and purposeful).

**3. Identification of imaginary play discourse.** Imaginary play was defined as the "voluntary transformation of the Here and Now, the You and Me, and the This or That, along with any potential for action that these components may have" (Garvey, 1977, p. 82). Classification of those monologic and dialogic topic-related discourse units as "imaginary play" depended on identification of the occurrence of any one of the following four types of transformation: (a) self-transformation; (b) other-transformation; (c) situation transformation; and (d) object transformation or substitution (Johnson, Ershler, & Bell, 1980). Twenty-five imaginary play monologues and 16 dialogues were identified. Children's monologic and dialogic imaginary play could be described as brief event sequences or role enactments. Examples are car crashes, policeman giving tickets, and characters buying food at town-center stores. Children frequently began and interrupted their event sequences only to continue or reintroduce them at a later point during their play session. These were repeated with slight modifications which included changes in character, object, or location as well as the deletion or addition of an event in the sequence. For purposes of this study, all repetitions, continuations, and modifications of an event sequence were included as part of the same discourse unit.

**4. Selection of monologic and dialogic imaginary play productions.** For each child the longest monologic and dialogic play productions were selected for analysis from the previously described corpus. Our initial decision procedure entailed restricting the choice of either a monologic or a dialogic play production to the one in which a topic was initiated and sustained by the target child in that particular discourse unit. This, however, was for the most part not possible. Topics evolved or developed in several ways. These included instances in which a topic was initiated as part of a dyadic interaction and, despite the departure of one of the participants, was sustained, repeated, and/or modified in the context of the solitary or parallel play of the other participant. Conversely, a topic was frequently enacted by a child engaged in monologic play and reintroduced or continued within a dyadic interaction. In describing activities within preschool ecological spaces, Cook-Gumperz and Corsaro (1976) refer to activities as taking on a "'life of their own' with alternating participants" (p. 15). Such a description could well apply to a sizeable proportion of these data.

For the purpose of this study, a monologic play production represented a production which incorporated a topic that was initiated by the target child in *either* his monologic or dialogic play. A dialogic production represented one in which the particular child in question introduced the topic in *either* his monologic or dialogic play discourse, initiated the dyadic interaction, and contributed at least one half of the segments produced by his/her dyad.

### Data Analysis and Dependent Variables

**Story and play productions.** To investigate children's competency in generating different kinds and levels of text structures in their story and play productions, we employed discourse analysis techniques to specify dependent variables indexing these levels. For a description of these techniques, the reader is referred to Frederiksen et al., (1984). Following segmentation, all production protocols were analyzed in terms of: (a) clausal structures; (b) propositional structures; and (c) an index of propositional density. These variables represent the lowest levels of semantic and text structures. Subsequent studies will focus on higher level structures, namely, frame and text linguistic structures.

*1. Clausal structures.* Clausal segments were coded as: (a) simple, (b) complex, and (c) fragments. Simple segments included single clauses containing no embedded clauses. Complex segments included single clauses containing embedded or secondary clauses. Fragments included the following segments, spoken in isolation: (a) isolated constituents or phrases (e.g., "off the tree"); (b) interjections (e.g., "yes," "no," "right"); (c) onomatopoeic sounds imitating objects and animals (e.g., "Grr, grr, grr"); (d) rhyming words consisting of sounds put together which rhyme or form jingles (e.g., "Shelley Poke-Poke"). Interjections, onomatopoeic sounds, and rhyming words incorporated within another segment, were counted as part of that segment.

*2. Propositional structures.* Techniques of propositional analysis were employed to specify the main propositional structures, explicitly encoded in the production protocols. A propositional system is an alternative representation of a semantic network, a labeled network consisting of a set of concepts (nodes in the network) and a set of semantic relations that connect pairs of nodes. Cognitive psychologists (e.g., Frederiksen, 1975, 1977; Kintsch, 1974) have proposed that these networks reflect the propositional structures represented in semantic memory. The propositional model used here is Frederiksen's (1975), recently simplified and formalized as a recursive transition network grammar of propositions (Frederiksen, 1985, in press). Frederiksen's model is chosen for purposes of this study because it provides a well-defined basis for explicit and fine-grained analyses of both recalls and productions. The following major types of propositions, as defined by Frederiksen (1975, 1977), were identified for each individual protocol:

a.   Event propositions, composed of an action or class of actions together
     with case relations that specify the nature of the action, any proposi-
     tions embedded in case slots, and identifying relations which specify
     information about the time, location, and manner of the action. Pos-
     sessives (e.g., "I have a car") were counted in the total number of pro-
     positions generated by a subject but were not included in the count for
     event propositions;
b.   Stative propositions, composed of an object or object class together
     with a set of identifying relations which specify information about the
     time, location, and manner of the object, and which distinguish an ob-
     ject from other classes of objects.
c.   Higher-order relations, composed of two or more propositions connected
     by means of relative, dependency, or identifying relations (includes
     measures (d) and (e) as well as other relations linking propositions);
d.   Relative relations, composed of two or more propositions connected by
     an algebraic relation or function as in comparatives, and relative time
     or location;
e.   Dependency relations, composed of two or more propositions which
     are connected by logical, causal or conditional relations.

*3. Propositional density.* To measure the encoding relationship between
propositions and clause structures, an index of propositional density was
computed by calculating the average number of propositions per clausal
segment. This "procedural" variable reflects the complexity of the propositional encoding process, and strictly speaking, is neither a semantic nor linguistic structural variable.

**Story comprehension.** Protocols obtained under the story comprehension task were analyzed, both as productions, following the procedures described earlier, and as story recalls, reflecting the percentage of propositions
in the original text which were recalled and those which generated inferences. Each segment in a child's recall protocol was scored directly against
the propositional structure of the original oral text. The criterion for scoring a segment as recalled entailed that it include in the case of an event one
concept–relation–concept triple, the head element being either the same,
synonymous, or, in the case of an event, in a superordinate or subordinate
relationship. In the case of other propositions, an identical or synonymous
concept–relation–concept triple was necessary. A segment containing a
change or addition made in the meaning of a concept or relation was scored
as an inference against the proposition to which it was most related, according to both its content and context. Segments, bearing no relationship to
propositions in the original text, were not scored but were marked as un-
coded on the subject's code sheet. These rules have been set down in a
detailed coding guide by J. D. Frederiksen (in Frederiksen, in press).

## Results

Multivariate repeated measures analysis of variance (ANOVA) was used to analyze children's: (a) comprehension, (b) story production, and (c) play production. This method of analysis permitted the study of interactions of between-subjects factors with within-subjects factors as well as of between-and-within-subject effects. Analysis 1, of story comprehension, investigated the equivalence of the two stories employed (with different groups of subjects). Analysis 2 examined effects of story-production task conditions on response modes, reflecting clausal and propositional structures, and on propositional density in subjects who differed in their story comprehension. Analysis 3 investigated similar effects for different play conditions: monologic or dialogic play.

### Analysis 1: Story Comprehension

The first analysis was conducted to assess: (a) children's comprehension as measured by the percentage of propositions recalled or on which inferences were based; and (b) any possible effects of the two versions of oral texts and picture sequences on these measures of story comprehension. The between-subjects factor was Story (S); the within-subjects factor was Response Mode (M). The results, typical of studies of text comprehension, demonstrated a significant main effect of Response Mode (M) $F(1, 10) = 37.2250$, $p < .0002$, indicating that for both stories a higher percentage of propositions had been inferred than recalled. The mean score for the percent of propositions recalled was 9.82, and 16.43 for those inferred. Since the main effect of Story and the interaction of Story with Response Mode were not significant, the two versions of oral text and accompanying picture sequences were treated as equivalent in subsequent analyses.

A grouping variable, Level of Comprehension (L), was established on the basis of children's recall scores. A median score was employed to classify children into high- and low-comprehension groups of 6 subjects each. This grouping variable was used in the following analyses to investigate the relationship of a child's level of story comprehension to measures of his/her text production abilities.

### Analysis 2: Story Production

The second set of analyses, of story production, was concerned with: (a) the extent to which the grouping variable, Level of Comprehension (L), interacted with the within-group factors Response Mode (M) and Task Conditions (C); and (b) the main effects of the within-group factors, Task Condition (C) and Response Mode (M); and (c) the interactions of the within-group factors. Analysis 2 consisted of a series of 6 multivariate analyses of variance, all conducted employing a repeated measures design with Response Mode (M) and Task Condition (C) as the within-group factors and Level of Comprehension (L) (High, Low) as the grouping variable. In Analysis 2, there were three levels of Task Condition (C): (a) story recall production (C1); (b) picture-elicited production (C2); and (c) free production (C3). The respective levels of Factor C in each analysis in set 2 remained the same. However, the particular levels of Response Mode (M) varied with each analysis. Three different sets of dependent variables were used to index children's production: (a) clausal structures; (b) propositional structures; and (c) propositional density. The series of multivariate repeated measures analyses of variance performed for the different dependent variables were as follows:

1. Clausal structures: Two separate multivariate repeated measures analyses of variance were performed. The sets of dependent variables were the percent of clausal structures analysed as (a) simple and complex (in the first analysis); and (b) complex and fragment (in the second analysis).
2. Propositional structures: The next three separate multivariate repeated measures analyses of variance were conducted with the dependent variables being the percent of propositional structures analyzed as (a) events and statives (in the third analysis); (b) events and higher-order relations (in the fourth analysis); and (c) relative relations and dependency relations (in the fifth analysis).
3. Propositional density: The final multivariate analysis employed propositional density as the dependent variable. The design included only the Task Condition factor (C) as the within-subjects factor in the design. Again, Level of Comprehension (L) was the grouping variable.

In all analyses, differences in the absolute number of propositional/ clausal structures produced were controlled by converting these numbers into percents of the total number of propositional/clausal structures produced.

**Clausal and propositional structures.** Mean percentages of clausal structures, for each task condition and level of comprehension are given in Table 1 and those for propositional structures are given in Table 2. Significant effects from each analysis are indicated in Table 3.

A striking feature of these data is that Level of Comprehension did not interact significantly with the within-group factors (Task Condition and Response Mode) when propositional and clausal structures were the dependent variables. These results indicated that there is little relationship between a child's comprehension ability, as measured by his/her level of recall, and these measures of text production. High and low recall children appeared to employ approximately the same percent of different types of clausal and propositional structures to generate their story texts in all task conditions.

Table 1. Mean Percent of Clausal Structures for Level of Comprehension
and Story Task

| Level of Comprehension | Story Task Condition | | | Pooled over Condition |
|---|---|---|---|---|
| | Condition 1 | Condition 2 | Condition 3 | |
| **Simple Clauses** | | | | |
| High | 76.40 | 83.33 | 80.71 | 80.15 |
| Low | 70.08 | 79.29 | 77.03 | 75.47 |
| Pooled | 73.24 | 81.31 | 78.87 | 77.81 |
| **Complex Clauses** | | | | |
| High | 20.80 | 14.71 | 10.40 | 15.30 |
| Low | 13.66 | 10.10 | 15.02 | 12.93 |
| Pooled | 17.23 | 12.41 | 12.71 | 14.12 |
| **Fragmented Clauses** | | | | |
| High | 2.80 | 1.96 | 8.89 | 4.55 |
| Low | 16.26 | 10.63 | 7.95 | 11.61 |
| Pooled | 9.53 | 6.29 | 8.42 | 8.08 |

*Note.* Condition 1: story recall; Condition 2: picture-elicited production; Condition 3: free production.

When the interactions of Task Condition (C) and Response Mode (M) were considered, a consistent pattern of significant findings was not obtained, providing evidence that overall, task conditions do not serve to constrain either propositional structures or their clausal encodings. The one exception to this general trend of nonsignificant results occurred in relation to relative and dependency propositional structures, $F(1, 10) = 7.0074, p < .0245$ (Table 3). This significant $C \times M$ interaction indicates that children employed significantly more relative structures (relations of temporal and locative order) in relation to dependency structures (relations of causality and conditionality) in generating their story texts in the picture-elicited productions (C2) than in the free productions (C3) (Table 2).

Significant main effects of Response Mode (M) were obtained when simple and complex clausal structures were the dependent variables, $F(1, 10) = 334.8469, p < .0001$ (Table 3), indicating that children generated a higher percent of simple than complex clausal structures (Table 1). Although the percent of complex clauses produced was greater than that for fragmented clauses, this difference was not sufficiently large to be statistically significant, $F(1, 10) = 1.600$, *n.s.* Significant effects of Response Mode (M) also were obtained, $F(1, 10) = 41.3296, p < .0001$; $F(1, 10) = 106.3237, p < .0001$, for events and statives and for events and higher-order relations (Table 3), but the effect of M was not significant for relative and dependency rela-

Table 2. Mean Percent of Propositions for Level of Comprehension and Story Task

| Level of Comprehension | Story Task Condition | | | Pooled over Condition |
|---|---|---|---|---|
| | Condition 1 | Condition 2 | Condition 3 | |
| **Events** | | | | |
| High | 51.30 | 47.75 | 46.60 | 48.55 |
| Low | 42.69 | 47.95 | 56.28 | 48.97 |
| Pooled | 47.00 | 47.85 | 51.44 | 48.76 |
| **Statives** | | | | |
| High | 23.11 | 29.03 | 19.27 | 23.80 |
| Low | 20.84 | 34.34 | 27.26 | 27.48 |
| Pooled | 21.97 | 31.69 | 23.27 | 25.64 |
| **Higher Order Relations** | | | | |
| High | 14.26 | 13.70 | 12.52 | 13.49 |
| Low | 13.92 | 11.91 | 7.88 | 11.24 |
| Pooled | 14.09 | 12.81 | 10.20 | 12.37 |
| **Relative Relations** | | | | |
| High | 9.77 | 9.11 | 7.24 | 8.71 |
| Low | 10.26 | 7.94 | 2.94 | 7.05 |
| Pooled | 10.01 | 8.52 | 5.09 | 7.88 |
| **Dependency Relations** | | | | |
| High | 3.78 | 4.58 | 4.72 | 4.36 |
| Low | 3.47 | 2.22 | 4.94 | 3.55 |
| Pooled | 3.63 | 3.40 | 4.83 | 3.95 |

*Note.* Condition 1: story recall; Condition 2: picture-elicited production; Condition 3: free production.

tions. Children produced a greater percent of events than statives, a greater percent of events than higher-order relations, and approximately the same percent of relative and dependency relations, (Table 2).

**Propositional density.** The significant effects obtained in the multivariate repeated measures analysis of variance for propositional density are reported in Table 3. The means appear in Table 4. In contrast to the reported findings, what emerged clearly from the data were highly significant effects for Level of Comprehension (L) when propositional density was the dependent variable, $F(1,10) = 15.4413$, $p < .0029$ (Table 3). Children who obtained high recall scores encoded a greater amount of propositions per clausal segment than low recall children in all story production tasks (Table

Table 3. Summary of Significant Effects of Repeated Measures Multivariate
Analyses of Variance

| Task Conditions | Dependent Variable | | | | | |
|---|---|---|---|---|---|---|
| | Clausal Structures | | Propositional Structures | | | Propositional Density |
| | Simple vs Complex (SS vs CC) | Complex vs Stative (CC vs FR) | Event vs Stative (EV vs ST) | Event vs Higher Order (EV vs HO) | Relative vs Dependency (BE vs DE) | |
| **C1** Story Recall Production **C2** Picture–Elicited Production **C3** Free Production n = 12 | M(SC > CC): F(1,10)=41.3 P < .0001 | | M( EV > ST): F(1,10)=41.33 P < .0001 | M(EV < HO): F(1,10)=106.32 P < .0001 | CxM: F(1,10)=7.01 P < .0245 | L(high > low): F(1,10)=15.4413 P < .0029  C(C1>C2): F(1,10)=5.13 P < .0471 |
| **C1** Monologic Production **C2** Dialogic Production n = 8 | M(SS>CC): F(1,6)=51.43 P < .0003 | M(CC<FR): F(1,6)=84.44 P < .0001  LxM: F(1,6)=17.81 P < .0056 | M(EV>ST): F(1,6)=12.43 P < .0125 | M(EV > HO): F(1,6)=110.43 P < .0001 | | L(high > low): F(1,6)=12.94 P < .0115 |

Note: L = significant level of comprehension effect (high and
      low recall groups);
      C = significant condition effect;
      M = significant modality effect for dependent
      variables indicated.

4). The implication is that a child's level of comprehension is associated with
his/her propositional density in discourse production.

In addition, when task condition effects were considered, a significant
effect for the comparison of the story recall productions (C1) and the picture-elicited productions (C2) was obtained, $F(1,10) = 5.1272$, $p < .0471$;
Table 3. This significant comparison was produced by a decrease in the
number of propositions encoded per clausal segment from (C1) to (C2)
(Table 4) indicating that both high- and low-comprehension children encoded a greater number of propositions per clausal segment on the story
recall productions than on the picture-elicited productions. A similar pattern was observed for the comparison of the picture-elicited productions
(C2) and the free productions (C3), but this effect was not statistically sig-

Table 4. Mean Propositional Density for Level of Comprehension and Story Task

| Level of Comprehension | Story Task Condition | | | Pooled over Condition |
|---|---|---|---|---|
| | Condition 1 | Condition 2 | Condition 3 | |
| High | 2.52 | 2.27 | 1.92 | 2.23 |
| Low | 1.95 | 1.66 | 1.61 | 1.74 |
| Pooled | 2.23 | 1.96 | 1.76 | 3.97 |

*Note.* Condition 1: story recall; Condition 2: picture-elicited production; Condition 3: free production.

nificant (Table 4). There were no significant Level × Conditions interactions for propositional density. Taken together, these results indicate that the story recall production task which provides adult textual input information prior to production appears to enhance the number of propositions encoded by both high- and low-recall children.

## Analysis 3: Play Production

Clausal and propositional structures. The third set of analyses of imaginary play production investigated: (a) the interaction of the grouping variable (Level of Comprehension (L)) with the within group factors: Play Condition (C) and Response Mode (M); and (b) the main effects and interactions of these within-group factors. The levels of Play Condition were: (a) monologic play production (C1); and (b) dialogic play production (C2). Response Mode values varied with specific analyses and were the same as for Analysis 2. Mean percentages for Play Condition and Level of Comprehension for clausal structures and propositional structures are in Tables 5 and 6, respectively. A summary of significant effects are given in Table 3.

Overall, the findings of Analysis 3 paralleled the findings of Analysis 2. First, only one significant interaction of Level of Comprehension (L) with Response Mode (M) was obtained, $F(1, 6) = 17.8088$, $p < .0056$; (Table 3). Here low-comprehension children produced more fragmented clauses than the high-comprehension children and fewer complex clauses (Table 5). However, there was little relationship between a child's comprehension level and his/her production of propositional structures (Tables 3 and 6).

Second, no significant effects were found for Play Conditions (C), and the effect of Play Condition did not interact significantly with Response Mode (M) for any set of dependent variables. These results lend additional support for the conclusions drawn from Analysis 2 that task/condition has little affect on the propositional and clausal structures children employ in generating their production texts.

Finally, the pattern of results that emerged when the effects of Response Mode (M) were analyzed, was similar, with one exception, to the pattern ob-

Table 5. Mean Percent of Clauses for Level of Comprehension and Play Condition

| Level of Comprehension | Imaginary Play Condition | | Pooled over Condition |
|---|---|---|---|
| | Monologic | Dialogic | |
| **Simple Clauses** | | | |
| High | 71.51 | 61.56 | 66.53 |
| Low | 56.95 | 59.50 | 58.22 |
| Pooled | 64.23 | 60.53 | 62.38 |
| **Complex Clauses** | | | |
| High | 6.78 | 14.23 | 10.50 |
| Low | 2.79 | 8.57 | 5.68 |
| Pooled | 4.78 | 11.40 | 8.09 |
| **Fragmented Clauses** | | | |
| High | 21.72 | 22.68 | 22.20 |
| Low | 40.18 | 34.31 | 37.25 |
| Pooled | 30.95 | 28.50 | 29.72 |

tained in Analysis 2: Children generated a significantly higher percent of events in relation to statives, $F(1, 6) = 12.4329$, $p < .0125$ and to higher-order relations $F(1, 6) = 110.4313$, $p < .0001$ (Tables 3 and 6)) but approximately the same percent of relative and dependency structures (Tables 3 and 6). As in Analysis 2, a significant modality effect for simple and complex structures was obtained $F(1, 6) = 61.4344$, $p < .0003$ (Table 3). However, in contrast to the results obtained in Analysis 2, a significant effect for complex and fragmented clausal structures also was obtained, $F(1, 6) = 84.4348$, $p < .0001$ (Table 3) indicating that, in the imaginary play productions, children generated more fragmented clausal structures in relation to complex structures (Table 5).

Propositional density. Table 3 displays the significant effects obtained in the multivariate repeated measures analysis of variance for propositional density. The means are given in Table 7. As in Analysis 2, a highly significant effect for Level of Comprehension (L) was obtained when propositional density was the dependent variable, $F(1, 6) = 12.9384$, $p < .0115$ (Table 3). Again, high-recall children appeared to encode more propositions per clausal segment than low-recall children (Table 7), further confirming our previous finding that a child's level of comprehension is associated with his/her propositional density in discourse production.

In contrast to Analysis 2, however, a significant effect of Play Condition (C) was not obtained. Children appeared to encode almost the identical amount of propositions per clausal segment in both their monologic (C1) and dialogic (C2) play productions (Table 7). The opportunity to engage in

Table 6. Mean Percent of Propositions for Level of Comprehension
and Play Condition

| Level of Comprehension | Imaginary Play Condition | | |
|---|---|---|---|
| | Monologic | Dialogic | Pooled over Condition |
| **Events** | | | |
| High | 62.83 | 55.69 | 59.26 |
| Low | 55.11 | 56.92 | 56.01 |
| Pooled | 58.97 | 56.30 | 57.64 |
| **Statives** | | | |
| High | 29.67 | 28.86 | 29.27 |
| Low | 31.74 | 29.93 | 30.84 |
| Pooled | 30.71 | 29.39 | 30.05 |
| **Higher Order Relations** | | | |
| High | 3.13 | 12.73 | 7.93 |
| Low | 4.25 | 6.90 | 5.57 |
| Pooled | 3.69 | 9.81 | 6.75 |
| **Relative Relations** | | | |
| High | 3.13 | 3.29 | 3.21 |
| Low | 4.25 | 2.99 | 3.62 |
| Pooled | 3.69 | 3.14 | 3.41 |
| **Dependency Relations** | | | |
| High | 0.00 | 8.97 | 4.49 |
| Low | 0.00 | 0.00 | 0.00 |
| Pooled | 0.00 | 4.49 | 2.24 |

Table 7. Mean Propositional Density for Level of Comprehension
and Play Condition

| Level of Comprehension | Imaginary Play Condition | | |
|---|---|---|---|
| | Monologic | Dialogic | Pooled over Condition |
| **Events** | | | |
| High | 1.40 | 1.35 | 1.37 |
| Low | 1.01 | 1.05 | 1.03 |
| Pooled | 1.20 | 1.20 | 1.20 |

social play did not appear to enhance the amount of propositional encoding.

## Discussion and Conclusion

The present research was concerned with applying cognitive discourse analysis techniques, derived from the study of text comprehension, to investigate the ability of preschool children to generate story and imaginary play texts and to relate measures of this production ability to story comprehension. Children's comprehension was assessed by coding story recalls, obtained in the comprehension task, against the propositional structures of the presented oral text and scoring for recall and inference of text propositions. Analyses of productions in this study focused on propositional and clausal structures and on propositional density, a measure of clausal encoding of propositions. Analyses of children's productions obtained in two different sequences of experimental tasks, story production and imaginary play, may be summarized.

First, both analyses demonstrated that a child's level of comprehension is associated with his/her propositional density in all story and play tasks. The major source of variation between high- and low-recall children lies not in the type of propositional and clausal structures they employ to construct their story and play texts but rather in the complexity of propositional encoding.

Second, evidence from both analyses indicated that children (with one exception) produce similar clausal and propositional structures under varied task conditions. However, with respect to propositional density, the story comprehension task which provided a structured adult text prior to production, enhances this measure of complexity of propositional encoding for both high- and low-recall children.

Thus, children did not differ systematically with respect to the propositional and clausal structures they employed to construct their text productions in the different task conditions, but in the number of propositions encoded per clausal segment. These findings require an explanation beyond the level of knowledge of clausal and propositional structures. The explanation may, therefore, be in terms of the *processes* involved in choosing propositional and clausal structures and in encoding propositions in clauses. These findings may also reflect differences in production of suprapropositional frame structures. Frederiksen's theoretical model (Frederiksen, 1985, in press) and the recent findings of Frederiksen et al. (1984) lend support to the latter explanation. Within this theoretical perspective, clausal, propositional, and text-linguistic structures reflect conceptual frame structures. Differences or similarities in production at these levels of analysis, therefore, are best understood with reference to the higher levels they reflect.

Within this context, Frederiksen et al. (1984) demonstrated that there were only minor differences between a grade-2 and grade-4 child in the propositional and clausal structures they produced under a picture-elicited production task, but striking differences with age in the extent and complexity of the narrative and problem frame structures generated. Moreover what differences there were in propositional and clausal structures and in text-level linguistic structures (topic-comment structure and cohesive devices) appeared to reflect the differences in frame structures produced. Similarly further analysis of our data at the level of conceptual (frame) and text-linguistic structures will enable us to relate our findings on propositional density to other text and discourse level processes.

Overall, task condition had little effect on the propositional and clausal structures children employ in generating their story and play texts. The finding of similar patterns of results (with one exception) when the effects of Response Mode were considered in both the story production and play production analyses further supports our conclusion that there is a high degree of consistency in children's production of propositional and clausal structures across a range of discourse productions and that task conditions involve similar constraints on these structures. The one exception to the general trend of nonsignificant task condition effects occurred in the comparison of the picture-elicited and free production tasks for relative and dependency propositional structures. Further analysis of our data, specifically the application of a narrative frame grammer, detailing the rules of formation in which events are linked by means of relative and dependency relations to form higher-order units such as episodes and episode sequences should permit us to relate this finding to other discourse level processes, as was found in Frederiksen et al. (1984).

With respect to propositional density, the results indicated the story comprehension task which made available to the child an adult discourse model prior to his/her production enhances the number of propositions encoded by both high- and low-recall children. However, a similar finding was not obtained for the comparison of monologic and dialogic discourse. The opportunity to engage in peer interactions did not result in an increased amount of propositional encoding.

The failure to find significant play condition differences in the imaginary play condition is surprising in view of recent observational studies of play discourse which have implicated social play in the production of complex linguistic structures (Garvey, 1979) and textual surface features (cohesion and topicalization patterns, Pellegrini, 1982). To explain this discrepancy in findings, we need to examine what aspects of social play would likely influence discourse structures. One component of social play believed to affect children's discourse is the negotiation of a common frame, particularly for fantasy play, prior to or during participants' narrative enactments. Elements central to fantasy play such as fantasy themes and symbolic transformations of roles and props require children to provide explicit verbal accounts and explanations for their ongoing play activities (Martlew et al., 1978; Pellegrini, 1982). It is this negotiation of a common frame for fantasy play that is believed to be one of the factors differentiating monologic from dialogic discourse (Martlew et al., 1978). However, social play, vis-à-vis its effects on discourse must be considered not only in terms of the type of play, but also in terms of children's world knowledge, and features of the environmental setting (Cook-Gumperz & Corsaro, 1976; Corsaro, 1983). In the social play interactions in our sample, the children, who were well known to each other, seem to have entered these interactions with a common notion of the play task as narrative production, a notion that appears to have been established in part by the floor toy environment. Given the nature of this play setting, which featured familiar social scenes and characters, and children's prior knowledge concerning the normative roles of these play characters, the children were able, without extensive negotiation, to cooperatively produce discourse structures that were similar to those produced in the monologic condition. Thus, the dialogic play strongly resembled the monologic play in its narrative enactments of brief event sequences and in its discourse characteristics. Within our theoretical perspective, differences or similarities in clausal and propositional structures are best understood with reference to the frame-level semantic structures they reflect. It will require further analysis at the level of narrative and conversational frame structures to establish whether such similarities are evident at these higher levels of discourse structure.

In summary, the similarities and differences we have identified in children's story and play productions lie at the propositional and clausal levels, and we have emphasized throughout the interpretation of these lower-level semantic and text structures in terms of higher-level text and discourse structures. Clearly then any conclusions concerning the issues of an oral/literate or play/school dichotomy in language development or the sources of literacy skills in preschool experiences will have to await completion of frame-level analyses. The results we have presented thus far seem to suggest continuity across the range of discourse tasks we studied rather than any major discontinuities. It would appear that similar cognitive skills associated with the production of semantic and text structures may occur across different task conditions. The search for "sources" of literate discourse skills in play may be misdirected. Rather, the problem may be one of examining the development and functioning of structure-building processes in discourse production and comprehension across a range of task environments representative of varied school, home, and community experiences.

## References

Bracewell, R. J., Frederiksen, C. H., & Frederiksen, J. D. (1982). Cognitive processes in composing and comprehending discourse. *Educational Psychologist, 17,* 146–164.

Brewer, W. F., & Lichtensten, E. H. (1980). *Event schemas, story schemas and story gram-mars*. (Technical Report No. 197). Champaign, IL: University of Illinois at Urbana-Champaign.

Bruce, B. (1980). Plans and social actions. In R. J. Spiro, B. C. Bruce, & W. F. Brewer (Eds.), *Theoretical issues in reading comprehension*. Hillsdale, NJ: Erlbaum.

Clements, P. (1979). The effects of staging on recall from prose. In R. O. Freedle (Ed.), *New directions in discourse processing: Vol. 2. Advances in discourse processes*. Norwood, NJ: Ablex.

Cook-Gumperz, J., & Corsaro, W. A. (1976). Social–ecological constraints on children's com-municative strategies. In J. Cook-Gumperz and J. J. Gumperz (Eds.), *Papers on lan-guage and context*. (Working Paper No. 46, Language Behavior Research Laboratory), Berkeley, CA: University of California.

Corsaro, W. A. (1983). Script recognition, articulation, and expansion in children's role play. *Discourse Processes, 6,* 1–19.

Doyle, A. B., Connolly, J., & Rivest, L. P. (1980). The effect of playmate familiarity on the social interactions of young children. *Child Development, 51,* 217–223.

Feitelson, D., & Ross, G. S. (1973). The neglected factor: play. *Human Development, 16,* 202–223.

Fine, J. (1976). *Notes on components in the study of oral communications*. Unpublished man-uscript.

Frederiksen, C. H. (1975). Representing logical and semantic structure of knowledge acquired from discourse. *Cognitive Psychology, 7,* 371–485.

Frederiksen, C. H. (1977). Semantic processing units in understanding text. In R. O. Freedle (Ed.), *Discourse production and comprehension: Vol 1. Advances in discourse pro-cesses*. Norwood, NJ: Ablex.

Frederiksen, C. H. (1981). Inferences in preschool children's conversations: A cognitive per-spective. In J. Green & C. Wallat (Eds.), *Ethnography and language in educational set-ting*. Norwood, NJ: Ablex.

Frederiksen, C. H. (1985). Cognitive models and discourse analysis. In C. R. Cooper & S. Greenbaum (Eds.), *Written communication annual: An international survey of research and theory: Vol. 1. Linguistic approaches to the study of written discourse*. Beverly Hills: CA: Sage.

Frederiksen, C. H. (in press). *Knowledge and inference in discourse communication*. Nor-wood, NJ: Ablex.

Frederiksen, C. H., & Frederiksen, J. D. (1982, March). *Frame construction and comprehen-sion of school-type texts*. Paper presented at the meeting of the American Educational Research Association, New York, NY.

Frederiksen, C. H., Frederiksen, J. D., & Bracewell, R. J. (1984). Discourse processing in chil-dren's written and oral production. In A. Matsuhasi (Ed.), *Writing in real time*. New York: Longman.

Frederiksen, C. H., Frederiksen, J. D., & Bracewell, R. J. (1985). *Frame construction pro-cesses in children's production: The effects of task demands on children's production of narrative and conversational text structure*. Manuscript submitted for publication.

Garvey, C. (1974). Some properties of social play. *Merrill-Palmer Quarterly, 20,* 163–180.

Garvey, C. (1975). Requests and responses in children's speech. *Journal of Child Language, 2,* 41–64.

Garvey, C. (1977). *Play*. Cambridge, MA: Harvard University Press.

Garvey, C. (1979). Communicational controls in social play. In B. Sutton-Smith (Ed.), *Play and learning*. New York: Wiley.

Garvey, C., & Hogan, R. (1973). Social speech and social interaction: Egocentrism revisited. *Child Development, 44,* 562–568.

Golomb, C. (1979). Pretense play: A cognitive perspective. In N. R. Smith & M. B. Franklin (Eds.), *Symbolic functioning in childhood*. Hillsdale, NJ: Erlbaum.

Gregory, M. (1967). Aspects of varieties differentiation. *Journal of Linguistics, 3,* 177–198.

Gregory, M., & Carroll, S. (1978). *Language and situation: Language varieties and their social context*. London: Routledge & Kegan Paul.

Gundlach, R. A. (1981). On the nature and development of children's writing. In C. H. Frederiksen & J. F. Dominic (Eds.), *Writing: Process, development, and communication*. Hillsdale, NJ: Erlbaum.

Halliday, M. A. K., & Hasan, R. (1976). *Cohesion in English*. London: Longman.

Hidi, S. E., & Hildyard, A. (1983). The comparison of oral and written productions in two discourse types. *Discourse Processes, 6,* 91–105.

Johnson, J. E., Ershler, J., & Bell, C. (1980). Play behavior in a discovery-based and a formal-education preschool program. *Child Development, 51,* 271–274.

Keenan, E. O. (1974). Conversational competence in children. *Journal of Child Language, 1,* 163–183.

Kintsch, W. (1974). *The representation of meaning in memory*. Hillsdale, NJ: Erlbaum.

Kintsch, W., & van Dijk, T. A. (1978). Toward a model of text comprehension and production. *Psychological Review, 85,* 363–394.

Mandler, J. M., & Johnson, N. S. (1977). Remembrance of things parsed: Story structures and recall. *Cognitive Psychology, 9,* 111–151.

Martin, J. R. (1983). The development of register. In J. Fine & R. O. Freedle (Eds.), *Developmental issues in discourse: Vol. 10. Advances in discourse processes*. Norwood, NJ: Ablex.

Martlew, M., Connolly, K., & McCleod, C. (1978). Language use, role and context in a five-year old. *Journal of Child Langauge, 5,* 81–99.

Olson, D. R. (1977). From utterance to text: The bias of language in speech writing. *Harvard Educational Review, 47* (3), 257–281.

Pellegrini, A. (1982). The construction of text by preschoolers in two play contexts. *Discourse Processes, 5,* 101–108.

Pellegrini, A. D. (1984). The effect of dramatic play on children's generation of cohesive text. *Discourse Processes, 7,* 57–67.

Pellegrini, A., & Galda, L. (1982). The effects of thematic-fantasy play on the development of children's story comprehension. *American Educational Research Journal, 19,* 443–452.

Rubin, A. (1980). A theoretical taxonomy between oral and written language. In R. J. Spiro, B. C. Bruce, & W. F. Brewer (Eds.), *Theoretical issues in reading comprehension*. Hillsdale, NJ: Erlbaum.

Rumelhart, D. E. (1977). Understanding and summarizing brief stories. In D. LaBerge & J. Samuels (Eds.), *Basic processes in reading: Perception and comprehension*. Hillsdale, NJ: Erlbaum.

Sachs, J. (1980). The role of adult–child play in language development. In K. H. Rubin (Ed.), *New directions for child development: Vol. 9. Children's play*. San Francisco, CA: Jossey-Bass.

Sachs, J., Goldman, J., & Chaille, C. (1984). Planning in pretend play: Using language to coordinate narrative development. In A. Pellegrini and T. Yawkey (Eds.), *The development of oral and written language in social context*. Norwood, NJ: Ablex.

Scinto, L. F. M. (1983). The development of text production. In J. Fine & R. O. Freedle (Eds.), *Development issues in discourse: Vol. 10. Advances in discourse processes*. Norwood, NJ: Ablex.

Scribner, S., & Cole, M. (1981). Unpackaging literacy. In M. F. Whiteman (Ed.), *Writing: The nature, development, and teaching of written communication: Vol. 1. Variation in Writing: Functional and linguistic-cultural differences*. Hillsdale, NJ: Erlbaum.

Singer, J. L. (1973). *The child's world of make-believe.* New York: Academic Press.

Smilansky, S. (1968). *The effects of sociodramatic play on disadvantaged preschool children.* New York: Wiley.

Stein, N. L. (1982). What's in a story: Interpreting the interpretations of story grammars. *Discourse Processes, 5,* 319–335.

Stein, N. L., & Glenn, C. G. (1979). An analysis of story comprehension in elementary school children. In R. O. Freedle (Ed.), *New directions in discourse processing: Vol. 2. Advances in discourse processes.* Norwood, NJ: Ablex.

Sutton-Smith, B. (Ed.). (1979). *Play and learning.* New York: Wiley.

Sutton-Smith, B. (1980). Children's play: Some sources of play theorizing. In K. H. Rubin (Ed.), *New directions for child development: Vol. 9. Children's play.* San Francisco, CA: Jossey-Bass.

Tannen, D. (1982). Oral and literate strategies in spoken and written narratives. *Language, 58,* 1–21.

Thorndyke, P. W. (1977). Cognitive structures in comprehension and memory of narrative discourse. *Cognitive Psychology, 9,* 77–110.

Tierney, R. J., Bridge, C. A., & Cera, M. J. (1979). The discourse processing operations of children. *Reading Research Quarterly, 14,* 539–573.

Trabasso, T., & Nicholas, D. W. (1980). Memory and inferences in the comprehension of narratives. In F. Wilkening, J. Becker, & T. Trabasso (Eds.), *Information integration by children.* Hillsdale, NJ: Erlbaum.

Weaver, P. A., & Dickinson, D. K. (1982). Scratching below the surface structure. Exploring the usefulness of story grammars. *Discourse Processes, 5,* 225–243.

Wimmer, H. (1980). Children's understanding of stories: Assimilation by a general schema for actions or coordination of temporal relations. In F. Wilkening, J. Becker, & T. Trabasso (Eds.), *Information integration by children.* Hillsdale, NJ: Erlbaum.

Winograd, T. (1972). Understanding natural language. *Cognitive Psychology, 3,* 1–191.

Yawkey, T. D., & Silvern, J. (1979, April). *An investigation of imaginative play and aural language development in young children, five, six and seven.* Paper presented at the meeting of the American Educational Research Association, San Francisco, CA.

# PART III
# PLAY AND LEARNING TO USE LANGUAGE

# 7

## Play Beyond Play: Its Role in Formal Informative Speech*

### Mary Ann Evans
University of Guelph

### Introduction

Play has proven to be a popular means for studying children's development. Through observing children's play activity and coding, counting, and selecting behaviors, psychologists have made inferences regarding such diverse issues as children's wishes and fears, attitudes, sex-role identity, and cognitive style. As this volume demonstrates, play has also been the principal context for studying adult speech to children (see Raffer-Engel & Lebrun, 1976; Snow & Ferguson, 1977) and the productive language of children themselves, ranging from their early symbolic development in infancy (e.g., Bates, Bretherton, Shore, & McNew, 1983; Fein, 1979; Shotwell, Wolf, & Gardner, 1979) to their conversational skills with their agemates as toddlers and preschoolers (e.g., Dore, Gearhart, & Newman, 1978; Garvey & Hogan, 1973; Shields, 1978). In these studies, the play interactions of the participants have provided a rich data base representative of naturally occurring language.

Unfortunately, however, while manipulative and pretend play between mothers and infants and among preschoolers is easily staged by providing age-appropriate toys and a comfortable setting, the play of older children is more elusive for observation. Among older children, free play is increasingly replaced by teacher-directed, structured lessons in the school and by formal games with rules in the home and on the street (Knapp & Knapp, 1976; Opie & Opie, 1969). It is, perhaps, for this reason that a major shift occurs in the way children's language and communication are studied once they enter

* This research was supported by the Social Sciences and Humanities Research Council. Grateful thanks is extended to the Wellington County Board of Education for its participation and to Karina Forsyth, Kathy Williamson, Janet Clewes, and Alice Sibal-Lim for their assistance with the tape transcriptions.

kindergarten, from naturalistic observation in realistic contexts, referred to by Dickson (1981) as the sociolinguistic tradition (see review by Shatz, 1983), to experimenter-directed testing in laboratory settings, or the referential tradition (see reviews by Asher, 1978; Dickson, 1981; Glucksberg, Krauss, & Higgins, 1975). Except for instructional interactions studied in the classroom (e.g., Cazden, Cox, Dickinson, Steinberg, & Stone, 1974; Cicourel, 1974; Griffin & Shuy, 1978; Mehan, 1979; Sinclair & Coulthard, 1975), spontaneous language, so much a part of play, is simply not as readily available after age five for research scrutiny.

These two different methodologies have created an incongruous characterization of preschool-aged children as competent communicators with a reasonably sophisticated understanding of discourse rules and conversational strategies, but slightly older beginning school-aged children as communicatively inept, hindered by limited processing skills which cannot meet the particular task constraints. In addition they have afforded little opportunity for an appreciation of the continuities within a given age range across contexts (see French, Lucariello, Seidman, & Nelson, this volume) or within a given context across age ranges.

What follows is an attempt to partially bridge the two research traditions by discussing how children in the early school grades spontaneously relate ideas to others during a classroom discussion period. A main focus will be to show how habits and elements of behavior during the contextually embedded interactions of play also appear within more formal and decontextualized informative speech in young children. The observations on which this discussion is based principally stem from a longitudinal study of children's participation in the classroom activity of "Show and Tell" which I have recently conducted. In this situation the children were asked to talk about something which was usually physically and/or temporally removed from its context and unknown to their listeners, that is, to engage in informative speech. It will be argued that while this is a relatively difficult process for preschool and primary-grade children, it is facilitated by communicative habits and strategies used earlier in play. A number of transcriptions of children's turns at Show and Tell have been included throughout the manuscript as qualitative illustrations of the quantitative patterns revealed by the coded data.

## The Course of Informative Speech

Those of us who study the development of informative speech may feel somewhat self-conscious, for much of our work requires the very thing we study. However, informative speech is not limited to conferences and colloquia. It pervades daily social interaction. In meeting others, both children and adults exchange details of their interests and backgrounds to establish a common ground (Gottman, 1983; Gottman & Parkhurst, 1980) and continue to exchange their ideas and experiences as part of their evolving social relationship. Informative speech may be conceived of as a kind of social currency for the trading of one's life view. Its value is further suggested by studies showing a positive relationship between peer popularity and the ability of children to sustain conversations (La Greca & Mesibov, 1979) and to produce informative messages (Gottman, Gonso, & Rasmussen, 1975; Rubin, 1972). Informative speech is also of prime importance in school, serving as the principal means by which the content of the curriculum is transmitted from the teacher, and in its written form as the principal means by which mastery of the curriculum by the student is evaluated. It has also been suggested that it has personal heuristic value, in that in "reaching out to touch others with our recollections, we give ourselves resources for mental activity when we are alone" (Rosen & Rosen, 1973, p. 56).

Although informative speech is the dominant function of adult speech, it is developmentally the last to emerge. In his account of "learning how to mean," Halliday (1975) describes two macrofunctions of speech encompassing several subfunctions. Initially children's speech is entirely "pragmatic" in that it demands some form of response in terms of goods and services, verbal, nonverbal, or material. Children state what they want and want others to do and ask about their environment. Toward the end of the second year it becomes more mathetic in function whereby children report on objects and events in the environment which impinge on their perceptions (Brown & Bellugi, 1963; Halliday, 1975). These assertions state nothing new for the listener but confirm common referential points between speaker and listener and the linguistic means for expressing them. The child covered in chocolate from ear to ear who says, "I got dirty face" is expressing given and not new information (Clark & Haviland, 1977). Similarly, the interpretation of the classic quote "Mommy sock" (Bloom, 1970) is based on what the listener already knows about the sock and its relationship to mommy and the child.

Gradually these commentaries on the here-and-now shift to being more truly informative, conveying a unique perspective to a listener who does not already posses it. And gradually, they become separated from the extralinguistic context which spawned them. Umiker-Sebeok (1979) observed that about one third of the conversations of 3- to 5-year-old children contained descriptions of past experiences, a form of informative speech. Similarly, Moerk (1975) noted that the conversations of mothers with their children age 2 through 5 increasingly dealt with past activities and future plans as the age of the child increased. This gradual separation of language from the environment and activity on which it is based and necessity of expressing one's meaning unambiguously with words is referred to as *decontextualization*

(Bates, 1979) and is viewed as an important transition for dealing with written text- and school-based learning (Olson, 1977). However, what children talk about during this transition period and how they go about it has remained largely unexplored.

## The Present Data Base

Observations of children's participation in Show and Tell afford some insight into both the topics and manner of young children's informative speech, for each child chooses his subject matter and participatory style. Show and Tell regularly occurs in primary grade classrooms and is an example of what Cazden (1975) calls a "concentrated encounter"—a situation that permits naturally occurring patterns of speech but is structured to maximize the occurrence of a particular type of speech. The data reported here are derived from 18 children, 11 boys and 7 girls in each of a kindergarten and second grade class. These children had been present during the five Show and Tell periods observed in each of the fall, winter, and spring terms. During each Shown-and-Tell period, the children sat in a circle on the floor. The kindergarten teacher began by asking who had something they would like to tell and then called upon individual children, choosing from among children when several of them raised their hands. In the second grade classroom, the children took turns from day to day in taking the teacher's role. Each session lasted about 25 minutes and continued until as many children who wanted had had at least one turn at sharing something with their classmates. The kindergarten teacher also made a point of calling upon children who did not volunteer, but they often declined to take a turn. A total of 205 turns at speaking and 305 topics were provided by the kindergarteners. The second graders contributed a total of 170 turns and 286 topics across the 15 sessions observed.

## The Rhythm of Show and Tell: The Role of Repetition

The initial examination of the children's speech involved noting which children participated in each session and the topic of their speech. As has been noted by Hurtig (1977) speech typically involves units larger than sentences, these units having a single logical or topical structure regardless of whether they are multiperson exchanges, dialogues, or monologues. Many of the kindergarten children spoke only one or two sentences before the teacher acknowledged their comment with a suitable phrase such as "Oh" or "Did you?" followed by further comments, and it was easy to identify the topic of their speech within these beginning sentences. Similarly second graders typically uttered a topic sentence within the first two or three sentences of their monologues.

The following listing outlines the topic sentences of a typical Show-and-Tell session within the kindergarten classroom. Each speaker is numbered in sequence, and multiple topics by a single speaker are distinguished by upper-case letters.

1. Holly R:    A. Today a bird came to my birdfeeder.
               B. Once I catched a bird by the wing.
2. John:       A. I saw a bird with a red wing.
3. Donald:     A. My sister got a silly doll at her birthday.
4. Emily:      A. We saw a bird once that couldn't fly.
               B. I have some tattoos on my arm.
               C. Gerald and Kevin threw snowballs at me.
5. Michael:    A. At my friends, [house] we made a giant snowman.
               B. I got hit by a snowball once.
               C. I rolled a giant snowball home.
6. Jonathan:   A. I got an animal book.
7. Billy:      A. My spaceship from McDonald's went crazy.
               B. I had a milkshake that took till midnight to drink.
8. Tamara:     A. Long time ago I watched a movie about dinosaurs.
               B. My brother has a library book about animals.
9. Saudia:     A. My brother has tattoos.
10. Holly T:   A. I got a new hat for my birthday.
11. Wendy W:   A. I know one dinosaur still lives today.
12. Michael:   D. We got a book about sea monsters.

Holly begins by describing the event of a bird coming to her bird feeder. The second speaker, John, offers a similar comment as does the fourth speaker, Emily, who then turns to describe some press-on tattoos she got on her arm at a birthday party. Five speakers later, Saudia talks about her brother's tattoos, a topic which never arose in any other session observed. Emily's third topic, being hit by a snowball, is echoed by the next speaker, Michael, who then talks about a *giant* snowman. Two speaker's later, Billy mentions the *giant* milkshake he had. The sixth speaker, Jonathan, tells that he has an animal book at home, a topic repeated by the eighth speaker, Tamara. The twelfth and last speaker, Michael, who had earlier had a turn, repeats this topic of books and incorporates the dinosaur theme of the eleventh speaker, Wendy, and eighth speaker, Tamara.

Such recurring topics were not unusual among the kindergarten children. During the fall, winter, and spring observations, 30%, 24%, and 23% of the speech topics, respectively, were shared by different speakers within the same session. Of the 73 instances observed, most formed sequences separated by fewer than three intervening speakers, and half were produced by adjacent speakers. This repetition and modulation of previous speech topics is reminiscent of the ritualized play sequences observed by Garvey (1977). According to Garvey, such sequences begin when one child picks up on a comment of another child and repeats it identically, or modifies it by substituting one item of the utterance by another, or completes and complements it in some form. However, unlike the ritualized sequences noted by Garvey which occurred in play dyads, the topical repetitions in Show and Tell typically involved two or three and sometimes five to seven children. One particularly long round emerged during one session after which the first speaker of the day, Emily, told about falling down on the sidewalk. She then asserted that her favorite color was pink. Speakers numbered 8, 10, 11, 12, 13, 14, 15, 16, and 17 then each stated their favorite colors. Then, in a grand coda, the round ended with speaker 18 stating her least-liked color, and Emily returning to assert, "I like all the colors," followed by her best friend who echoed, "And I like all the colors too."

Such topic repetitions were rarely observed among the second grade children. Only 12%, 6%, and 2% of the topics in the fall, winter, and spring terms, respectively, were common among the speakers. The fact that topics were repeated less frequently in the second grade classroom suggests that the older children came with something specific to tell, independent of what others said, whereas the younger children were influenced in their choice of speech topics by what had been said before. With respect to the play sequences she observed, Garvey (1977) commented, "Such interaction is relatively inexpensive: No new topics, ideas or opinions are required" (p. 120). Similarly, with respect to Show and Tell, no new topic need be thought up to relate, enabling the kindergarten children to more easily participate in this activity. As long as the imitative turn is not too distant from its source, it may be perceived as interactional rather than simply copycat.

### The Topics of Show and Tell: The Role of Objects

A description may be defined as speech by which the speaker asserts his perspective about a state of affairs in order to turn his listener's attention to it and to create some shared understanding of it (Evans & Carr, 1984). Laboratory studies of referential communication require children to describe experimenter-chosen topics such as abstract designs, games, and specific personal events, with the principal assigned goal being to express oneself clearly and unambiguously. Show and Tell also primarily requires descriptions from the children, but the children may choose to comment on any object or event, and the goal is as much social participation as unambiguous communication. Thus the topics of children's turns and the ideas they express provide insight into what is significant and conversationally manageable for them.

Six categories were used to designate the topics of the children's speech. *Object descriptions* dealt with possessions such as toys and clothes; *activity reports* consisted of one or two utterances about something they (or another) had done or were going to do; *activity narratives* told about something that had happened; *mastery comments* expressed what the child could do (e.g., "I can tie my shoes"); *observations* commented on something in the environment (e.g., "Holly and I have the same pants on"); and a miscellaneous *other* category allowed for any other type of remark.

Table 1 displays the percentage of topics falling into each classification by grade. Second graders more often told their classmates stories about what they had seen or what had happened to them but were comparable to the younger children in the number of activity reports, some of which had the potential for becoming full-blown narratives. On the other hand, kindergarten children more frequently talked about objects, 78% of which were their toys. Usually they held the toy right in front of them for their classmates to see. Their behavior explains the comment of one school administrator who commented, "So you want to watch Drag and Brag." Further, the proportion of object descriptions decreased across the year in the second-grade class from 50% in the fall to 20% in the spring in favor of an increasing number of narratives. In contrast, the proportion remained at 50% in the kindergarten class across the school year.

Just as object-focused contacts serve as the basis for social interaction among toddlers during play (Eckerman, Whatley, & Kutz, 1975; Mueller, 1979; Mueller & Brenner, 1977; Wellman & Lempers, 1977), they appear to be a major basis for participating in this more formal communicative activity. At face value, talking about objects would appear to be relatively simple. Rather than having to order a series of events in a cohesive and unambiguous fashion as when telling a narrative, the child need only comment on a static item. Moreover, holding the object forward is an easy way to introduce the

Table 1. Distribution of Topic Categories Among Kindergarten and Second Grade Speakers

| Grade | | Object Descriptions | Activity Reports | Activity Narratives | Mastery Comments | Observations | Other |
|---|---|---|---|---|---|---|---|
| Kindergarten | | | | | | | |
| | *n* | 117 | 64 | 62 | 26 | 22 | 14 |
| | % | 38 | 21 | 20 | 9 | 7 | 5 |
| Two | | | | | | | |
| | *n* | 79 | 63 | 112 | 5 | 10 | 17 |
| | % | 28 | 22 | 39 | 2 | 3 | 6 |

topic (Keenan & Klein, 1975) and keep the attention of one's listener. Of particular note is the fact that those children who rarely participated almost always talked about objects when they did take a turn. In short, objects appear to be easier to talk about, allowing younger children, especially the more reticent ones, to participate in Show and Tell and facilitating the transition to more elaborate informative spech in the form of extended narratives among second graders.

### Showing in Show and Tell: The Role of Nonverbal Channels

The apparent ease of using objects as something to talk about is misleading, however. While holding an object forward is an effective and simple way of unambiguously introducing a topic (a strategy employed in three quarters of the object-related descriptions by both kindergarten and second-grade children), further elaboration may pose problems. Kindergarten children's descriptions about objects were only half as long (about 26 words) as their descriptions of events. In contrast, this discrepancy was not shown by the grade-two children.

Remarks which the kindergarten children offered about objects spontaneously, without any specific teacher queries, of course were even briefer, an average of about 17 words. Substantial variation was shown, depending on whether the object was present or absent. Of the 18 kindergarten children, 9 always had the objects with them that they were describing. When their speech about present objects was contrasted with that of their classmates who spoke about both present and absent objects, the mean number of spontaneous words for present objects was only half as large, 6.51 versus 19.98, respectively. In addition, the latter children were more fluent in talking about objects that were absent than those that were present. They spontaneously spoke an average of 40.04 words for absent objects compared to the aforementioned 19.98 words of present object speech. This pattern again suggests that holding forth the object to be spoken of is a strategy which less fluent speakers may use to participate in Show and Tell, but paradoxically, it also suggests that it is a strategy which constrains the speech of the more able kindergarten speakers.

The objects which kindergarten children described were most often symbolic toys (44%) such as dolls, cars, and stuffed animals. Clothes (22%), books (8%), organizational toys (6%), sports and game items (4%), and miscellaneous articles (11%) such as craft items, photographs, and found objects (e.g., feathers, rock collections) were also topics. In 50% of the descriptions of objects held in view, the speaker said either nothing or only a single spontaneous utterance. Frequently, kindergarten children held the object forward and said nothing, prompting their teacher to say, "Tell us what you brought" or "Can you tell us about it?" This was especially true for children who did not also talk about absent objects and accounted for a full third of their object-related descriptions. A single spontaneous utterance which labeled the object (e.g., "I got two racing cars"; "A Rubik's Cube"; "It's a picture") was offered by all the kindergarteners about a third of the time. Spontaneous comments which the children did offer beyond a simple label most often concerned what the objects could do or what they did with them, what hidden components there were (e.g., batteries), and where they got the object. In contrast, when the object was not present, the children spontaneously spoke five or six utterances which described the origin, appearance, and components of the object, and what to do with it.

To illustrate the difference between these two types of object descriptions, the transcripts of a kindergarten boy talking about two representational transport toys are provided. During one November session, he takes his turn by describing a boat he has at home:

> Child:    You know what I got for my birthday? A boat with a—with a truck.
>           And you can put the boat in the water. And then...a man can go in
>           the water and—and the motor. You could go up with it on yourself.
> Teacher:  You can? Would you use it in the bath?
> Child:    Yep. And it's sold in the mall.

In this description he begins with a rhetorical gambit which includes when he got the boat. He then labels the item and relates its affiliated components—what one can do with it and where it is sold. None of this information is directly solicited by the teacher. The verbal spontaneity shown in this turn at talking stands in direct contrast to the same child's performance when showing a dinky car he has brought for Show and Tell.

> Child:    (Holds out dinky car)
> Teacher:  Can you tell us what you brought?
> Child:    A...car.
> Teacher:  And where did you get it?
> Child:    At Christmas.
> Teacher:  Can you tell us anything about it?
> Child:    It can drive.
> Teacher:  Do you have any more at your house?
> Child:    (Nods)
> Teacher:  Oh.

This transcript consists entirely of teacher-query, student-answer exchanges with only a minimal response on the part of the child.

The greater reticence on the part of kindergarteners when the object was in view may be attributed to the prominence of the nonverbal channel. Showing the object calls attention to it. Once seen by the listener, the child may feel that it speaks for itself and that little more can be said. Alternately, the child may feel that little more need be said, in which case he is relieved of much of the burden of having to convey information through words in this relatively formal and unfamiliar school setting. Reliance on the non-verbal channel is most apparent among toddlers who frequently point to, hold up, and place objects in their mother's laps (Anderson, 1972; Buhler, 1935/1937; Clarke-Stewart, 1973; Rheingold, Hay & West, 1976) as a means of establishing a shared focus with their social partners. Increasingly with age, the burden of communication is shifted away from the nonverbal activity of sharing the object itself to sharing one's comments on the object. As Piaget (1926/1971) has noted, discussions can "take place on the verbal plane without actions, without the aid of the material object with which the speakers might have been playing or working, without even the present spectacle of the phenomenon or of the events about which they are talking" (p. 77). Words gradually supplant gestures, but in situations which stress emergent verbal ability, communicators, in this case kindergarten children, fall back on an earlier communicative strategy—showing.

Kindergarteners not only frequently showed objects but in a third of these instances demonstrated what to do with them without any accompanying words. The reliance on gesture is well-illustrated in the following transcript of a kindergarten boy.

| | |
|---|---|
| Child: | (Holds out toy gun) |
| Teacher: | Tell us about it. |
| Child: | (Holds gun above head and cocks it) |
| Teacher: | But can you tell us what you brought, Tom. |
| Child: | A gun. |
| Teacher: | Is it a special kind? |
| Child: | (Nods) |
| Teacher: | What kind? |
| Child: | And you have to put balls in it. |
| Teacher: | Can you tell us anything else? |
| Child: | (No response) |
| Teacher: | Do you play with it a lot? |
| Child: | (Nods) |
| Teacher: | When you put in the balls, do they fire? |
| Child: | (Nods) |
| Teacher: | Oh. |

In this case, he holds the gun above his head and cocks it in answer to "Tell us about it." When his teacher insists that he use words, he resorts to a simple labeling of the item.

The importance of demonstration as a supplement to what is said is illustrated by another kindergarten child talking about his toy movie camera.

Child:      (Puts together film pack)
Teacher:    Tell us what you brought, Donald.
Child:      A film.
Teacher:    Uh huh. Can you tell us some more about it?
Child:      Well, you put it in like that. (Demonstrates) And you turn it around.
            (Turns handle) And then it opens the doors. And then water comes
            out and the ghost comes out. And the ship.
Teacher:    Do you have more films at your house?
Child:      One more. (Holds up one finger)
Teacher:    One more?
Child:      It's a Sesame Street one.

The observations here are not unlike those in a study by Evans and Rubin (1979) in which kindergarten children relied on demonstrating the actions of a board game to supplement the ambiguous and inadequate information conveyed by their words. The older second grade children, in contrast, more adequately explained the game without relying on the board game itself. Likewise, for the older second grade children of the present study who had had more practice and experience in the formal informative speech context of Show and Tell, the presence of the object had relatively little impact on the verbalizations about it.

### The Content of Show and Tell: The Role of Action

Intimately associated with gestures and demonstrations are the actions which children perform upon the objects. Over half of the descriptions of objects, both present and absent, included some spontaneous remark concerning what was done with the item, this being the most frequent type of information offered aside from a simple label. Even the less fluent children of whom the teacher asked a number of questions in an attempt to solicit further speech, volunteered this type of information. A very quiet kindergarten girl, for example, says this about the doll she has brought to Show and Tell.

Teacher:    Tell us what you brought today.
Child:      (Pulls rag doll out of bag; does button up on doll's dress) A doll.
Teacher:    Can you tell us about it?
Child:      It can stand up.

Teacher: Can you tell us anything else?
Child: (No response)
Teacher: Does she have a name?
Child: (No response)
Teacher: Where did you get her?
Child: From Christmas.
Teacher: Did you? She's very nice.

A description by a more fluent kindergarten girl follows.

Teacher: Can you tell us what you brought?
Child: It's for measuring.
Teacher: It's a ——?
Child: For measuring. For measuring. You put it together and push it around like this. (Demonstrates) And you look at the little numbers on this little thing here. And that's how many feet it is. It would be right here.
Teacher: So that would be a really good thing for use in measuring a long distance.
Child: I measured my Dad today.
Teacher: Oh did you? And how long was he?
Child: Ooh. He was about...ten feet even.
Teacher: And where did you get that measuring thing?
Child: I got it from McDonald's.
Others: (A chorus of "I got one too", etc.)

Both children, like many of their classmates in talking about objects, focused on what one does with the object. This was not an isolated phenomenon. In studying the manner in which kindergarten, grade one, grade four, and grade eight children describe common childhood games, Evans and Rubin (1983) observed the same emphasis on "what you do" by the kindergarten and first grade children. When asked to explain how to play musical chairs, hide-and-seek, Simon Says, and Doggie, Doggie, Who's Got the Bone, the younger children rarely mentioned the physical resources required such as the props, number of players, or their designated roles. In addition, they less often volunteered how the games came to a conclusion. However, this information was equally well known by the younger and older children when they answered later questions. What the younger children concentrated on was the performance feature of the game (Sutton-Smith, 1959), what the players *do* in the game. For example, to explain hide-and-seek, a first grade boy, age 7;2, proceeded as follows:

Like you start off by going and hiding—hiding somewhere where you can fit. And then a person counts to 20 or—. And then he says, "Ready or not. Here I come." And then the person says, if he's not, "Wait a minute, and count to 3 and let me have one more chance." So he does, "Ready or not." And then they say, "Ready." And then whoever wants to find and finds them, they're out and can't play for a little while. And then if he finds them again, they're out.

Older children, on the other hand, began by specifying the players and props needed and proceeded through the game preparations and actions to the determination of a winner. It was especially noteworthy that this pattern held true for both the games played throughout middle childhood and the game Doggie, Doggie, Who's Got the Bone, which was played only in nursery school and more familiar to the younger children.

From these data it is apparent that primary grade children use a somewhat different and less complete internal framework, which guides their descriptions of objects and events. Until the present study, the importance of actions has been demonstrated with reference to game explanations (Evans & Rubin, 1983), the narration of personal episodes (Kernan, 1977; Labov and Waletsky, 1967; Menig-Peterson & McCabe, 1978), the retelling of narratives from memory (Brown, 1975; Mandler & Johnson, 1977; Stein & Glenn, 1979) and the description of general events (Nelson & Gruendel, 1979). With increasing age, children are more likely to describe the persons, place, time, and behavioral situation of the central core of events they describe, and the emotions, reactions, and evaluations of the characters, rather than simply relating the events as they unfold. The observations made of Show and Tell suggest that the prominence of actions is a more general phenomenon which extends to the description of objects. Kindergarten children less frequently stated where or when they acquired the object, the parts comprising it, or what they thought of it than the actions associated with it. This was true not only of toys but of clothes ("I put my scarf in my coat sleeve"), a birthday cake ("You hold it in your fingers and chomp on it"), ornaments ("It fell off my door"), ponytails ("It goes like this and then makes it go like that"), and pictures ("They're walking in the picture"). It might be noted that a similar bias in young children toward function and action has also been observed in semantic retrieval tasks (Heidenheimer, 1978; Moran, 1973; Prawat & Cancelli, 1977).

Why the actions associated with an object (or the people in a game or characters in a story) have such salience for young children can only be speculated upon. They appear to comprise the central core around which other elements are added in the formation of increasingly elaborate schemata. Nelson (1977) has suggested that this functional core is the initial meaning of the concept for the child and "may include what the object does, the set of its possible actions, as well as what can be done with it and the results of the actions on it" (p. 229). This core is experienced based and for the young child much of it is play-based. Furthermore it is a core which plays a predominant role in what children spontaneously relate to others even after other features have been added.

## Conclusion

Within the formal context of Show and Tell in which children describe objects and events to their classmates, several basic components of informal play were observed to have a prominant role. Kindergarten children most often brought objects to show and to talk about which assisted them in gaining their listener's attention and in taking their turn. In attempting to describe an object, regardless of the type of item or whether it was or was not in view, the children most often spontaneously related the actions associated with it and frequently used gestures to supplement or replace their speech in conveying those actions. The objects that they most often talked about were their toys, testifying to the importance of toys both to the owners and to the peer group as a whole. When not talking about objects which they had planned in advance to bring, the kindergarten children frequently imitated and modified a previous speech topic within the same session. This pattern was evidenced by all kindergarten children, even the more fluent speakers, but it was particularly prominent among those children who appeared to find it very difficult to take a turn at speaking in front of their classmates. When doing so, they almost invariably held up a toy and manipulated it to show what it could do.

Play with toys thus appears to provide the young child with basic resources for participating in formal informative speech activities. Through play children may acquire the beginning kernel of a framework for the act of describing. It is as though they follow the rule, "Tell your listeners what you do with it," something which may be accomplished through words, gestures, or a combination of both. Repeated questions from the teacher such as "Where did you get ———?" "How does it feel?", "Do you have more at home?", "Does it have a name?", and "What kind of a ——— is it?" serve to solicit further ideas from the children and to provide more comprehensive models for future descriptive attempts. As Brown (1977) has suggested, school plays an important role in grafting a more context-free conceptualization onto the basic script structures which children bring to the classroom. With repeated teacher input and practice at describing their possessions and the things that have happened to them, more deliberate, systematic and informative descriptions would be expected to be produced. The one possible negative effects of this socialization in "how to describe" is that descriptions may become so leaden and rigid as to arouse little genuine interest from an audience. I suspect this, in fact, had partly happened in the second grade classroom in which relatively little variety was shown in both the topics and speech style of the children's turns at talking. The illusory, dynamic, paradoxical, ephemeral, uncertain,—in short nonliteral—nature of play is not easily rendered into words.

# References

Anderson, J. W. (1972). Attachment behaviour out of doors. In N. Blurton Jones (Ed.), *Ethological studies of child behavior.* Cambridge England: Cambridge University Press.

Asher, S. (1978). Referential communication. In G. J. Whitehurst & B. J. Zimmerman (Eds.), *The function of language and cognition.* New York: Academic Press.

Bates. E. (1979). *The emergence of symbols: Cognition and communication in infancy.* New York: Academic Press.

Bates, E., Bretherton, I., Shore, C., & McNew, S. (1983). Names, gestures, and objects: The role of context in the emergence of symbols. In K. Nelson (Ed.), *Children's language (Vol. 4).* Hillsdale, NJ: Erlbaum.

Bloom, L. (1970). *Language development: Form and function in emerging grammars.* Cambridge, MA: MIT Press.

Brown, A. L. (1975). Recognition, reconstruction, and recall of narrative sequences by preoperational children. *Child Development, 46,* 156-166.

Brown, A. L. (1977). Development of schooling and the acquisition of knowledge about knowledge. In R. C. Anderson, R. J. Spiro, & W. E. Montague (Eds.), *Schooling and the acquisition of knowledge.* Hillsdale, NJ: Erlbaum.

Brown, R., & Bellugi, U. (1964). Three processes in the child's acquisition of syntax. *Harvard Educational Review, 34,* 133-151.

Buhler, C. (1937). *From birth to maturity: An outline of the psychological development of the child.* (E. Menaker & W. Menaker, Trans.) London: Kegan Paul. (Original work published 1935).

Cazden, C. (1975). Concentrated vs. contrived encounters: Suggestions for language assessment. *The Urban Review, 8,* 28-34.

Cazden, C. B., Cox, M., Dickinson, D., Steinberg, & Stone, C. (1979). "You all gonna hafta listen": Peer teaching in a primary classroom. In W. A. Collins (Ed.), *Children's language and communication. The Minnesota Symposia on Child Psychology (Vol. 12).* Hillsdale, NJ: Erlbaum.

Cicourel, A. V. (1974). *Language use and school performance.* New York: Academic Press.

Clark, H., & Haviland, S. E. (1977). Comprehension and the given-new contract. In R. O. Freedle (Ed.), *Discourse processes: Advances in research and theory: Vol. 1.: Discourse production and comprehension.* Norwood, NJ: Ablex.

Clarke-Stewart, K. A. (1973). Interactions between mothers and their young children: Characteristics and consequences. *Monographs of the Society for Research in Child Development, 38,* (6-7, Serial No. 153).

Dickson, W. P. (1981). Referential communication activities in research and in the curriculum: A metaanalysis. In W. P. Dickson (Ed.), *Children's oral communication skills.* New York: Academic Press.

Dore, J., Gearhart, M., & Newman, D. (1978). The structure of nursery school conversation. In K. Nelson (Ed.), *Children's language (Vol. I).* New York: Gardner Press.

Eckerman, C. O., Whatley, J. L., & Kutz, S. L. (1975). Growth of social play with peers during the second year of life. *Developmental Psychology, 11,* 42-49.

Evans, M. A., & Carr, T. H. (1984). The ontogeny of description. In L. Feagans, C. Garvey, & R. Golinkoff (Eds.), *The origins and growth of communication.* Norwood, NJ: Ablex.

Evans, M. A., & Rubin, K. H. (1979). Hand gestures as a communicative mode in school-age children. *Journal of Genetic Psychology, 135,* 189-196.

Evans, M. A., & Rubin, K. H. (1983). Developmental differences in explanations of childhood games. *Child Development, 54,* 1559-1567.

Fein, G. G. (1979). Echoes from the nursery: Piaget, Vygotsky, and the relationship between language and play. In E. Winner & H. Garner (Eds.), *Fact, fiction, and fantasy in childhood*. San Francisco, CA: Jossey-Bass.

Garvey, C. (1977). *Play*. Cambridge, MA: University Park Press.

Garvey, C., & Hogan, R. (1973). Social speech and social interaction: Egocentrism revisited. *Child Development, 44,* 562–568.

Glucksberg, S., Krauss, A., & Higgins, E. T. (1975). The development of referential communication skills. In F. Horowitz (Ed.), *Review of child development research, (Vol. 14)* Chicago, IL: University of Chicago Press.

Gottman, J. M. (1983). How children become friends. *Monographs of the Society for Research in Child Development, 48,* (3, Serial No. 201).

Gottman, J. M., Gonso, J., & Rasmussen, B. (1975). Social interaction, social competence and friendship. *Child Development, 46,* 709–718.

Gottman, J., & Parkhurst, J. T. (1980). A developmental theory of friendship and acquaintanceship process. In W. A. Collins (Ed.), *Development of cognition, affect, and social relations. The Minnesota Symposia on Child Psychology (Vol. 13).* Hillsdale, NJ: Erlbaum.

Griffin, R., & Shuy, R. (1978). *Children's functional language and education in the early years.* Final report to the Carnegie Corporation of New York: Arlington, VA: Center for Applied Linguistics.

Halliday, M. A. K. (1975). *Learning how to mean.* London: Edward Arnold.

Heidenheimer, P. (1978). A comparison of the roles of exemplar, action, co-ordinate, and superordinate relations in the semantic processing of 4- and 5-year-old children. *Journal of Experimental Child Psychology, 25,* 143–159.

Hurtig, E. (1977). Toward a functional theory of discourse. In R. O. Freedle (Ed.), *Discourse processes: Advances in research and theory (Vol. 1): Discourse production and comprehension.* Norwood, NJ: Ablex.

Keenan, E. O., & Klein, E. (1975). Coherency in children's discourse. *Journal of Psycholinguistic Research, 4,* 365–380.

Kernan, K. T. (1977). Semantic and expressive elaboration in children's narratives. In S. Ervin-Tripp & C. Mitchell-Kernan (Eds.), *Child discourse.* New York: Academic Press.

Knapp, M., & Knapp, H. (1976). *One potato, two potato... The secret education of American children.* New York: Norton.

Labov, W., & Waletsky, J. (1967). Narrative analysis: and versions of personal experience. In J. Helm (Ed.), *Essays on the verbal and visual arts.* Seattle: WA: University of Washington Press.

LaGreca, A. M., & Mesibov, G. B. (1979). Social skills, intervention with learning disabled children: Selecting skills and implementing training. *Journal of Clinical Child Psychology, 8,* 234–241.

Mandler, J. M., & Johnson, N. S. (1977). Remembrance of things parsed: story structure and recall. *Cognitive Psychology, 9,* 111–151.

Mehan, H. (1979). *Learning lessons: Social organization in the classroom.* Cambridge, MA: Harvard University Press.

Menig-Peterson, C. L., & McCabe, A. (1978). Children's orientation of a listener to the context of their narratives. *Developmental Psychology, 14,* 582–292.

Moerk, E. L. (1975). Verbal interactions between children and their mothers during the preschool years. *Developmental Psychology, 11,* 788–794.

Moran, L. (1973). Comparative growth of Japanese and North American cognitive dictionaries. *Child Development, 44,* 862–865.

Mueller, E. (1979). Toddlers + Toys) = (An autonomous social system). In M. Lewis & L. A. Rosenblum (Eds.), *The child and its family.* New York: Plenum Press.

Mueller, E., & Brenner, J. (1977). The origins of social skills and interaction among playgroup toddlers. *Child Development, 48,* 854–861.

Nelson, K. (1977). Cognitive development and the acquisition of concepts. In R. A. Anderson, R. J. Spiro, & W. E. Montague (Eds.), *Schooling and the acquisition of knowledge.* Hillsdale, NJ: Erlbaum.

Nelson, K., & Gruendel, J. M. (1979, March). *From personal episode to social script: Two dimensions in the development of event knowledge.* Paper presented at the Biennial Meeting of the Society for Research in Child Development, San Francisco.

Olson, D. R. (1977). The language of instruction: the literate bias of schooling. In R. C. Anderson & R. J. Spiro (Eds.), *Schooling and the acquisition of knowledge.* Hillsdale, NJ: Erlbaum.

Opie, P., & Opie, I. (1969). *Children's games in street and playground.* Oxford: Clarendon Press.

Piaget, J. (1971). *The language and thought of the child.* (M. Gabain and R. Gabain, Trans.) London: Routledge & Kegal Paul. (Original work published in 1926).

Prawat, R. S., & Cancelli, A. A. (1977). Semantic retrieval an young children as a function of type of meaning. *Developmental Psychology, 13,* 354–358.

Raffer-Engel, W., & Lebrun, Y. (1976). *Baby talk and infant speech.* Lisse, Netherlands: Swetz & Zeitlinger.

Rheingold, H. L., Hay, D. F., & West, M. J. (1976). Sharing in the second year of life. *Child Development, 47,* 1148–1158.

Rosen, C., & Rosen, H. (1973). *The language of primary school children.* Harmondsworth, Middlesex, England: Penguin Educational.

Rubin, K. (1972). Relationship between egocentric communication and popularity among peers. *Developmental Psychology, 7,* 364.

Shatz, M. (1983). Communication. In J. H. Flavell & E. M. Markman (Eds.), *Handbook of child psychology (Vol. 3).* New York: Wiley.

Shields, M. M. (1978). Some communication skills of young children: a study of dialogue in nursery school. In R. N. Campbell & P. T. Smith (Eds.), *Recent advances in the psychology of language (Vol. III:4a).* New York: Plenum.

Shotwell, J. M., Wolf, D., & Gardner, H. (1979). Styles of achievement in early symbols use. In B. Sutton-Smith (Ed.), *Play and learning.* New York: Gardner Press.

Sinclair, J., & Coulthard, R. (1975). *Toward an analysis of discourse: The English used by teachers and pupils.* London: Oxford University Press.

Snow, C. E., & Ferguson, C. A. (Eds.) (1977). *Talking to children.* Cambridge, England: Cambridge University Press.

Stein, N., & Glenn, C. G. (1979). An analysis of story comprehension in elementary school children. In R. O. Freedle (Ed.), *Discourse processing: Multidisciplinary perspectives.* Norwood, NJ: Ablex.

Sutton-Smith, B. (1959). A formal analysis of game meaning. *Western Folklore, 18,* 13–24.

Umiker-Sebeok, D. J. (1979). Preschool children's intraconversational narratives. *Journal of Child Language, 6,* 91–109.

Wellman, H., & Lempers, J. (1977). The naturalistic communication abilities of two-year-olds. *Child Development, 48,* 1052–1057.

# 8

# Narrative Play in Second-Language Learning

## Shirley Brice Heath
## (with Hey-Kyeong Chin)
### Stanford University

## Introduction

Only a few sentences of a child's reenactment of a past episode or directions to a playmate for a housekeeping game will usually be sufficient to identify these narratives as part of sociodramatic play, different from all other kinds of talk during children's play. In sociodramatic play, children use language to create an imaginary situation in which objects, other children, or adults, and the initiator of the play are made to assume make-believe identities. Forms of dramatic play vary from society to society, and some groups have less of this play than others. Children in nursery schools or other types of preschool settings in the United States, however, have numerous props, occasions, and models for dramatic play. For these youngsters, the first clue that they are about to engage in dramatic play is most often a child's verbal frame for the reenactment or ensuing dramatic play; this frame usually takes the form of an announcement such as "OK, I'm David and you're Goliath" or "Let's play house." Besides these openings, intonation, ensuing speech acts, discourse form, and types of cohesion will distinguish dramatic play from other types of play. In this study, the primary purpose is to explore dramatic play as language play and to consider its role for children learning a second language.

The primary data for this study are from recordings made over the six weeks just prior to the third birthday of SooJong, a Korean girl born in the United States. The recordings were made from mid-April until the end of May, 1983; SooJong began attending a half-day nursery school with English speakers when she was 2;4; she had been uttering Korean words distinguishable to her Korean-speaking parents since she was 18 months old. SooJong's parents had graduate degrees from an American university and were fluent in English, but they spoke almost exclusively Korean at home. The family consisted of SooJong, her parents, and a 5-year-old brother who spoke English at home only when he brought home English-speaking friends to play. In the first six months of nursery school, SooJong participated in all of the school's activities enthusiastically, but she talked at school primarily in routinized activities when she could join the other children in a chorus. She volunteered little talk at school during the first year. At home, she usually played either alone or with her brother.

By the time SooJong was 2;9, her mother noticed that she was speaking English at home but almost entirely in replays of routine school activities and in dramatic play. Her mother took field notes describing the contexts and utterances during these occasions and tape-recorded the 20- to 40-minute play sessions she had nearly every afternoon with SooJong. SooJong's favorite toys were puzzles, blocks, and her Raggedy Ann doll. During the six weeks of data collection, her voluntary play at home consisted primarily of dramatic play, in which she announced verbally a new identity for blocks or puzzle pieces and narrated social roles for herself and her doll. Her mother did not initiate activities during the play period, except to invite SooJong to listen to stories read in English and to talk about the stories. The summary of types of play during these play sessions appears in Table 1. These data were supplemented by observations made of SooJong's uses of dramatic play just before going to sleep and just after awakening.

### Play and Language Learning

Linguists have long been fascinated by children playing with language as they learn their mother tongue. Since the classic (1962) study by Ruth Weir of her son's language play in his crib, linguists have reported in detail on the sound play, secret languages, and lexical inventions of children (Ferguson & Macken, 1983; Sanches & Kirschenblatt-Gimblett, 1976; Sherzer, 1976). Evidence from children's language play indicates that children may apply precise phonological rules to the word shapes of a language (Ferguson & Macken, 1983), attend to the formal features of one another's utterances, and converse cooperatively by attending to each others' topics (Keenan, 1974). Without explication or formal teaching, children create and impose rules for language play.

Table 1. Types of Dramatic Play, April 11 to May 23, 1983

| Language | Noncooperative Play | Cooperative Play | Pretend Book Reading | Singing with Props |
|----------|---------------------|------------------|----------------------|--------------------|
| Primarily English | 9 | 6 | 15 | 10 |
| Primarily Korean | 4 | 4 | 4 | 0 |

*Note:* Figures indicate numbers of instances of use of each language.

Some of these rules may apply to only one speaker, who will engage in certain "response cries," or self-talk (Goffman, 1981) which may remain stable for several weeks or months, become progressively more complex, or stop entirely (Weir, 1962; Black, 1979). For some speech communities, play in self-talk may be socially accepted behavior and even a type of language use expected by members of the community. For example, preschool girls in the black working-class community of Trackton in the Piedmont Carolinas play at being conversationalists, talking to themselves in mirrors and taking both sides in a mock conversation, which may be either a replay of talk they have heard or an original creation (Heath, 1983, pp. 96–97). For all speech communities, we can hypothesize that some form of language play is part of the total repertoire of language structures and uses, and some forms of language play are specific to children learning their mother tongue.

A common response to the fact of language play by children is the judgment that such play affords opportunities to practice language. Even when the primary function of play is regarded as enjoyment, its secondary function is characterized as mastery (Kuczaj, 1982). Many of the forms of language play closely resemble the structures which provide practice in formal language instruction. Crib language play may be closely akin to the pattern practice of second-language classes (Weir, 1962; Black, 1979). The repetitive imitations of the early morning interactions of twins (2;10) when they were by themselves resemble substitution drills found in foreign-language textbooks. One twin's "You silly" is followed by the other's "No, you silly," and such repetitions with negations of the first twin's utterance occur throughout their play with language (Keenan, 1974). The Trackton children, when they first learned to talk, repeated unanalyzed chunks of phrasal and clausal utterances of speakers around them, imitating intonation contours; they later repeated pieces of conversation going on about them and played with particular themes, as they began to apply productive rules, inserted new words for those used in the chunks being repeated, and varied their intonation patterns (Heath, 1983, pp. 91–93). These routines are parallel in structure to those that appear in foreign-language textbooks, asking students to manipulate set portions of the text to show their application of grammar rules.

In addition to these more conventionalized types of language practice, within some communities language play takes on a "nonordinary" form. Within some communities, sociolinguistic routines such as teasing, singing games, and gibberish rhymes are based on the manipulation of "ordinary" language according to cooperatively acknowledged, but rarely explicated, rules (Ochs & Schieffelin, in press). Analyses of such routines stress the synchronicity of these encounters as well as their interdependence with judgments about role relationships and suspension of customary conventions of interaction (e.g., Abrahams, 1964; Dundes, Leach, & Özkok, 1970). Second-language and foreign-language instructors have long advocated the use of role-playing, engagement in sociolinguistic routines, and sociodrama to develop vocabulary, discourse strategies, and to elicit oral production from hesitant students (e.g., Scarcella, 1978).

If language play provides practice for first-language learners and is advocated in the formal instruction of second- or foreign-language learners, does it occur naturally in the play of children who are learning a language other than their mother tongue? Relatively little research answers this question for children alone at play, but there is some evidence on the language of second-language learners when they are engaged in play either with other children or with adults. Peck (1978) provides an account of Angel, a Spanish speaker of 7;4 at play with Joe, an English speaker of about the same age; Angel and Joe's discourse closely resembled that of the 2-year-old English-speaking twins reported by Keenan (1974). The second speaker, Angel, focused on some constituent of Joe's previous utterance, and either repeated it as it appeared in the original or modified its phonological or syntactic form. Angel responded in a greater variety of ways but with shorter answers to Joe than to an adult. In play with Joe, Angel worked hard to get "into" the discourse and also seemed to feel freer to play with the language. He often parroted prefabricated routines and created patterns from these (cf. Hakuta, 1974), but he rarely initiated a topic; he had to be a follower in the language surrounding the play of the two boys.

Other researchers have identified second-language learners' use of "discontinuous frames with multiple slots" to describe ways in which children pick up certain sentence frames and then expand or substitute within these frames (Peters, 1983, p. 52). Wong Fillmore (1976) characterizes Nora, a native Spanish speaker learning English as a second language, as extracting chunks such as "how-do-you-do-dese" from sentences containing this unit and adding her own noun phrase or prepositional phrase (e.g., "How-do-you-do-dese in English?"). Many of these chunks surrounded play activities, which lent themselves to the learning of routines as chunks. Termed by Peters (1977; 1983) the "gestalt" style, this approach is one in which learners try to use whole utterances in socially appropriate and usually conversationally defined contexts. This style is distinguished from the "analytic" style used for labeling, referential functions, and characterized by one-word-at-a-time learning. Other studies of second-language learners reported in Huang and Hatch (1978) and Vihman (1982) describe similar aspects of the gestalt style exhibited by children acquiring a second language in play conditions such as school playgrounds, sibling play, or mother–child play routines.

## Dramatic Play as Narrative Context

Most of the literature reviewed here for first- and second-language learners at play with language focused on small units of language: sounds, words, intonation, phrases, or clauses. Though formal language learning often urges memorization of longer units such as poems, dialogues, or brief narratives, no studies that we know of report either first- or second-language learners' playing with long stretches of discourse that may be called narratives. Of the "extended stretches of cooperative talk" in her twins' early morning exchanges in the crib, Keenan (1974) noted:

> Novel utterances may appear as topically relevant comments on an antecedent utterance. But normally such exchanges are short-lived. Extended sequences of novel utterances in adjacent turns are either part of a routine (e.g., lines of a rhyme or song), or they are nonattentive or egocentric speech (e.g., narratives). (p. 183)

The twins' narrative, stretches of discourse—usually by a single sepaker—on a single topic, are described as either repeats of established routines derived from another source or, if original, as "nonattentive," that is, appearing not to take into account the listener and to express only the self-chosen topic and style of discourse of the speaker.

Children's dramatic play, in which youngsters must invite others to take part in their make-believe world, is a type of narrative which depends on being attentive—both to the mental image of the situations or actions and to the coparticipants. In essence, dramatic play is a form of problem-solving behavior which depends for its success on cooperation from other participants. This point is underscored by numerous studies of dramatic play which have examined the extent of dramatic play by children of different cultures and socioeconomic class backgrounds, links between engagement in dramatic play and achievement in prereading activities, the cohesiveness of the texts children use to frame the play, and the extent to which children explain their plans for pretend play. Following the conclusion of Smilansky (1968) that "disadvantaged" Israeli youngsters engaged in less dramatic play and role-playing of poorer quality than "advantaged" children, several scholars tested these results with other populations (e.g., Feitelson & Ross, 1973, with white, lower-middle-class kindergarten children in the Boston area; Rosen, 1974, with black lower-class children in the southeastern United States; Schwartzman, 1978, pp. 116–120, provides a review of such studies; Sutton-Smith & Heath, 1981, argue against the enthnocentricity of studies which seek to apply universal definitions of make-believe to children of different cultures). The links between dramatic play and the requirements of acceptable performance of prereading tasks in school are suggested by researchers who have experimentally examined the components of dramatic play (Pellegrini, 1980; Pellegrini, DeStefano, & Thompson, 1983). Other detailed analyses of the language of dramatic play episodes have indicated the ways in which their texts are cohesive (Pellegrini, 1982; Pellegrini, 1984) as well as how children develop structure, sustained focus, and decontextualization in their verbal explications of plans for dramatic play (Sachs, Goldman, & Chaillé, 1984).

Previous research suggests that sociodramatic play must contain: imitative role play, make-believe with objects, future mental images of actions and situations, persistence, interaction with other children, and verbal communication (Smilansky, 1971, pp. 41–42). Several scholars (e.g., Pellegrini, 1980, 1982, 1984; Sachs, 1980, and others reported in Pepler & Rubin, 1982) have investigated ways in which these features of dramatic play are accomplished linguistically. Generally omitted from consideration in linguistic studies of such play, however, is discussion of where such episodes fit on a continuum of types of narrative. Though "narrative" has since the late 1970s been a popular topic for study by linguists, literary theorists, cognitive scientists, psychologists, and anthropologists, ambiguities still surround its definition, structure, and even taxonomies of narratives. Stories as a type of narrative have been a favorite subject for investigation (e.g., Stein, 1982); forms of exposition have received far less attention, except in discussion of differences between oral and literate language (Olson, 1977; Geva & Olson, in press).

As a framework for examining the data to be presented in this chapter, we review types of narratives which account for a large proportion of those that children of the mainstream middle-class, school-oriented communities in the United States produce. These types are based on the definition of narrative as the expression of remembered events through a structure which reveals what the speaker (or writer) has chosen for attention out of stored memories and within an organization which can be anticipated by listeners (or readers). The four types are: recounts, accounts, "eventcasts," and stories (Heath, in press). *Recounts* are retellings, which are voluntary or in response to others' promptings, of experiences or information known to both teller and prompter. Occasions for such recounts occur when a parent asks a child to tell someone else about an activity in which the parent and the child have participated or when an adult asks a child to retell the story which has just been read aloud. *Accounts* are narratives which the teller gives of experiences in which listeners may not have participated. Such narratives provide new information or new interpretations of information which may already be known to both teller and listeners. Children may tell parents about a friend's birthday party, a hole discovered in the back of the garage, or a story read to them at nursery school.

*Eventcasts* are running narratives on events currently in the attention of both teller and listeners; this type of narrative may be either simultaneous with events or precede them. A child's running narrative of how she is preparing a cake in the sandbox or a youngster's elaborate verbal planning for the sequence of events to take place at his birthday party are all eventcasts (cf. Ferguson, 1983, on sportscasts). *Stories* are fictional narratives which include an animate being moving through a series of events with goal-directed behavior. Children learn about stories through either oral tales of events in the past or through reading books with adults or older siblings. They create stories when they fictionalize themselves or others and attribute animacy, goals, and ways of overcoming obstacles to the characters within their stories.

In this discussion, we identify the narrative which accompanies dramatic play as a form of eventcast, and we examine how the data from a learner of English as a second language illustrate the essential components of this type of narrative. In the talk which frames dramatic play and sustains its activities, children must establish as the topic the joint actions of self and others in acting out a mental image of a future imagined event. Several types of activities such as dialogues either repeated from others or created anew and fictionalized talk about characters in books are sometimes preparatory to the full development of the narrative which precedes and accompanies the scripting of cooperative dramatic play.

## Learning to Symbolize a Script

In March 1983, when she was 2;9, during the hours of the day when she was at home, SooJong began in rapid succession to volunteer four varieties of noncooperative scripts, scripts in which she was not inviting another child or adult to take part. In the transcripts which follow, those portions which SooJong said in Korean are enclosed in brackets; the remaining portions she said in English; the dates of the recordings follow each entry.

The first variety of noncooperative scripts were *replays*—monologues or dialogues in which she played the role(s) of others—most frequently her teacher. It was these replays in which SooJong's mother first noticed her daughter repeating the English dialogues of her nursery school teacher. In the following episode, SooJong replays the end of rest period during story time at school. While they rest, the children must remove their name tags and wait for the surprise celebration of birthdays which may take place after the story:

> this is the end of the story, put away your pillow, I need your name take [tag], and so will give surprise for you (3-20)

SooJong said this just after her bedtime story and before going to bed at home. In the next few weeks, this routine and others drawn from school appeared at boundaries of activities at home which paralleled those of her school day. She modified school rules to make them apply to her own play, announcing to her dolls: "Raise your hand if you want——" and admonishing them with "No, you already have one."

Other varieties of noncooperative scripts followed rapidly in the next weeks, with different varieties sometimes appearing for the first time within the span of a 24-hour period. The next to appear after replays were simple *role announcements* without extensive directions regarding actions to be taken: "It's you, Raggedy Ann. It's you, hurry!" (4–11), said in mixed English and Korean. A few days later, she put her hand into a sock and announced in English: "Hello, my name is Koko," "Hi, my name is Popo," and laughed (4–18). The third variety was the *restatement* of fictionalized characters in books. In response to her mother's explanation that the doll pictured in a book wore glasses because the sun hurt her eyes, SooJong said, "She hurts her eyes and she has glasses on her" (4–11). The fourth variety were *scene setters* in which she both announced a role and established a situation for the role play. After spreading a small quilted cover on a tea table and placing a chair at the table, she held her doll and sat down on the chair: "Good morning, Raggedy Ann, I am your mommy. It's not dark. It's morning" (4–12).

In expansions of the second and fourth varieties, SooJong volunteered to her mother eventcasts describing her perception of her dolls' feelings and her own actions with her doll. Holding her doll, she said, "My baby cried a lot." When her mother asked why, she answered, "Because she went to the doctor and got a shot." Her mother continued to prod:

| | |
|---|---|
| Mother: | [What's wrong?] |
| SooJong: | She hurt here. (Pointing to doll's neck) |
| Mother: | [What happened?] |
| SooJong: | She got cold and hurt here. |
| Mother: | [Is she OK now?] |
| SooJong: | Um, Um. (Followed by laughter) (4–16) |

Within a few days, SooJong seemed, without her mother's actual questions, to script her own talk to answer the why, what's-wrong, and what's-happening questions her mother had asked of her play only a few days earlier. SooJong appeared to anticipate and answer such queries without prodding from an adult.

| | |
|---|---|
| SooJong: | Mommy! Raggedy Ann is dirty. I am making bath for her. [Where is soap? I shampoo baby] Mommy! Bath is [cold. Close the door.] |
| Father: | Is your baby cold? |
| SooJong: | Ya! My Raggedy Ann cold. |

In these examples, SooJong seems to give in English the major portion of that information which others would need to know, if they were playing with her. She names activities (making bath), past events (went to the doctor, got cold), and internal states which are not observable to others (internal hurt—she says "cold" the first time in Korean, then picks up the English word from her father's question). She followed this principle as well in scripting her own activities:

> SooJong: (Playing with paper and drawing her hand on the paper) Tape?
> Mother: [Where is it?]
> SooJong: [Where is it? I don't see it.]
> SooJong: I make a something. Mommy, I want to make a something (She folds papers, trying to make a shape)
> SooJong: How I do it? I need tape.
> Mother: [There a tape.]
> SooJong: (Putting tape on paper) I am putting bandaid on my hand because it hurt me. (Putting a piece of tape on her finger) Mommy! Give me one more tape. (4–28)

Here she explains verbally her future mental image (her projected desire to make "something"), the objects she needs, how she will pursue her actions, what she is doing, and how she feels about that activity. In English she has learned to manipulate productively the rules and lexical items she has heard in joint activities of play at school. At play in her home in the afternoon, she has practiced these first as she (a) replayed others' directions, then as she (b) announced the topic of her play with objects, (c) answered queries from her mother, and (d) narrated eventcasts with her dolls. A transcript from May 3 shows the full development of this fourth variety, in which she incorporated the second variety as well.

(It is 8:30 in the evening, and SooJong is playing on the floor with small plastic blocks. She has announced that she has two cars and four people—one car with daddy driving, the other car with the other three people. Her father is preparing to leave the house to go to class)

> SooJong: Mommy! Look at this.
> Mother: Oh! What is it?
> SooJong: This is a car. We are going to Pemco. Daddy is driving. Everybody have seatbelt, police get you. (She then sings a seatbelt song she has learned from an older cousin; the words are mumbled, but the melody is distinguishable.)
> SooJong (to her father as he leaves): Dad! You have it, you get it to school (handing her father the "one car with daddy." (She then took the remaining figures from the second car and laid them down on the lid of a plastic bowl.)
> SooJong: Mommy, they are sleeping. Sheeeee. It's time to sleep.

In this eventcast, she announces the opening of the play, actors, props, future goal, conditions to reach the goal, the internal states of the actors, and a closing boundary for the action. She interrupts this solo play by inviting her father into the play and telling him what to do—take the blocks, which is his car, to school. This is the first occasion in which SooJong tried to initiate cooperative dramatic play, and the first to have what we term the key components of dramatic play eventcasts:

1. *Opening Announcement.* This boundary marker stops the "ordinary" flow of action and establishes that dramatic play is going to take place. Included in this frame for play are the optional naming of the scene and the mandatory naming of parts actors are to play and identities that objects will take on as props. This frame focuses the attention of all players on a mental image of future events.
2. *Action Sequence.* This talk establishes the actions in which the actors are to engage and often includes the ways in which they are to use the props that surround them. This talk takes place simultaneously with the play activities.
3. *Goal.* Laying out the objective of the actions and the desired outcome, this talk provides the "truth value" or "possible world" base against which children test their specific activities and the changing identities of actors and objects. In cooperative dramatic play, if one child wants to change the identity of an actor or prop, such a change will be considered by others against the goal announced. If the alteration in actors, props, or even scene is accepted, the goal can be shifted as well. This talk may precede or be simultaneous with the play.
4. *Closing Boundary.* This announcement shifts children from the non-ordinary back to the ordinary and gives permission for children to use objects with their real-world identities without cries of protest from other participants in the dramatic play.

On May 6, in play with a young neighbor boy, SooJong tried to initiate an opening boundary for her narrative of cooperative dramatic play. Her playmate, however, rejected the terms of the designation of actors, and the dramatic play was abandoned. The children were playing in the living room of SooJong's home with the same small plastic blocks SooJong had used in the transcript of May 3 given earlier. She appears to want to continue the motif of that dramatic play, but her playmate reminds her that the cast of actors has changed—he must now be a part of the sociodrama.

SooJong:   This is my daddy, this is my mommy, this is my brother, and this is me (pointing to four plastic pieces).

Playmate:  (Pointing to the block designated as brother) This is me.

SooJong:   No! This is my brother.

Playmate:  I want this become me.

SooJong:    No, no, this is my brother.

Playmate:   But I am your friend.

SooJong:    OK, then this is you. (Picking up three plastic pieces and putting them in a box, leaving the disputed "brother" piece behind)

Playmate:   Wait for me. (Holding up disputed piece to try to place it in the box)

SooJong:    No, no, no, we'll go without you.

Playmate:   No, no. (Putting the disputed piece in the box)

SooJong:    You are not my brother, you can't come with us.

Playmate:   But I am your friend.

SooJong:    Yes, but you cannot be with us (taking out the disputed piece, laying it on the table, and leaving the room with the box).

In this transcript, SooJong's familiar routine of creating family rides for the four members of her family cannot tolerate the intrusion of a new actor. Her friend tries to negotiate that his role as friend is acceptable as a replacement for her brother in the play, but SooJong rejects this idea and leaves the room.

During the weeks since early April, SooJong's mother had read to her in English at bedtime and tried to encourage SooJong to listen to stories during her play periods in the afternoons. However, SooJong was not patient with reading and talking about books, except at bedtime. During the week of the previously described play incident, SooJong's mother asked SooJong to narrate or "read" to her doll the stories that she had just heard her mother read (in English). On her first attempt at doing this, SooJong negotiates each point of the action, testing her background knowledge and trying to clarify her understanding before she "reads" to her doll. The following transcript was recorded on May 7, after her mother had read her a book entitled *Busy Man* and had asked SooJong to read to her doll.

SooJong:    I'll read this book for you, my baby, this is a busy man, this is his house. (Shift of intonation and gaze) Mommy, this is not a teapot house, this is different house (referring to contrast between the picture of a house in this book and another her mother often read to her) (Shift of intonation and gaze) This is a house. (shift of intonation and gaze) Mommy, what *is* this house?

Mother:     Busy house.

SooJong:    This is a busy house, three door, three window. (shift of intonation and gaze) Mommy, what is this? (Pointing to picture of chimney in the book)

Mother:     They are chimneys.

SooJong:    What is chimney? (Her mother did not answer the question, but encouraged her to go on reading.)

SooJong:   Turn the page, busy man, he is busy man, clean the house, brush his teeth. (Pointing to man on the page) (shift of intonation) What is it, mommy?

Mother:    Slow man, he is busy man's neighbor.

SooJong:   Slow man, slow man has a green hat, yellow nose, he is sleeping like me, he is not hiding. (Casting ahead to the end of the story where slow man hides; she then skips several pages in turning.) Busy man, he is cleaning the garden. Busy man, he is sleeping. (Shift of intonation and gaze) Mommy, what is he doing here?

Mother:    He is taking a rest.

SooJong:   No, he is [close] his eye. He is sleeping. What is this, mommy?

Mother:    He is slow man.

SooJong:   Slow man, slow man, he is angry (imitating the facial expression of the picture), busy man, busy man, he is cleaning the house, busy man, busy man, he open the door, nobody there, busy man, go to the room, he—Mommy (shift of intonation and gaze) what is his name?

Mother:    Slow man——

SooJong:   ——is hiding under the bed. No, Mommy, he is hiding under the [quilt] like me, when I hide under my [quilt], nobody find me.

In this first extended book-reading episode in which SooJong focused her attention on the text for more than a few pages, she takes on the "mother" role in reading, and shifts her gaze and intonation when she needs to get information from her own mother to play her role. At points during her "reading," she contrasts items and objects with those in other stories she has heard read to her, and she focuses several times on the names and specific actions of characters. At the end of the reading, she slips out of the mother role and compares the fictional character's behaviors with her own in a direct conversation with her mother.

These play-at-book-reading occasions in English provided SooJong an opportunity to take the script given by someone else and interpret it. In her solitary play, she had not had to negotiate the meaning of narrative eventcasts of her play, except in response to the straightforward information-seeking, but nonthreatening questions of her parents. Implicit in their questions to her was their acceptance of her power over decision making in her play; she did not have to change her play in accord with their wishes. At school, Soo-Jong watched other children in dramatic play and other types of negotiations at play, but she had rarely taken direct part in verbally negotiating or challenging any roles in play at school.

During the second week of May, SooJong's mother began to ask her to read to her doll, providing occasions in which she could step into the words and roles of others. Quite unexpectedly, during this same week and immediately after the attempt at joint dramatic play noted for May 6, SooJong shifted almost entirely to Korean in play with her dolls and toys. On May 9, in a long play session with her toy kitchen set, SooJong used almost exclusively Korean. Her mother, as was customary, prodded her in Korean with questions about her play ("Who is the mommy?" "What's your baby's name?"), and SooJong answered in Korean. Unlike the pattern established in the previous days of naming actions, stating goals, and describing internal states in English, she used Korean for all utterances which served these functions. She used English only to ask for items from her mother ("I want a spoon"). Near the end of the play, she began songlike language play based on the substitution of words which could follow the numeral "one."

| | |
|---|---|
| SooJong: | one hammering, one hammering |
| | you want a *one* cup |
| | one hammering |
| | one cup, one cup |
| | one hammering, one hammering |
| | one plate, one plate |
| | one cup, one cup |
| | one plate, plate |
| | one cup |
| | one of music, more music, play, more bike, please |

She continued her song, gibbering in English, seeming to play at putting words together and occasionally involving an imaginary other ("You want a *one* cup," "more bike, please"). For the next week, she used very little English in her play, but she asked her mother to read to her in English, and she then read the story to her doll in English. Initial readings of the books by SooJong focused on naming items, providing simple information about the items, and labeling events. Subsequent readings of the same book shifted to talk about why and how characters were carrying out certain actions and how they felt about the course of events.

In her reading of *Busy Man* on May 14, SooJong does not play the part of mother reading, but instead focuses on the causes of actions and the evaluations of the characters' feelings. After asking about the name of the character and his initial actions, SooJong continues:

| | |
|---|---|
| SooJong: | Mr. Slow, what he is doing? |
| Mother: | Nothing. |
| SooJong: | Then, why he is standing up? |
| Mother: | Just they show Mr. Slow. |
| SooJong: | Why? |
| Mother: | Because they know how he looks like. |
| SooJong: | Why he got a green hat? |
| Mother: | Um. Um. |

| SooJong: | He got a green hat. I don't understand. Mommy, looking to him, where is him? |
|---|---|
| SooJong: | He want to go up to stairs like Mr. Busy. Now, it's him. Now, Mr. Busy |
| Mother: | And who else? |
| SooJong: | And Mr. Slow. Mr. Slow, Mr. Slow, he got up, let him go to swing and clean up here. |
| Mother: | Where is a swing? |
| SooJong: | This way, over there right behind our house. |
| Mother: | What is he doing? |
| SooJong: | He is cleaning Mr. Slow house, and Mr. Slow house—— |
| Mother: | ——And what are they doing right now? |
| SooJong: | Why he sleeping? |
| Mother: | He is just taking a rest. |
| SooJong: | Then, why he closing her eye? He don't like, he don't like to go somewhere, right? |

In this text, SooJong tries to "make sense" of the pieces of the text in terms of cause and effect relations and the links between characters' feelings and their portrayals in the book. Since the book does not have a storyline but simply names male characters who are at work in a house, SooJong tries to get enough information to narrate a story. At one point, she brings the characters into her world—the swing in her backyard, but she abandons this familiar scene almost immediately.

At the end of this "reading," SooJong declares she does not like Mr. Slow, and she settles into talk with her mother about her doll. In this episode, carried out entirely in English, she puts her doll in many of the same situations the characters of the book had been in, declaring after each activity why the episode occurred and how her doll felt about the episode.

Until May 23, she continued to use Korean during play, and English while reading books and talking afterwards about the books' stories with her doll and mother. On May 23 in play with HaeWon, a 4-year-old Korean playmate, SooJong used the first English in dramatic play around dolls and kitchen sets she had used since May 6.

| SooJong: | He (she) is a sister (pointing to her doll). I am the mommy. |
|---|---|
| Mother: | [How about HaeWon?] |
| SooJong: | (Looks at HaeWon) You are the sister. |
| HaeWon: | (Taking off the doll's panties) He do pupu. |
| Mother: | ["You need to wash the baby's bottom. What are you doing, Soo-Jong?] |
| SooJong: | I am making a water for sister. |

Mother:      [Are you going to give that to sister?]
SooJong:     Cold, it's cold. Can you drink this? (Offering a cup of water to HaeWon)
HaeWon:      My baby crying.
SooJong:     Why?
HaeWon:      Because——
SooJong:     Can you, mommy?
HaeWon:      Yea——
SooJong:     ——people come to mommy.
HaeWon:      He is crying.
SooJong:     He is crying. Bring to mommy.

This episode continues with SooJong counting the number of cups on the table and asking her mother for another so that the number of cups matches the number of players—including children and dolls. The play is interrupted by SooJong's brother who comes in and wants to join the play. He volunteers to be "the dad" but wants to bring in his friends from outside as well. SooJong refuses and announces: "I am the mommy." The boys counter by saying *their* mothers have said "yes." Two of her brothers' friends come into the house to join the play.

Brother:     My mom say yes.
SooJong:     My daddy say no.
Brother:     My brother say yes.
SooJong:     My mommy, my daddy don't say, my daddy say no. When you hit me, I am going to my daddy, and you are not gonna go with
                . . .
Two new boy playmates: No, no, my daddy say no, too; My daddy say no, too.
Brother:     But we are not hitting you.
Playmates:   But we are not hitting you.
SooJong:     When you fight with me, you can't come to movie with me. . . .

In this episode, initiated with a Korean-speaking playmate, SooJong reverts to her earlier pattern of using English in solitary dramatic pay and making some attempts at using English in cooperative play. During the opening of her dramatic play on May 23, SooJong announces the casts of characters, clarifies the role of HaeWon in response to her mother's query, and directs the rest of the play to maintain her role as the mother. When her brother and his friends interrupt, she tries to continue her own dramatic play script. The boys contest, she shifts from a mother to a daddy role, and she then steps out of the dramatic play altogether, announcing the consequences if the boys hit her. Having done this, she then steps back into the role as mother, and the children continue to play together until one of the boys decides he wants to read instead.

## Conclusions

It has been the purpose of this study to demonstrate how one Korean-speaking child learning English used long stretches of narrative discourse in dramatic play. This play was both noncooperative—without invitation to others to join in—and cooperative. Forms of noncooperative play included replays of the dialogues of others, role announcements, restatements of characters and actions from both books and ongoing play, and scene-setters which announced a situation in which she was engaged. In the first of these varieties —the replays—she seemed to practice the dialogues which formed the boundaries of activities at school. In role announcements, she framed nonordinary action by verbalizing the assumed roles of toys, herself, and her dolls. Her restatements were in response initially to her own or her mother's questions; later she volunteered information while she played just as though she were answering her mother's questions about who she and her dolls were and what they were doing. Subsequently, she also verbally described conditions which could not be observed by an onlooker, because they existed only in her symbolic representation of how her doll felt, where she hurt, etc. Through scene-setters, she named the situation in which she was involved and announced her role and that of others in the ensuing play.

In her cooperative play in English, she focused on establishing dramatic play as the frame, naming actors, and establishing a goal. The play broke down when she could not negotiate the cast of characters she had named or include her playmate in the script she internally had, but did not verbalize, about an ensuing "family" trip in which only a brother and not a friend could be included. After this aborted dramatic play, she reverted to Korean in her noncooperative play, using English only when she needed items from her mother for her play.

Although she stopped using English in her solitary play, she still spoke English when, at her mother's request, she took the role of mother reading to her dolls. In these episodes, she used English, following the intonation patterns of her mother's reading style when she was addressing the doll, and shifting to her own "voice" when she asked her mother to clarify actors and actions in the book. In these episodes, she followed a developmental pattern similar to that described by Snow and Goldfield (1982) for a mainstream native English-speaking boy reading with his mother. She used item and event labels most frequently at first, and then elaboration of these items and events. Only in the later episodes did she discuss motives and causes or evaluations and reactions. In play, she talked about real-world events only when the fantasy world broke down for her—when she failed to get a story-line from the reading or when she negotiated with her brother and his friends as they tried to enter her ongoing dramatic play.

SooJong seemed to recognize the basic components of dramatic play and to find ways to perform these in English initially in her solitary play. When her routines did not work successfully in cooperative play, she reverted to Korean for her solitary play but enthusiastically engaged in the coached dramatic play of reading to her dolls. The "dropping out" of use of certain forms is well-documented in the first- and second-language acquisition literature; several scholars report children who seem to have mastered one form only to omit it from their repertoire for a period of time and then resume using it (e.g., Leopold, 1939–1949). Similarly SooJong apparently dropped one language out of use for certain functions for a short while.

During her pretend book-reading with her mother and her doll, SooJong often interrupted to collect general knowledge about the categories of information necessary for narrating an eventcast in English about the actions and feelings of the characters pictured in the book. When the book provided no evidence for causes and effects or motivations, she tried to create these in dialogue with her mother.

After approximately a week of using English primarily during pretend reading and not in her own noncooperative play, SooJong went back to using English in cooperative play. While playing with a bilingual Korean-speaking playmate, SooJong appeared willing to try in English to negotiate cooperative dramatic play. She announced the play and cast of characters, named the props, and monitored others' actions so they would fit the goal of playing house. When her play was interrupted, she announced closure of the play through another future eventcast—her brother will hit her. In protest, her brother reasoned for the "reality" of the current situation: He had not hit her. SooJong reluctantly agreed, and reannounced "I am mommy" to begin the houseplay again with HaeWon and the three boys who had entered the play.

We conclude from the data presented here that SooJong unconsciously recognized the eventcast in dramatic play as a type of discourse she would have to learn to handle in English. She practiced precursors of dramatic play alone, "tried out" her eventcasts in cooperative play, and recognized her lack of success. She then turned to another type of play—role-playing in book reading to her dolls, dropping her use of English in her noncooperative play. After more than a week of practice of pretend reading in English, she tried her English again in cooperative dramatic play. Some degree of purposiveness in using English in this event seems indicated by the fact that her playmate was Korean-speaking. On this occasion, she successfully drew her playmates into her script for the dramatic play. When the play seemed threatened by intruders, she stepped out of her play role, announced terms, and then shifted back to the play with a cooperative group.

As the oral prescripting of events to come or reporting of ongoing activity, the language of dramatic play is one type of narrative—an eventcast. The language of dramatic play is a monologue or dialogue which makes clear that the interactants perceive the world about them as nonordinary. All become performers, often without spectators. To perform in synchrony, all players must recognize the initial communicational frame which sets the coming play apart from the ordinary. The director must verbalize ahead of current actions, so that actors can monitor each other's behaviors and ensuing events according to the script for accomplishing either the established or frequently renegotiated goal. For nonnative-English-speaking children whose playmates are English-speakers, the need to learn to handle dramatic play narratives must soon become painfully obvious. We suggest that Soo-Jong did not want to risk such narratives at school and chose to try them out and practice them at home until she felt secure to try her English with playmates. When her first attempt failed, she found a substitute type of narrative, through which she could build up similar types of skills to those required in successful dramatic play narratives. She turned her use of English to these.

We suggest that further research with young children acquiring a second language may verify that, once they have mastered some of the basic structures and routines of the second language ($L_2$), these children will focus on longer stretches of discourse. These stretches will be selected in part because of their relevance to preparing for participation in the social play of $L_2$ speakers. In other forms of play such as object play, imitation, and even many games, verbalization is not absolutely necessary for all parties. However, in dramatic play, the child who wishes to direct the script *must* verbalize, and the others are usually also expected to contribute some dialogue during play; thus children must have more than a receptive knowledge of the $L_2$ to engage in dramatic play. Moreover, since the basis of the play is cooperative negotiation of key elements such as scene, actors, props, actions, and goals, the narrative in such play must be attentive to the others' talk, and it cannot be merely routines. Thus, children have to learn to manipulate stretches of language productively and to consider how language can be used to accomplish immediate and future social ends. This kind of language use is not explicitly taught but is picked up by observations of other children (cf. Corsaro, 1979, on English-speaking children trying to negotiate their way into ongoing play).

We suggest that for second-language learners, there will be typical developmental sequences in their acquisition of types of discourse. That is, in the developmental stages of acquiring narrative dramatic play, they will use replays first, announce boundary markers (especially beginnings) of episodes next, and follow with talk about internal aspects of the full script. Children at play have strong motivations to monitor their own success rates and practice occasions for certain language uses. There are, no doubt, factors such as personal styles of leadership, extent of opportunities with book-reading, and encouragement of fantasy by parents which will lead particular children to adopt certain strategies of discourse acquisition (cf. Faerch & Kasper, 1983, on adult speakers' strategies of purposefully avoiding certain forms and types of language uses until they feel their linguistic skills are appropriate). This study of SooJong has shown us how valuable it is to look at a child's use of particular forms of discourse as part of the strategies children can employ as second-language learners.

## References

Abrahams, R. (1964). *Deep down in the jungle: Negro narrative folklore from the streets of Philadelphia.* Chicago, IL: Aldine.

Black, R. (1979). Crib talk and mother–child interaction: A comparison of form and function. *Papers and Reports on Child Language Development, 17,* 90–97.

Corsaro, W. A. (1979). "We're friends, right?" Children's use of access rituals in a nursery school. *Language in Society, 8,* 315–336.

Dundes, A., Leach, J. W., & Özkok, B. (1970). The strategy of Turkish boys' verbal dueling rhymes. *Journal of American Folklore, 83,* 325–349.

Faerch, C., & Kasper, G. (Eds.). (1983). *Strategies in interlanguage communication.* London: Longman.

Feitelson, D., & Ross, G. S. (1973). The neglected factor—play. *Human Development, 16,* 202–223.

Ferguson, C. A. (1983). Sports announcer talk: Syntactic aspects of register variation. *Language in Society, 12,* 153–172.

Ferguson, C. A., & Macken, M. (1983). The role of play in phonological development. In K. E. Nelson (Ed.), *Children's language (Vol. 4).* Hillsdale, NJ: Erlbaum.

Geva, E., & Olson, D. (in press). Children's story-retelling. In K. E. Nelson (Ed.), *Children's language (Vol. 5).* Hillsdale, NJ: Erlbaum.

Goffman, E. (1981). Response Cries. In *Forms of Talk.* Philadelphia, PA: University of Pennsylvania Press.

Hakuta, K. (1974). Prefabricated routines and the emergence of structure in second language acquisition. *Language Learning, 24,* 287–298.

Heath, S. B. (1983). *Ways with words.* New York: Cambridge University Press.

Heath, S. B. (in press). The book as narrative prop in language acquisition. In B. Schieffelin & P. Gilmore (Eds.), *The acquisition of literacy: Ethnographic perspectives.* Norwood, NJ: Ablex.

Huang. J., & Hatch, E. (1978). A Chinese child's acquisition of English. In E. Hatch (Ed.), *Second language acquisition.* Rowley, MA: Newbury House.

Keenan, E. (1974). Conversational competence in children. *Language in Society, 1,* 163–183.

Kuczaj, S. (1982). Language play and language acquisition. *Advances in Child Development and Behavior, 17,* 198–232.

Leopold, W. F. (1939-1949). *Speech development of a bilingual child.* (4 volumes). Evanston, IL: Northwestern University Press.

Ochs, E. & Schieffelin, B. (in press). *Language acquisition and socialization across cultures.* New York: Cambridge University Press.

Olson, D. (1977). From utterance to text: The bias of language in speech and writing. *Harvard Educational Review, 47,* 257–281.

Peck, S. (1978). Child-child discourse in second language acquisition. In E. Hatch (Ed.), *Second language acquisition: A book of readings.* Rowley, MA: Newbury House.

Pellegrini, A. (1980). The relationship between kindergartners' play and achievement in pre-reading, language, and writing. *Psychology in the Schools, 17,* 530–535.

Pellegrini, A. (1982). The construction of cohesive text by preschoolers in two play contexts. *Discourse Processes, 5,* 101–108.

Pellegrini, A. (1984). The effect of dramatic play on children's generation of cohesive text. *Discourse Processes, 7,* 57–67.

Pellegrini, A., DeStefano, J. S., & Thompson, D. L. (1983). Saying what you mean: Using play to teach "literate language." *Language Arts, 60,* 380–384.

Pepler, D. J., & Rubin, K. H. (1982). *The play of children: current theory and research (Vol. 6); Contributions to human development.* Basel: Karger.

Peters, A. (1977). Language learning strategies. *Language, 53,* 560–573.

Peters, A. (1983). *The units of language acquisition.* New York: Cambridge University Press.

Rosen, C. E. (1974). The effects of sociodramatic play on problem-solving behavior among culturally disadvantaged preschool children. *Child Development, 45,* 920–927.

Sachs, J. (1980). The role of adult–child play in language development. *New Directions for Child Development, 9,* 33–48.

Sachs, J., Goldman, J., & Chaillé, C. (1984). Planning in pretend play: Using language to co-ordinate narrative development. In A. Pellegrini & T. Yawkey (Eds.), *The development of oral and written language in social contexts.* Norwood, NJ: Ablex.

Sanches, M., & Kirschenblatt-Gimblett, B. (1976). Children's traditional speech play and child language. In B. Kirshenblat-Gimblett (Ed.), *Speech play.* Philadelphia, PA: University of Pennsylvania Press.

Scarcella, R. (1978). Socio-drama for social interaction. *TESOL Quarterly, 12,* 41–46.

Schwartzman, H. B. (1978). *Transformations: The anthropology of children's play.* New York: Plenum.

Sherzer, J. (1976). Play languages: Implications for (socio) linguistics. In B. Kirshenblatt-Gimblett (Ed.), *Speech play.* Philadelphia, PA: University of Pennsylvania Press.

Smilansky, S. (1968). *The effects of sociodramatic play on disadvantaged preschool children.* New York: Wiley.

Smilansky, S. (1971). Can adults facilitate play in children? Theoretical and practical consider-ations. In *Play: The child strives toward self-realization.* Washington, DC: National Association for the Education of Young Children.

Snow, C., & Goldfield, B. (1982). Building stories: The emergence of information structures from conversation. In D. Tannen (Ed.), *Analyzing discourse: Text and talk* (GURT, 1982). Washington, DC: Georgetown University Press.

Stein, N. (1982). What's in a story: Interpreting the interpretations of story grammars. *Discourse Processes, 5,* 319–335.

Sutton-Smith, B., & Heath, S. B. (1981). Paradigms of pretense. *The Quarterly Newsletter of the Laboratory of Comparative Human Cognition, 3,* 41–45.

Vihman, M. M. (1982). Formulas in first and second language acquisition. In L. Obler & L. Menn (Eds.), *Exceptional language and linguistics.* New York: Academic Press.

Weir, R. H. (1962). *Language in the crib.* The Hague: Mouton.

Wong Fillmore, L. (1976). *The second time around: Cognitive and social strategies in second language acquisition.* Ph.D. dissertation, Stanford University, CA.

# 9

## Assessing Children's Knowledge About Book Reading*

Catherine Snow
Debra Nathan
Rivka Perlmann
Harvard University

### Introduction

Book reading during the preschool period has been identified as a source of information to children about vocabulary (Ninio, 1983), about other aspects of language (Ninio & Bruner, 1978; Snow & Goldfield, 1983), about the conventions of print (Anderson, Teale, & Estrada, 1980; Snow, 1983), and about the nature of narrative forms (Heath, 1982; Snow & Goldfield, 1982). Although most of the research has been directed to analyzing the structure of interactions during book reading, a few studies (Snow & Goldfield, 1982, 1983) have also demonstrated that children learn specific things about language and about literacy from reading books with adults (see Goldfield & Snow, 1984, for a review).

Prior, however, to being able to learn vocabulary, language structures, or literacy conventions from a book-reading experience, a child must first learn *how to read books,* i.e., how to participate in the interaction format that occurs during book-reading sessions. It has been argued (Snow, 1983; Snow & Goldfield, 1983) that the beneficial effects of book reading on children's language and literacy skills are made possible by the routinized nature of book reading, and the opportunity to reread certain books many

* This paper was prepared while the first author was a Fellow at the Institute for Advanced Studies, The Hebrew University. Thanks are due to the Institute for its generous support, to the Spencer Foundation, which funded the research, to the observer/transcribers (Andrea Senkowski, Susan Bertram, Cheryl D'Amelio, and Carol Johnson), and to the pseudonymous Alex, Jim, Josh, and Ben and their mothers.

Address correspondence to Catherine Snow, Harvard University, Graduate School of Education, Larsen 7, Cambridge, MA 02138.

times, thus building progressively richer knowledge structures around them. Book reading is a highly "routinizable" activity, and descriptions of it suggest that it is typically highly routinized for any mother–child pair. Across mother–child pairs, however, the nature of the routine can vary considerably, though these individual differences may well be confounded with developmental change and with differences produced by the nature of the book being read (see Snow, Dubber, & DeBlauw, 1982 for some evidence concerning book effects). Descriptions in the literature (e.g., Ninio, 1980) suggest just some of the variation that occurs, e.g., requiring production (What's that?) versus comprehension (Where's the bunny?) versus imitation (Look at the bunny. Say "bunny.") in reading picture books; concentrating on labeling items in pictures versus developing narratives around the pictures; talking about the pictures versus reading the text; expecting the child to "fill in" bits of the text versus asking questions. Presumably different children learn whatever routines their caretakers emphasize and then, having learned the routine, are able to go and learn whatever it is about language or literacy that routine is well-designed to teach.

The purpose of this study is to assess children's knowledge of the book-reading routine their caretakers use in two ways: (a) by showing how the children's behavior changes from an early to a late session of reading one particular book, reflecting the demands being placed on the child by the caretaker, and (b) by looking at the children's behavior when they assume the adult role and read the book to a puppet. The measures taken of child and of maternal behavior were designed to reflect each partner's discharge of responsibility for initiating topics and providing information about topics relevant to the book (see Snow & Goldfield, 1982, for an earlier use of a similar scoring procedure). Telling a story requires introducing certain categories of information (who the characters are, what objects are involved, where and when the action takes place, what the main event consists of, why the event occurred, what the consequences of the event are) and making sure that the information relevant to each of those categories for the narrative under discussion is made explicit. The task of introducing the categories of information (e.g., by a directive to attend to something, and by a question) can be separated from the task of providing the information, though the two are both fulfilled by a traditional, noninteractive storyteller. We assumed that, at least during the early sessions, the mother would have primary responsibility for introducing information units and for providing information, that with time one or both of these responsibilities would be shifted to the child. We also were interested to discover whether mothers had consistently different styles for introducing information units (e.g., question vs. directing attention) and for level of dominance in the interaction and, if so, whether the children would mimic their own mothers' patterns if asked to "play mother's role."

## Sample

The data presented are drawn from series of naturalistic interactions at home between four mothers and their children, Alex, Jim, Josh, and Ben, aged 1; 11.0, 1; 10.28, 1; 8.20 and 1; 7.20 respectively, at the start of the observations. The interactions were audiotaped at approximately weekly intervals over a period of four to six months. Transcriptions included all mother and child speech and contextual notes made by the observers.

The interactions analyzed here were collected as part of a study designed to capture routinized situations in the child's life—caretaking and play activities that were recurrent, rule-governed, and somewhat predictable. For these four of the five children in the larger study, book reading was identified by the mothers as fulfilling our criteria for routines. We provided each of these mother–child pairs with a book (or they selected a previously unread book), so that the sessions would record the child's increasing knowledge of the book starting from zero. We asked the mothers not to read the selected book with the child outside our recording sessions.

Childish obstinacy, sickness, and holidays made it impossible to standardize exactly the recording intervals and frequencies across children. However, after a minimum of five sessions (for Josh; seven for Alex and Jim; and nine for Ben) in which the routine book was read by mother and child, we instituted a role-reversal procedure. The observer brought a puppet and asked the child to read the by-now-familiar book to the puppet (the mother having been previously warned to talk as little as possible). If feasible, we repeated the role-reversal procedure at subsequent sessions to collect as large as possible a set of utterances from the child in role as "competent reader." Needless to say, "reader" is meant to be taken metaphorically; neither mothers nor children paid much attention to the texts of the books, and all spent most of their time discussing and explaining the pictures. This interaction style, which has been reported previously, may be limited to books like those used here (*Richard Scarry's Best Word Book Ever, Richard Scarry's Color Book, Nicky Goes to the Doctor* by Richard Scarry, and *The Sesame Street Pet Show,* put out by Children's Television Workshop) in which the pictures are more compelling than the text. Dr. Seuss books, are, for example, much more likely to produce reading aloud than picture discussion (see Snow, Dubber, & DeBlauw, 1982).

We were interested in analyzing the transcripts in such a way as to provide information about the competence of the child to contribute to the picture discussions and changes in that competence with time, and the child's ability to take the adult role in book reading. Accordingly, the first and at least one late session of reading the book with the mother were analyzed as well as all role-reversal sessions. The measures taken are now discussed.

## Language Measures

**Number of information units.** Information unit (IU) is defined as the smallest topical unit isolated by the exchange between the conversation partners (see Snow & Goldfield, 1982). The units are of variable "size," depending on the density of conversational exchange. A typically sized unit is defined by a wh—— question and its answers (What's that? A big car. Where's the elephant? Right here. What happened? Dingo had an accident), but an answer to a question or a statement can be "split" into more than one information unit by subsequent conversational moves. For example, the exchange:

| C: | What's that? | M: | A little tiny fire. |
|----|--------------|----|---------------------|
| C: | Tiny. | M: | Yes, it's so tiny. |

would define *fire* and *tiny* as separate IUs, because the second exchange isolates *tiny* as a separate unit of semantic information. Conversely, however, an IU can extend over several utterances if no new semantic information is isolated, e.g.:

> M: Look at that teeny tiny fire. It's so little. Just a tiny little flame.

The information unit is defined by semantic intention rather than by specific form of expression. Thus, the following exchange contains only one IU:

| C: | Dat a slide. | M: | No, it's not a slide, it's a ladder tipping over. |
|----|--------------|----|---------------------------------------------------|
| C: | Ladder tipping over. | | |

**Percent of information units introduced by mother/by child.** Introducing an IU can be accomplished in a number of ways, some of which require no specific lexical reference. Thus, it is quite possible that the child introduces the majority of IUs, for example, by questioning extensively; if the child did so, he/she could be seen as dominating the discussion, even if he/she provided very little of the information about the pictures.

**Total number of utterances.** An utterance was defined as a segment of speech with a final intonation contour, followed by a pause.

**Percent utterances produced by mother/by child.** It seemed likely that as the children got more competent with the books, they would produce a higher percentage of the utterances during the picture discussions.

**Number of utterances per information unit for mother/child.** More utterances per IU indicates that the picture discussions are getting longer by virtue of more elaborated conversations around each topic rather than simply by adding new topics.

**Method of introducing information units.** Each information unit introduction was classified as one of the following three types:

1. Providing information (PI). Giving the informative content of the IU: "That's a fire truck." "It's all messy." "Look at all that water for that little tiny fire."
2. Questioning. Introducing an information unit without providing the relevant information: "What's what?" "Who's that on the fire truck?" "What's happening to this car?"
3. Direction attention. Introducing an IU which is subsequently elaborated by the exchange without in its introduction either providing information or questioning it: "Look at this." "Isn't that interesting!" "This is a funny picture."

After identifying the method by which each IU was introduced, it was possible to calculate in what percentage of the cases each mother and child used each of the three methods.

## Results

### Changes Across Sessions

Table 1 presents data on changes in the children's behavior from an early to a later book reading session. It can be seen that three of the four children became more dominant participants in the book reading, increasing the proportion of IUs they introduced by at least 30% and also increasing the number of utterances per information unit. In addition, all the children in-

**Table 1. Changes in Children's Behavior From First to Last Mother-Child Session**

| Subject | N of IUs Total | % of IUs introduced by Child | % of Utterances by Child | Utterances/IU Adult | Child |
|---------|--------|----------|----------|-------|-------|
| Alex | + 2 | +30 | +12 | − .7 | + .3 |
| Jim | − 80 | +34 | + 5 | + .4 | + .5 |
| Josh | +31 | +31 | +25 | + .5 | +1.0 |
| Ben | − 27 | −11 | + 1 | − .3 | − .2 |

creased the proportion of utterances they contributed to the conversation, but that proportion increased less than the proportion of IUs introduced. In other words, they talked more, but the increase in talk is not enough to explain their increased responsibility for introducing IUs.

Ben was the only child who showed no improvement whatsoever in terms of amount of participation in the book reading. Because the data comparing his first and last mother–child sessions showed a decline which contrasts sharply with the other children's increasing participation, we analyzed two additional intermediate sessions for Ben. The data from all four mother–child sessions taken together suggest that there was really no change at all in Ben's behavior over time. The sharp decline at session 6 reflects lower than usual level of participation at that session, for no apparent reason, but sessions 1, 3, and 4 were all quite similar, with Ben introducing 11–17% of IU's and producing 24–27% of utterances.

It is not clear why Ben failed to take over greater participation in the book reading. It may have been that the book he was reading was too difficult to give him much opportunity for increased participation, especially in light of his mother's tendency to concentrate on the overall plot line of the book rather than letting each picture be discussed on its own terms as the other mothers were more likely to do. As we will see in the next section, Ben's mother used a style of interaction very similar to Jim's mother, so her style cannot by itself explain the difference in effect.

## Maternal Style

It has been suggested in the literature that mothers have "a style" for book reading which remains somewhat constant in their interactions with their children. On the other hand, the children's increasing competence to participate and to initiate, documented in the previous section, might lead one to expect that mothers' styles will also change in adaptation to the children. The data on continuity and change in mothers' styles of introducing IUs are presented in Table 2.

A major dimension of maternal style is the degree to which mothers dominate the book-reading session by selecting topics themselves as opposed to letting the child initiate IUs. The first column in Table 2 indicates rather large differences among the mothers in their ability and/or willingness to cede control of the session to the child. Josh and Alex's mothers started out by dominating the topic selection but allowed the children to take over as they became more competent. Jim's mother, similarly, let Jim progressively take over, but since he was starting from a position of much greater control, he reached a level of initiating 74% of the information units by the last session. Ben's mother started off at a moderately high level of control but did not cede control at any point to Ben (perhaps because Ben did not show any attempt to take over the task of topic selection). Thus, only Ben's mother showed continuity rather than change in this aspect of maternal style.

Table 2. Maternal Style During Book Reading: Percent and Type of IU Initiations

| Mother of | Session | % of IUs Initiated by Mother | Type of IU Initiation | | |
|-----------|---------|------------------------------|------------------------|---------------------|--------------------|
| | | | % Providing Information | % Directing Attention | % Asking Question |
| Alex | 1 | 96 | 7 | 4 | 89 |
| | 3 | 73 | 16 | 6 | 78 |
| | 7 | 67 | 17 | 10 | 73 |
| Jim | 1 | 60 | 44 | 27 | 29 |
| | 6 | 26 | 57 | 10 | 33 |
| Josh | 1 | 100 | 42 | 25 | 33 |
| | 2 | 67 | 27 | 8 | 65 |
| Ben | 1 | 83 | 64 | 14 | 22 |
| | 3 | 89 | 47 | 10 | 43 |
| | 4 | 85 | 41 | 5 | 54 |
| | 6 | 99 | 58 | 6 | 36 |

Mothers have three options for how to initiate IUs—asking questions about them, providing the relevant information, and directing attention to them without either questioning or providing information. The mothers differed considerably from one another in the extent to which they favored these various strategies (see Table 3), with Alex's mother showing a strong preference for questions, while Jim's mother favored the provision of information. Josh's mother, like Ben's to some extent, increased the percentage of questions asked as her child became more familiar with the book, and used questions and the provision of information about equally.

It seems clear, then, that mothers differ in the degree to which they dominate topic selection during book reading and in the devices they use for topic selection. The question to be addressed in the next section is whether children in any sense mirror these differences in maternal style.

## Comparison of Mother and Child

We have seen that three of the four children were learning about how to read these books, as revealed by their increasing ability to initiate topics and to contribute to the conversation. Is there any evidence that the children were learning the specifics of their mothers' book-reading styles? We can answer this question by looking at the children's methods for topic-initiation, both while in interaction with the mother and during role reversal.

Neither in the last session with mother nor in the role-play session did any of the four children match their own mothers in relative frequency of the three initiation strategies, although Jim and Josh matched their mothers in most preferred strategy (see Table 3). The major deviations of the children's from the mothers' patterns were caused by the children's relatively

**Table 3.** Maternal and Child Preferences for Providing Information (PI), Directing Attention (DA), and Asking Questions (Q) as Techniques for Introducing IUs

|  | Mother | Child During Last Mother–Child Session | Child During Role Reversal |
|---|---|---|---|
| Alex | Q>>PI>>DA | PI>Q=DA | PI>Q=DA |
| Jim | PI>Q≳DA | PI≳DA>>Q | DA>PI>>Q |
| Josh | Q>PI>>DA | Q>DA>>PI | Q>DA>PI |
| Ben | PI>Q>DA | DA>>PI=Q | DA>PI=Q |

>> means more than 3 times as often.
> means 1.8–3.0 times as often.
≳ means 1.2–1.8 times as often.
= means .8–1.2 times as often.

much greater preference for directing attention as a way of introducing information units. All the mothers used this strategy less than any other, whereas all the children except Alex made it their first or second choice. If the attention-directing is left out of consideration, then both Jim and Josh do match their mothers, while Alex shows the opposite preference. Ben used only directing-attention with any frequency—his general lack of participation in the book-reading interaction makes it difficult to assess whether he learned anything at all about the book being read.

It should be noted here that directing attention is the least demanding strategy in terms of linguistic and cognitive resources. Providing information as an initiation strategy requires at least naming some aspect of the picture. Questioning requires having control over the appropriate question forms—What's that? Who's that?; Where's X?; What's happening?—and knowing which of the various questions is appropriate. Directing attention requires only pointing and vocalizing or forms like *look*. It is, thus, not surprising that the children use it with relatively greater frequency than their mothers, nor that Ben used it more than the other children.

## The Children as Readers

Until now, we have considered the children in their roles as children being read to by their mothers. Although they could become increasingly dominant (i.e., motherlike) in terms of talking, introducing information, and initiating topics in the later mother–child sessions, after they had gotten to know the book better, they nevertheless retained their roles as child listeners. The last session was designed to seduce them into another role, that of adult reader, reading the book to an incompetent puppet.

Table 4 presents the data comparing the child in his last session reading the book with his mother to his role-play session(s). It should be pointed out that the role play is a difficult task for children as young as these, and that Josh and Ben were reluctant and somewhat puzzled by requests that

Table 4. Child Behavior During Last Mother–Child Session Compared to Role-Reversal Sessions

| Child | Session (n) | N of IUs Discussed | % of IUs Introduced by Child | % of Utterances Produced by Child | Utterances per IU | |
|---|---|---|---|---|---|---|
| | | | | | Adult | Child |
| Alex | Mother–child | 117 | 34 | 30 | 2.32 | .99 |
| | role reversal (3) | 242 | 47 | 43 | 1.85 | 1.40 |
| Jim | Mother–child | 82 | 74 | 43 | 2.04 | 1.56 |
| | role reversal (2) | 143 | 33 | 42 | 2.43 | 1.64 |
| Josh | Mother–child | 55 | 31 | 35 | 2.07 | 1.13 |
| | role reversal (1) | 17 | 29 | 34 | 2.41 | 1.24 |
| Ben | Mother–child | 33 | 6 | 21 | 1.45 | .39 |
| | role reversal (2) | 107 | 15 | 29 | 1.58 | .65 |

they tell the puppet about the book. They simply were not able to slip into the other role and then keep it up as Alex and Jim were. The observers who played the puppet role attempted to maintain a very noninitiating position, saying only things like "read to me" or "tell me about this picture," but in fact with all the children to some extent, and with Josh and Ben to a large extent, were unable to avoid asking specific questions, thus introducing information units or providing information.

The figures in Table 4 suggest that Alex was the best able to take responsibility when cast in role of reader. He increased the percentage of IUs he introduced, the percentage of utterances he produced, and the number of utterances per IU, over the levels of the final adult–child session. Josh performed as well during role play as during the last mother–child session. Ben actually improved during role play but from such a low level of participation that it is difficult to analyze how much he really learned. Jim, who had been promoted to a very high level of participation and dominance during the late mother–child sessions, retreated, leaving more than usual of the topic initiations up to his new conversational partner, the incompetent puppet. He did, however, participate willingly in the role reversal, as did Alex. Josh, although the data suggest he was quite competent during role reversal, was very reuctant, terminated the session after only 17 IUs had been discussed, and refused to participate in later sessions.

## The Children's Role Play: Content

It seems that the children do not match their mothers' styles of book reading very exactly, perhaps because their linguistic resources do not enable them to. It is still possible, though, that the content of the children's speech during role reversal—the nature of the IUs the children discussed and the kind of information they offered about them—reflected the mothers' choices during earlier sessions.

In order to assess whether the content of the mother–child sessions determined the topics and information presented during children's role play, we analyzed in some detail Jim's discussions concerning four frequently read pages (actually 2-page spreads) in his book, Richard Scarry's *Cars and Trucks and Things That Go*. The pages were selected because they were discussed elaborately enough during role reversal to be reasonably analyzed and had been discussed at least three times during the mother–child sessions, again at some length. They vary in the degree to which they lend themselves to listing and labeling versus a narrative; pages 40 and 41 present a miniature narrative of a tiny fire in a bug-car being put out by 4 fire engines, despite considerable misdirection of water hoses, tripping over errant hoses, and other distractions, whereas pages 36 and 37 shows 13 assorted vehicles with no relation to one another except location on the same road. The presence of a narrative theme greatly increased the proportion of information units that recurred during discussion of a picture, so we decided to select pictures across the entire range of narrativity.

Table 5 presents the data derived from analyzing Jim's reading of these four pages. Each page was analyzed by identifying the IUs introduced by

**Table 5. Data from Jim's Recurrent Reading of Several Pages from "Cars and Trucks"**

|  | **Pages** | | | |
| Data | **10–11** | **36–37** | **40–41** | **60–61** |
| --- | --- | --- | --- | --- |
| N of mother–child sessions in which page was discussed | 5 | 4 | 4 | 3 |
| N of role-reversal sessions in which discussed | 2 | 2 | 2 | 1 |
| N of IUs during mother–child sessions | 21 | 29 | 25 | 19 |
| N of IUs discussed more than once | 4 | 3 | 10 | 5 |
| % initially introduced by mother | 24 | 41 | 64 | 63 |
| % of information initially provided by mother | 24 | 45 | 60 | 68 |
| % of IUs from mother–child sessions discussed during role reversal by child | 29 | 28 | 44 | 32 |
| % of IUs discussed more than once during mother–child sessions that were introduced during role reversal by the child | 75 | 100 | 70 | 60 |
| % IUs during role reversal not previously discussed | 40 | 38 | 0 | 50 |
| % of mother-introduced IUs which Jim learned | 57 | 30 | 63 | 46 |

the child during the role reversal, and all IUs during the mother–child sessions. Many IUs were, of course, discussed during only one session of reading a particular page, whereas others recurred once or several times. The basic questions guiding the analysis were whether (a) most of what Jim said about the pictures during the role reversal could be traced to his mother's selection of topics and presentation of information during the mother–child session, (b) the IUs that recurred during the mother–child sessions were more likely to emerge during role reversal than the ones that occurred only once, and (c) there was better evidence from the mother–child sessions or the role-reversal sessions that Jim was learning to select the topics and provide the information his mother had modeled for him.

It can be seen from rows five and six of Table 6 that mother and child shared the task of initiating topics and of providing information about those topics rather evenly, though at very different rates for the different pictures. The seventh row indicates that 28–44% of the IUs discussed during mother–child sessions emerged druing a role-reversal session. This percentage is much higher though (60–100%) for thɔse IUs discussed two or more times during mother–child sessions. Row 9 shows that a minority of the IUs that the child used during role play had not been previously discussed, clear evidence that Jim's role-playing behavior was modelled on the specifics of his mother's behavior. The final row gives evidence that an IU which Jim's mother had introduced or provided information about was taken over by Jim at a later session, whether a mother–child or a role-reversal session; 30 to 66% of the IUs that Jim initially did not introduce were "learned" by him.

We present in Table 6 a few examples of the talk relevant to particular IUs on pages 40 and 41 (the fire trucks and small fire) to give an indication of how Jim followed his mother's lead, both in selecting topics for discussion and in providing information about them.

## Conclusion

We have demonstrated in this study that mothers use individualized styles of interaction with their children while reading books, but that they also can adapt their style, particularly their ratio of questioning to provision of information, as the child becomes a more competent discussant of the book. When the situation is held constant, it is possible to see that the complexity of maternal speech is quite finely tuned to children's levels of understanding and production. Children are thus given a great deal of support in learning to understand the stories they hear in the context of these book-reading sessions. Children who have many such experiences might be expected to develop, after some time, a generalized "sense of story" or set of expectations concerning the nature of a complete narrative. This set of expectations will

Table 6. Conversations between Jim and his mother concerning four recurrent information units demonstrate how the child relies on adult models in selecting topics to discuss and in deciding what information to provide.

| Session | Fire Trucks | Water Misdirected into Truck | The Dog that Tripped | The Mess | The Fire |
|---|---|---|---|---|---|
| 2 | A: Oh look, what are these?<br>C: Right here.<br>A: Right, what are they?<br>C: Fire truck.<br>A: That's right. | | | | A: But where's the fire? (child turns page) |
| 3 | C: Fire truck. | A: And look, they goofed. They got the water of the hose going into the truck instead of onto the fire.<br><br>C: Water/in it/in<br>A: Yes, water in the truck. | A: Look, this doggy fell down trying to get out of his car. He was in too much of a hurry. | A: What a mess!<br>C: Mess.<br>A: What a mess!<br>C: Messy. | A: Where's the fire though?<br>Where's the fire? (2x)<br>You help me find the fire. I wonder where the fire is.<br>(Pointing) Right there.<br>C: No.<br>A: Look, see the fire?<br>C: Fire.<br>A: It's a little fire. |
| 4 | C: Fire truck. | A: Look, the water flowed all inside the truck. | C: Fall down the doggy.<br>A: Yeah, that doggy fell down. He opened the door and fell right out. I think he might have tripped over that hose. | A: Oh look!<br>C: Messy, uh very messy.<br>A: Very messy. | A: They're spraying the water on this tiny little fire. |

178

Table 6 (Continued)

| Session | Fire Trucks | Water Misdirected into Truck | The Dog that Tripped | The Mess | The Fire |
|---|---|---|---|---|---|
| 6 | C: Fire trucks. Fire trucks.<br>M: That's what they are, Fire trucks. | A: Big mess of spilled water.<br>C: Not the water.<br>A: No spilled water in that truck. The spilled water in this truck. | A: What's happening here?<br>C: Up fall down.<br>A: Yeah, that doggie fell down. | A: Oh, Jim, what do we have here?<br>C: A mess, oh mess. | A: Do you remember where the fire is?<br>C: (pointing) A fire.<br>A: Right there, a tiny fire. |
| 8 (RR) | C: Fire truck.<br>A: Wow.<br>C: Fire truck. | A: What's all this?<br>C: A water.<br>A: Why water?<br>C: A go in there. | | C: Oh messy. | A: What's that?<br>C: A fire. |
| 11 (RR) | C: A fire truck. Fire trucks... This is a fire truck, doggie... Where a fire truck? Where's the fire truck? Where's the fire truck go? | C: A water in it. A water in it. | C: Fall down/doggie... That doggie fell down on top car... A fall doggie. | | |

179

be of help in their early efforts to understand stories they hear and read; it constitutes the acquisition of a bit of their culture.

We have replicated in this analysis earlier findings that children can learn specific expressions and informative content from recurrent reading of one book. It is quite clear from the results reported here that more frequent presentation of information in the routinized context leads to better learning. For example, Jim was best able to present in his role-play sessions the IUs that had been discussed more than once by him and his mother. At the same time, however, children are able to incorporate some IUs (presumably ones they find especially salient or interesting) into their retellings after only one exposure.

We have, furthermore, extended the former findings by showing that some children are capable of switching to the "adult-reader" role, at least after they have become somewhat familiar with a book. In the reader role they can become more dominant in selecting conversational topics, though without shifting their strategies for introducing information units from those used in the child-listener role to those typically used by their mothers.

Microanalysis of one child's reading shows that the topics selected and information provided during the role reversal were largely, though not entirely, limited to those modeled by the mother during earlier sessions. When the situation is held constant, we can see very specific effects of adult speech on children's learning.

It is surprising and impressive that any children only 22 to 25 months old could carry out the task required during the role-reversal sessions, given the shift in perspective demanded. It may well be that Alex and Jim succeeded precisely because they had received rich and extensive modeling of how to read books to children; alternatively, they may have been able to reverse roles because they had had so much recent experience as child-listeners of precisely the books they were asked to read. Their knowledge of how to read the book in question was broad and detailed enough to carry them through the task, despite its demanding nature.

## References

Anderson, A. B., Teale, W. H., & Estrada E. (1980). Low income children's preschool literacy experiences: Some naturalistic observations. *The Quarterly Newsletter of the Laboratory of Comparative Human Cognition, 2* (3), 59–65.

Goldfield, R., & Snow, C. E. (1984). Reading books with children: The mechanics of parental influence on children's reading achievement. In J. Flood (Ed.), *Understanding reading comprehension.* Newark, DL: IRA.

Heath, S. B. (1982). What no bedtime story means: Narratives at home and school. *Journal of Communication, 30,* 123–133.

Ninio, A. (1980). Picture book reading in mother–infant dyads belonging to two subgroups in Israel. *Child Development, 51,* 587–590.

Ninio, A. (1983). Joint book-reading as a multiple vocabulary acquisition device. *Developmental Psychology, 19,* 445-451.

Ninio, A., & Bruner, J. (1978). The achievement and antecedents of labelling. *Journal of Child Language, 5,* 1-15.

Snow, C. E. (1983). Literacy & language: Relationships during the preschool years. *Harvard Educational Review, 53,* 165-189.

Snow, C. (1983). Saying it again: The role of expanded and deferred imitations in language acquisition. In K. E. Nelson (Ed.), *Children's language (Vol. 4).* New York: Gardner Press.

Snow, C., Dubber, C., & DeBlauw, A. (1982). Routines in parent–child interaction. In L. Feagans & D. Farran (Eds.), *The language of children reared in poverty.* New York: Academic Press.

Snow, C., & Goldfield, B. (1982). Building stories: The emergence of information structure from conversation and narrative. In D. Tannen (Ed.), *Analyzing discourse: Text and talk.* Washington, DC: Georgetown University Press.

Snow, C., & Goldfield, B. (1983). Turn the page please: Situation specific language acquisition. *Journal of Child Language, 10,* 551-570.

# Author Index

Italics indicate bibliographic citations.

## A

Abelson, R., 1, 10, *27,* 46, 53, *61*
Abrahams, R., 149, *165*
Anderson, A.B., 167, *180*
Anderson, E.S., 30, 32, 41, *42,* 55, *60*
Anderson, J.W., 138, *143*
Applebee, A.N., 52, *60,* 92, *95*
Aschenbrenner, J., 32, 41, *42*
Asher, S., 130, *143*

## B

Bartlett, E., 64, *76*
Bartz, K.W., 40, *42*
Bates, E., 32, *42,* 129, 132, *143*
Baumrind, D., 40, *42*
Bell, C., 112, *127*
Bellugi, U., 3, 8, *25,* 131, *143*
Berndt, T.R., 22, 24, *26,* 45, *60*
Bernstein, L., 56, *60,* 91, *95*
Black, J.B., 10, *25*
Black, R., 149, *165*
Bloom, L., 32, *42,* 56, *60,* 131, *143*
Botvin, G., 51, *61*
Bower, G.H., 10, *25*
Boynton, M., 9, 14, 17, 18, 22, 23, *25, 26*
Bracewell, R.J., 103, 105, 106, 110, 113, 123, *125*
Brenner, J., 135, *145*
Bretherton, I., 129, *143*
Brewer, W.F., 104, *126*
Bridge, C.A., 103, *128*
Brown, A.L., 6, *25,* 141, 142, *143*
Brown, R., 3, 4, 8, 131, *143*
Bruce, B., 105, *126*
Bruner, J.S., 13, *25, 26,* 66, 69, *76,* 167, *181*
Buhler, C., 138, *143*

## C

Cancelli, A.A., 141, *145*
Carni, E., 5, *25*
Carr, T.H., 134, *143*
Carroll, S., 111, *127*
Cazden, C., 130, 132, *143*
Cera, M.J., 103, *128*
Cerbone, M.J., 9, *26*
Chaillé, C., 45, 46, 48, 52, *60, 61,* 93, *96,* 102, *127,* 152, *166*
Cicourel, A.V., 130, *143*
Clark, E.V., 3, 4, *25*
Clark, H.H., 3, 4, *25,* 131, *143*
Clarke-Stewart, K.A., 138, *143*
Clements, P., 103, *126*
Cole, M., *96,* 99, *127*
Connolly, K., 82, *96,* 101, 109, 111, 125, *126, 127*
Cook-Gumperz, J., 31, *42,* 79, 91, *95,* 102, 112, 125, *126*
Corsaro, W.A., 102, 112, 125, *126,* 164, *165*
Coulthard, R., 130, *145*
Cox, M., 130, *143*
Cromer, R.F., 4, *25*
Cross, T.G., 41, *42*

## D

DeBlauw, A., 168, 169, *181*
De Stefano, L., 45, 52, *60,* 151, *166*
Devin, J., 31, 40, *43*
Dickinson, D.K., 104, *128,* 130, *143*
Dickson, W.P., 130, *143*
Dore, J., 129, *143*
Doyle, A.B., 109, 111, *126*
Dubber, C., 168, 169, *181*
Dundes, A., 149, *165*
Dunn, J., 9, *25*

# Subject Index

**A**

Accommodation, 80–81
Adult–child interaction, 7–13, 68–69, 142, 168
Assimilation, 80–81
Autonomous text, 63–76, 131–132

**B**

Book reading, 167–180
    child style, 174–177
    maternal style, 172–174
Boundary-making strategies, 66–67, 70–73, 75

**C**

Communicative competence, 46, 55–60, 130–131
Componential model, 4
Comprehension, 4, 5, 99–125
Conflicts, 50–51, 82, 83, 86–87, 90
Conjunctions, 87, 92–93
Context, 1–27, 58–59
Conversational turns, 56–58

**D**

Decontextualized language, 64, 65, 101, 131–132
Decontextualized play, 81, 82

**E**

Egocentrism, 14, 49, 80, 81
Endophora, 87, 90
Event casts, 152, 153, 156, 164
Exophora, 87

**F**

Frames, 104–106, 162
    construction of, 104–106

**G**

Goals, 11, 12

**H**

Hypothetical reasoning, 6

**I**

Information units, 170–172
Informative speech, 129–142
Intrusions in play, 69

**L**

Language play, 148, 149, 158, 159
Literate behavior, 75, 79–95

**M**

Metanarrative, 93
Monologue, 111, 112, 147
    collective, 147

**N**

Narrative line, 46, 50, 51, 59, 74, 75
Nonverbal channels, 136–139
Noun phrases, 87, 91

**O**

Object talk, 8
Objects, role of, 49, 74, 134–135, 139–142
    in play, 49, 74
    in informative speech, 134–135, 139–142

**P**

Peer interaction, 13–22
Pragmatic rules, 65–66

**R**

Roles in play, 29, 31, 36–41, 48–49, 73–74
    narrator role, 73–74

**S**

Scripts, 1–27, 46, 53–55, 59, 141
Second-language learning, 147–165
Sex difference, 52–53
Social-cognition, 30–32, 84, 85